THE
LONG DETOUR

THE
LONG DETOUR

*The History and Future
of the American Left*

JAMES WEINSTEIN

A Member of the Perseus Books Group

Copyright © 2003 by James Weinstein, A Member of the Perseus Books Group

Published in 2003 in the United States of America by Westview Press, 5500 Central Avenue, Boulder, Colorado 80301-2877, and in the United Kingdom by Westview Press, 12 Hid's Copse Road, Cumnor Hill, Oxford OX2 9JJ.

Find us on the World Wide Web at www.westviewpress.com

Westview Press books are available at special discounts for bulk purchases in the United States by corporations, institutions, and other organizations. For more information, please contact the Special Markets Department at the Perseus Books Group, 11 Cambridge Center, Cambridge, MA 02142, or call (617) 252-5298, (800) 255-1514 or e-mail j.mccrary@perseusbooks.com.

Library of Congress Cataloging-in-Publication Data.
Weinstein, James, 1926-
  The long detour the history and future of the American left / James Weinstein.
    p. cm.
  Includes bibliographical references and index.
  ISBN 0–8133–4104–3
  1. Socialism—United States—History. I. Title.
HX83.W43 2003
335'.00973—dc21

                                                            2003000941

The paper used in this publication meets the requirements of the American National Standard for Permanence of Paper for Printed Library Materials Z39.48–1984.

10   9   8   7   6   5   4   3   2   1

CONTENTS

PREFACE

T HE FOLLOWING ESSAY IS THE RESULT of half a century's
experience on the political left and in academia. The most productive of these years were those spent working on the three journals with
which I have been most closely associated. The first was *Studies on the
Left*, published in Madison, Wisconsin, from 1959 to 1963—and then in
New York from 1963 to 1967. That journal came to an end when the editors concluded that it had served its initial objectives and that, as the New
Left began to disintegrate, it was time to move on. The second was *Socialist Review* (originally *Socialist Revolution*), which I initiated in 1969 and
worked on intensively until 1974. And the third is *In These Times*, originally a weekly newspaper and now a bi-weekly newsmagazine, which I
started in Chicago in 1976.

These three publications shared one underlying imperative: to help integrate the left and its principles into the mainstream of American political and intellectual life. Each of these journals made a bit of progress in
that direction. And working with their editors, while sometimes frustrating, was always intellectually stimulating. This was especially so in regard
to my symbiotic relationship with Martin J. Sklar, who greatly influenced
my thinking about all three journals, and my occasionally divergent relationship with John B. Judis, who joined the staff of *Socialist Review* when
he was a graduate student and also worked for many years as a senior editor of *In These Times*.

In writing this book, as the following pages make abundantly clear, I have relied heavily on the work of dozens of historians, political activists, and philosophers. But I have also relied on the advice and opinions of friends who have read all or parts of the manuscript to help me clarify arguments and unravel the many examples of my tendency to write in shorthand. They have made this essay more readable, and, I hope, more accessible to the uninitiated. My greatest debt here is to my wife, Beth Maschinot, a person who insists on explanations or clarifications when they are needed. Others who have read all or part of the manuscript, and who have made helpful suggestions include my old friend Bill Domhoff at U.C. Santa Cruz; my friend and former colleague at *In These Times*, Miles Harvey; and my sister, Lois Sontag. My agent, Sam Stoloff, made me scrap one chapter and suggested the book's title after I sent him some terrible ideas of my own, and Jill Rothenberg, my editor at Westview Press, made many useful suggestions. They have helped to make the book more intelligible and reader-friendly, for which I am deeply grateful.

James Weinstein

INTRODUCTION

I

FOR A FEW BRIEF MONTHS, after the Soviet Union's peaceful collapse, streams of vacuous babble about the "end of history" flooded the media. The Cold War ended so swiftly and effortlessly that simple minds were filled with dreams of unchallengeable power and eternal American world domination. According to the promoters of this idea, American-style capitalism fulfills human needs so well that a century of struggle against capitalism's underlying social principles has ended, and a future of imperturbable American hegemony lies ahead. But History was not impressed. As events in the Middle East have made all too clear, history's end is nowhere in sight.

In fact, it was the Cold War that in retrospect seems more like an end—or rather a detour from history—a time when the left was disoriented and the political life of the nation became one-dimensional. Promoted by our nation's leaders and the media as a period of historical contestation—a fight to the death between capitalism and communism—the Soviet threat (and its identity with socialism) now appears to have been grossly exaggerated. Now, the Cold War itself can be seen as an historical hiatus—a ritually choreographed standoff that afforded the American ruling class with protection from dissent and an organizing principle for its retrograde foreign and domestic policies. Similarly, the Cold War provided the Soviet Union with a rationale for the Communist Party's unquestioned rule at home and in Eastern Europe. In short, the fear and conformity of the Cold War was a godsend to the rulers on both sides of the Iron Curtain.

True, at times the threat of war seemed real enough, and at times military confrontations were devastating. The war against Vietnamese independence alone cost several million Indochinese lives, as well as the death of more than 58,000 American youth. But even in that situation underlying priorities were never challenged. Indeed, Cold War and the threat of nuclear annihilation were the health of the state on both sides of the Iron Curtain. And while the Vietnam War did create an ephemeral left, it did so only after Americans became aware of the toll it was taking on both sides. When the war was over, things went back to business as usual.

All that has now changed. The difference between ritual Cold War tensions and the terrors of the new era—real and faux—is all too clear. Now we confront a true enemy, an unpredictable, amorphous, almost intangible seething mass of freelancers, many of them highly educated and civilized, others feral, but all acting out of rage against the enhanced American Empire. These popular forces confront American-style capitalism spontaneously, through nongovernmental groups that ignore national boundaries and operate with little institutional control. Unlike the old enemy, the new ones mount deadly terrorist attacks on symbols of American military and commercial power, are secretly and informally organized, and are widely dispersed. As such they offer few clear targets for political or military engagement.

This represents a real threat to the social stability that post-industrial capitalism requires to function smoothly. And it offers the opportunity for megalomaniacal right-wingers to promote their militarist policies and dreams of perpetual world domination—as the Bush administration's actions show all too well. For all of democratic society, and especially for the left, this new (and certainly transitory) stage of history is costly and frightening. It is the price we pay for fifty years of political and intellectual stagnation, a time when the political dynamic of capitalism was detoured and frozen onto a Cold War sidetrack.

As I will argue, communism never posed a challenge to capitalism in the United States. Quite the contrary, the Russian Revolution and the formation of the Communist International disrupted and distorted the socialist policies and ideas that had engaged corporate capitalism before 1917. In those earlier years socialists had created an influential movement, one that played a major role in humanizing American society as it emerged from the period of ruthlessly competitive industrialization into the era of corporate domination. During this process, class-conscious capitalists had accommodated and assimilated many socialist ideas and programs as they rationalized and stabilized their changing society. And many socialist principles, once denounced as un-American, came to be seen as natural characteristics of our social system. The source of these ideas and programs, however, has been obscured. The role played by the once robust and dynamic left has faded from our collective memory.

But what about the threat from Russia and China? Didn't these Communists menace capitalism? Certainly, that is what the revolutionaries who seized power in Russia intended, and that is what the Bolsheviks attempted immediately following their revolution. Except in Hungary, however—where Bela Kun led an ephemeral Communist regime in 1919—these attempts were total failures. After 1920 the Russians established a non-market, nominally socialist, inward-looking, defensive regime, much as China would do after 1949, when the Communists took power there.

The Soviet and Maoist regimes did discard their native capitalists. But they neither could nor did realize socialist principles. Instead, they created highly centralized, bureaucratic societies in which the party acted as a surrogate for the capitalist class and mimicked many of the more retrograde methods of Western industrialization. Under its own monopoly control, the Russian party established a closed non-market system and called the result "real existing socialism." Similarly, the Chinese under Mao Tse-tung followed suit. But—as their defensive formulation implies on its face—Soviet leaders must have understood that while their revolutions were made by socialists, their regimes had little in common with Marx's ideas or the underlying principles of the traditional world movement.

For the most part, the Soviet Union (and later China) functioned outside the world capitalist market, but their unique systems never threatened the West. True, Western capital could not invest in the Soviet

Union or China or trade freely with those gigantic countries, and that did appear hostile to Western capitalists. And, of course, the Soviets and China supported anti-colonial movements in the undeveloped world, which also was experienced as hostile by Western colonial and neocolonial powers. But while communist support and rhetoric initially served some colonial independence movements well, none of the newly independent former colonies created a government along Soviet or Chinese lines, and none followed the Soviet lead in organizing its economy. On the contrary, from their inception all but two newly independent countries—Cuba and North Korea—sought to integrate themselves into the world market dominated by the Western powers and Japan.

In fact, while Soviet and Chinese leaders might rage and threaten the West, they, not the West, have been the true "paper tigers." Incapable of fighting an aggressive war of conquest against any Western power, even had they wished to, the Soviets and Chinese have always followed a strategically defensive foreign policy. Stalin, the poster child of paranoid nationalism, did see enemies everywhere. Many were real, but his overriding principle was the protection of his own turf. As World War II ended, he feared that his country—which had lost 20 million citizens and seen most of its industry reduced to rubble—would once again fall prey to the hostility of the West. He especially feared the United States, whose industry and military power had grown greatly during the war, and who had dropped atomic bombs on Hiroshima and Nagasaki in an apparent first step of a new war aimed at him.

Stalin's solution to this fear after World War II was an agreement with the Western powers that created a massive Soviet buffer under strict Soviet control in Eastern Europe and left the rest to the West. In his own way, Stalin observed this agreement. When Communists in Italy and Greece moved to take power after the second World War, for example, he ordered them to pull back. Even in regard to China, he pursued a policy of not antagonizing the West by discouraging Mao Tse-tung's efforts to defeat the pro-Western Chiang Kai-shek. (Of course, Stalin also opposed Mao because he feared him as a rival who, unlike his domestic enemies, real and imagined, couldn't be killed at will.)

The Cold War was widely seen as a titanic struggle for world domination, and certainly in terms of the weapons with which each side confronted the other it appeared to be just that. But while the military and political leaders on both sides needed the Cold War and made much of it, the military standoff was never more than an insanely dangerous bluff. In short, despite its frequently aggressive bombast and its overt and covert support of foreign Communist movements, the Bolsheviks had neither the ability nor the desire to fight a war. Nor were their proclamations—no matter how real in the minds of many on both sides of the political fence—more than a mask for a backward society whose espousal of socialism was politically indispensable but essentially cynical. After seventy years of Soviet power, Soviet communism fell peacefully of its own dead weight, having succeeded in doing little more than paving the way for a corrupt replay of what Karl Marx called the primitive accumulation of capital. (Similarly, with greater success, the Chinese are undergoing a more controlled transition to capitalism.)

II

As a lifelong Socialist, and one-time Communist, I have always been concerned about the movement of history. And as a pathological optimist, I have always viewed American history as tending inexorably, if fitfully, toward a more inclusive democracy. Like many Americans who experienced the twentieth century, I see history moving forward, driven by the progressive interaction between capitalist and socialist principles. Before World War II, labor's right to organize and the extension of civil liberties were foremost. During the Cold War, African-Americans and their allies on the left finally won an end to legal segregation and a modicum of social equality, women made impressive social and political gains, and—inspired by those movements—gays and lesbians came out of seclusion and demanded recognition in the mainstream of American culture.

Still, as these movements on the left struggled for a more egalitarian society, progress was impeded by the politics of the Cold War. By equating opposition to corporate domination of public life with disloyalty, our country's rulers disoriented the left, stifled public discussion of the most basic public policy issues, and transformed the left into a plethora of single-issue movements. This removed the progressive dialectic from our political culture and has steadily narrowed the difference between the major parties. Without vigorous debate over alternative values and principles, the left has receded from view. Our political system has been converted to one focused on personality, appearance, and the ability to raise money for trivial, brain-numbing television and radio commercials. Candidates for national office, chosen by small cabals of people with access to the huge sums of money needed to run media-driven election campaigns, dominate the electoral arena. People who can throw several million dollars of their own money into campaigns for public office push to the fore.

In short, it has become more and more difficult for working people, or associations who represent their interests, to participate meaningfully in national politics. As working people are excluded from this process, fewer and fewer of them bother to vote. Those concerned about popular disinterest in politics implore people to do their duty as citizens, and the corporate media pompously insist that if you do not vote you have no right to complain about the result. But with few differences between the major parties or their candidates, and with the left and the socialist ideas that shaped it absent from popular discourse, more citizens retreat into private life, increasingly ignorant of the impact of public policies on their lives.

III

What then has socialism meant to those who have appreciated the virtues of the Western democracies while simultaneously being repelled by the pervasive militarization, corruption, inequality, and superficiality of our market-driven system? And what, if anything, does socialism mean now that its once-dominant perverters have collapsed or peacefully turned to their own forms of capitalist accumulation? In proper historical context, the argument is simple. From capitalism's earliest beginnings, two sets of principles have provided the social dynamic of modern society. Especially after industrialization began in earnest, socialists challenged the heartlessness of raw competitive capitalism and fought for the kinds of reforms that at first were seen as threatening capitalism's existence, but that in the end saved the system from itself.

In capitalism's earliest years, it is true, utopian socialists did not contest capitalists in the public arena, but simply removed themselves from the mainstream of capitalist development. As the social solidarity of feudalism was dismantled and capitalist individualism developed, utopians came to America not as individuals or families who would integrate into society, but as fully formed artisanal communities intent on escaping the social fragmentation that followed the breakup of feudal estates. These utopians did not want to make capitalism more humane, but only to avoid it by isolating themselves in their own traditional communities. In the pre-industrial years of the new nation, the social capital that these communities brought with them served them well. But the utopians' initial advantage over frontier individualism did not last. As industrial development accelerated, the self-contained utopian communities were surpassed by the more dynamic world around them. Their communities dissolved, and their members sought opportunity in the dominant society. I will look briefly at this experience in Chapter 1.

The next wave of socialism shared with its predecessor the principles of democratic egalitarianism. But it emerged in tandem with industrialization, and, like children of abusive parents, socialists had a love-hate relationship with capitalism. Early on, this second wave of socialists was barely noticed by the larger society. But it was not for lack of effort on their part, nor—in the long run—were their efforts wasted. By the early twentieth century, socialists and their ideas had not only gained a wide following among working people, but also the attention of America's rulers as they helped to shape the new system of large-scale corporate capitalism and its transformation of the country from a backwater of small-scale competitive businessmen—urban and rural—into the industrial behemoth that it is today.

In this process, capitalists epitomized the principle of market-driven rapacious individualism, while the socialists' first principle was the promotion of humane social policy. Karl Marx explained again and again that socialists' long-range goal was to create a society based on democratic principles. But he understood that a fully developed capitalism alone could create the technological and social basis for such a society. Advanced industrial capitalism, in other words, was a prerequisite for socialism. Within American capitalism, therefore, socialists were the most consistent—and insistent—advocates of reforms that moved society toward greater equality and democracy.

By 1914, when World War I erupted, the Socialist Party of America had reached its greatest strength. Many of its ideas and much of its program had already been assimilated by progressives of both major parties and were helping to rationalize and stabilize the new corporate system. Later, in the New Deal and post–World War II years, many programs first proposed by Socialists became mainstays of American public policy. Indeed, as we will see, the Socialist Party's success on the programmatic level was so great that it led many adherents to question the party's further usefulness.

But to those steeped in its principles, socialism was more than specific policy proposals. The party's "immediate demands" were an expression of its principles as they applied to the current stage of capitalist development, but were neither its ultimate goal, not its driving force. As American capitalism accepted and internalized many socialist principles it reached industrial maturity. But as capitalism moved into its current period as a post-industrial, consumer-driven society, socialists have had little new to say.

This is not entirely their fault. From the perspective of the left's long-range viability, moving forward was made extremely difficult, if not impossible, by the ways in which the Russian Revolution inspired a worldwide political movement that not only split the left, but also redefined socialism in the popular mind to mean (at best) a lower standard of living minus democracy. As the journalist John Reed wrote, the Russian Revolution "shook the world," but not in the manner he perceived. While hundreds of millions of people throughout the world initially hailed the Bolshevik victory as a democratic overthrow of Russia's despotic czarist regime, the revolution occurred in a country that had none of the industrial, cultural, or social prerequisites for democratic egalitarianism. In short, the Soviet experience forced socialists in the West to engage in a hopeless rear-guard effort to move forward just as popular interest in socialism—in conformity with Soviet reality—moved backward.

To me—even when I was a Communist—socialism has meant the fulfillment of the promise of American democracy. And as an historian, I have studied the ways in which socialist principles of associational democracy have gained meaningful expression in our society and helped to democratize our nation's advance from the laissez-faire individualism of the late nineteenth century to the corporate liberalism of the twentieth century. The Soviets' not-entirely-unsuccessful attempt to industrialize under tightly centralized state control could not transcend American reality. Indeed, its often-expressed goal of catching up with the West was a long step backward from this process. Clearly, the Soviets had little to offer those who had reached the level of industrial development to which the Bolsheviks aspired. Communist domination of the American left, therefore, stifled socialist thought and creativity and diverted it into barren disputes over the nature of the Soviet Union and into sterile debates over revolutionary strategy among self-styled Marxists of various sects.

Fortunately, such debates have now passed away. History has dissolved them (though the habits they encouraged still survive on the margins of the left). In any case, my purpose is to circumvent the old debates and to take a fresh look at the ways in which the movement for socialism contributed to social progress in the United States during the Progressive Era (1900–1917) and the New Deal years (1932–1940). I also look at the movement's weaknesses and limitations, and, perhaps more important, how the left might contribute to the next stage in our democratic development. This will require brief examination of the movement from the early years of utopian communities, through the heyday of engagement

with the makers of corporate America, and into the future of our dein-
dustrializing era.

The possibility of a new beginning now exists—if not for a movement
that calls itself socialist then for one embodying the underlying principles
that gave the old movement its impetus. That, ultimately, is what this
book is about.

1

THE FIRST ROUND:
A HOME OF THEIR OWN

I

WHEN MOST AMERICAN HISTORIANS think of socialism, the labor struggles of the late nineteenth century and the early years of the twentieth spring to mind. In these decades industrial capitalism changed the face of the United States. Our modern trade union movement took shape. Industrial workers formed political parties. And the Socialist Party of America come together and grew rapidly. Those years were also a period of raw, violent strikes—and the strikes' more-deadly suppression—a time when new class relations took shape and the political movement for socialism emerged alongside the labor movement as a new entry in the political life of the nation. In America, as in Europe, socialism was a spectre haunting the new corporate ruling class.

But the first wave of socialism was different. It began migrating to America more than a century before Karl Marx's work became available in the United States in the late 1860s. These early utopian socialists, unlike their successors, had little interest in changing society at large. They came, mostly in the early 1800s, as self-contained communities attempting to escape the social fragmentation and the individualist ethos that accompanied the gradual emergence of capitalism at the end of the Middle Ages. This was a defensive and conservative period in socialism's trajectory. It was a response to the breakup of feudal estates and the earliest stages of industrial development in Europe, when the traditional communitarian protections of the old order were under attack and when peasants, thrown off their estates, were left to fend for themselves as individual wage earners bereft of the social support afforded by the old system.

Marx shared the utopians' fierce opposition to the harsh and often brutal conditions of life and work imposed by total dependence on wages. But his attitude toward the new entrepreneurs differed from theirs in one fundamental respect. While the utopians sought to escape capitalism's unrestrained individualism, Marx welcomed the revolutionizing of production that capitalism entailed. To him capitalism was an unprecedented progressive force that was creating the social and material conditions for a post-capitalist society of equality and abundance.

II

Feudal society, of course, had not been idyllic. In feudalism, lords of the manor were, well, lords of the manor. Born to their dominant roles they "naturally" enjoyed superior claims to the surplus created by the labor of serfs and artisans. And, of course, they lorded it over those born to lesser stations. Still, feudal estates upheld the ideals of social responsibility, and utopian communitarianism echoed the more humane aspects of life on the manor. Not surprisingly, therefore, utopian communities were inward-looking and apolitical. They sought to preserve their traditions by erecting barriers between themselves and the new, more dynamic but also cold-hearted, society that surrounded them.

In feudal society private capital had hardly existed. The lord of a manor did not own "his" land or its resources in the modern sense of individual ownership. Instead, as historian E. Harris Harbison has pointed out, "a human chain of holders of rights, from serf through lord of the manor to overlord and king" bound all together in a largely static community. Each person had a fixed relationship to the land, and each was bound to others in a web of traditional duties and obligations. Common ownership coexisted alongside traditional individual rights in the holding and use of productive property. Peasants' rights, either to land on agricultural manors or to the means of their trade in urban guilds, were considered inalienable—they could neither be bought nor sold. These rights might look to us like modern individual property rights—the peasant possessed his house, his garden, and his strips of arable land, and the artisan, likewise, possessed the tools of his trade—but these rights existed only as long as peasant and artisan lived on (and belonged to) the manor. Because individual ownership of land—protected by codified property law—was an anomaly before capitalism undermined feudalism, the peasant could not sell his house or his land, nor the artisan his shop.

Other rights were more obviously communal. Peasants had the right to use parts of the manor's common land for grazing their stock and for gathering their firewood, which was their only fuel for cooking and heating. Artisans had the right to an equal share of the available raw materials, as well as equal opportunities in the carefully protected local markets.

In this society, economic individualism—the private ownership of investable capital—was a radically new idea. Capitalism destroyed established common rights, and as it did, communities were broken up and peasants were thrown off their ancestral estates and left to fend for themselves. Therefore, when utopian socialism appeared in Europe, Harbison tells us, it did so largely as a reactionary defense of traditional communities against the development of the small-scale private ownership that preceded the development of the modern national state. Utopian communities, therefore, were inward-looking and apolitical. And because utopian movements preceded the formation of national states and civil society, religion provided their main social bond, as well as the context for their ideology. Thus Protestant sects, with their new, more egalitarian interpretations of the New Testament, were the basis of early communist societies seeking to create the kingdom of God on earth.

In short, while Marx's followers in the late nineteenth century sought to engage capitalism and to create a society that transcended it, the early socialist communities simply wanted to be left alone. They wanted only to pursue communal agriculture and artisan production, and America was an ideal place for them to do so. America abounded in large tracts of cheap, sparsely populated land, ideal for the establishment of the self-contained societies that utopians desired. And America's principle of religious freedom provided escape from the persecution that radical Protestant sects had endured in the rigid, church-dominated societies of their old countries.

These conditions acted as a magnet for many of Europe's communitarians. Until the mid-nineteenth century, this country's numerous socialist communities came fully formed from Europe. Only after the European movements inspired them did immigrants and converts organize new socialist communities in America. These latter groups became significant by mid-century when the Oneida colony, led by John Humphrey Noyes, and several Fourier and Icarian colonies took root in the context of widespread native religious revivalism, but few prospered and fewer lasted.

III

Even though they suffered discrimination and religious persecution in Europe, many immigrant communities had become wealthy in their native lands. Indeed, after selling their property in Europe, some brought a good deal of money with them. But the social capital these sects brought with them was just as important to their success in the New World. These groups came with the advantage of strongly shared beliefs, high levels of mutual trust, and the experience of working closely together on coordinated projects. In the chaotic, disorganized frontier, where most colonies located, these characteristics initially gave the utopians strengths that the isolated small farmers and artisans of the individualistic frontier lacked. And although the religious colonists established largely subsistence economies, their standards of living were high, and their property well-improved and developed. They were, however, averse to change and bound by tradition. As time went on the rapidly developing world around them caught up and surpassed their level of development. By the mid-1800s, pressures from the larger society—and the opportunities and new technologies it provided—began to draw many utopians away from their own communities and into the world at large.

The first of these transplanted communities, the Ephrata colony, came early, some sixty years before the American Revolution. It was brought from Germany to Pennsylvania in 1713 by its spiritual leader, Conrad Beizel. These radical Christians, with the gospels as their guide, held all things in common and lived a strictly celibate life. Without children to distract them from their daily labors, they worked efficiently and were highly productive. Their high standard of living and well-organized community eventually attracted nearly a thousand more followers from the Old World. Beizel was a strong, inspiring figure who ran Ephrata largely as a one-man show. Since he lived to a very old age the settlement prospered for many years. His successor was less charismatic, and the colony slowly ran down after he died. By the 1850s its property was in the hands of trustees and the community had all but dissolved.

Sixty years later, in 1774, an English import, "Mother" Ann Lee, arrived with a handful of followers. She soon established the first Shaker society, at Watervliet, New York. She died ten years later, but her successors were more talented and fortunate than Beizel's. They founded eleven new Shaker settlements within five years of her death, and by the 1830s there were many more, with a total of some 5,000 members. A. Jacobi, an author who visited four of these and lived for a while in two others, wrote that "in point of order, neatness, regularity and economy," the Shaker colonies were "in advance of all the other societies."

The Shakers, too, were strictly celibate. They were "of such a nature," Jacobi wrote, "as Christ said should be among his true followers." To become a senior member of the church order, one had to surrender all personal property to the "family" (as each separate community was called), but each Shaker family was an autonomous entity. Some were very prosperous, others merely comfortable. A celibate community, however, could maintain itself only by recruitment, and after a generation, as recruiting fell off, the Shakers' numbers dwindled. Toward the end of the twentieth century only one Shaker community remained and it had only two surviving members, both of them very old.

Mother Lee was followed in 1804 by George Rapp, who came to America with 600 adherents to escape severe persecution in Germany.

Rapp bought 5,000 acres of land in eastern Pennsylvania, where he and his flock established a settlement called Harmony. It grew to number some 1,800 souls. Like the Shakers, they, too, were industrious. And, like some other transplanted religious colonies, the Rappites prospered, outgrew their first location, and went west—to a larger tract of land that Rapp bought for them in Indiana.

Another German, Joseph Bimeler, founded the colony of Zoar in Ohio in 1817. Zoar was named after the town to which Lot fled seeking refuge from Sodom. Its articles of association were signed by fifty-three men and 104 women and provided equal political rights. Initially too poor to raise children, the members adopted celibacy so that they could pour all their energies into developing their land and industries. This was not a matter of principle, but "an indispensable matter of economy." At first, as John Humphrey Noyes wrote in his *History of American Socialisms*, "Their little town presented the anomaly of a village without a single child to be seen or heard within its limits." By 1874, however, Zoar's three hundred-odd members had accumulated more than a million dollars worth of property. Prosperity allowed them to give up celibacy—but it also weakened the Zoarites' commitment to communalism. In 1898, well past the heyday of American utopianism, the community divided its assets among its members and dissolved.

The most successful and long-lived of the utopian experiments began in 1846, when yet another German—Christian Metz—brought his flock to Buffalo, New York. Metz and his followers, who called themselves the "society of inspired people," were guided by the New Testament, as interpreted through their spiritual mediums. They had prospered for a hundred years in Germany, but as radical Protestants had been increasingly harassed for their religious beliefs. When the pressure became too great, they came to America to enjoy the religious freedom of the New World.

Metz and his sister, the two primary "mediums," led the society for more than thirty years. During the 1850s their colony swelled to about a thousand members and, like the Rappites, outgrew its first settlement. So Metz and his followers also decided to move west. After buying 25,000 acres of land in Iowa they relocated and changed their name to the

Amana colonies, which from their inception in Iowa constituted the largest and richest utopian community in America. One member was said to have brought $100,000 to it, a huge sum in those days; others contributed as much as $60,000.

Operating under the principle—adopted from the French philosopher St. Simon—of "from each according to abilities, to each according to needs," and handing down skills in the "Old World Tradition—from father to son and from mother to daughter"—Amana's residents established a large, self-contained community of farms, woolen mills, a calico plant, meat shops, cabinet shops, wineries, community kitchens, and many other industries, including household appliances. The colonies lasted in their communal form until 1932, when by a vote of the people they dropped the communal way and, as their current guidebook says, "took the great step into the system of free enterprise that surrounded them." Only then did they separate religious and secular matters. They transferred ownership of homes to individual families, closed up the communal kitchens and dining rooms, auctioned off their commonly held tools, and distributed their garden seeds to individual families. Today, the Amana colonies still exist as seven prosperous villages in Iowa. Proud of their heritage, the colonists are nevertheless very much a part of capitalist America.

The first wave of utopian colonies succeeded for many years because of their religious and social coherence. A second, more secular, wave of communitarian experiments was different. They were open and diverse and were meant to be examples for others to reproduce. And even though none of this secular second wave of utopian colonies survived long enough to establish itself on a sound footing, these later communities not only became better known to contemporaries, but their ideas also had a more lasting impact on later socialist development.

IV

The first of these second-wave communities was established by Robert Owen, a British industrialist who has been widely credited with coining the word *socialist* in 1827. Owen was the most successful of the European utopians in propagating his ideas in America. (John H. Noyes called him the "father of American Socialisms.") Yet his attempt, in 1826, to establish a socialist community at New Harmony, Indiana, collapsed in its first year.

Owen initially gained fame and fortune as a benevolent employer at his textile mill in New Lanark, Scotland. He claimed that his success as a manufacturer was based on the belief that a person's character is shaped by his environment. "Man," Owen wrote, "becomes a wild, ferocious savage, a cannibal, or a highly civilized and benevolent being according to the circumstances in which he may be placed from his birth." At New Lanark, he put this idea to the test by improving the conditions under which his employees worked and lived, and by doing so transformed his workforce, to their benefit as well as his own.

The New Lanark mill that Owen took over was typical of its time. Work was so hard and wages so low that few adult employees could be recruited. Instead, the mill was operated by some 500 children taken from orphanages in Edinburgh. Some were as young as six years old. Working from six in the morning until seven at night, many of the children did not long survive, while many who did grew up stunted or deformed. The village was no better than the mill. Many of its residents fell deeply in debt to the local usurer, or to the tavern-keeper or store-keeper. The village, as described by Owen, was filthy and the inhabitants were a drunken, brutal, and criminal lot.

As resident manager and major stockholder of the mill, Owen had the power to introduce reforms. He started by remodeling the village. First, he banished village merchants who sold inferior goods at exorbitant prices and replaced them with company stores that sold high-quality goods at cost. Then he removed the taverns to the village outskirts, had comfortable new houses built, and cleaned the streets. Next he stopped recruiting pauper children and established model schools for all those remaining in New Lanark. In the mills, he shortened hours of work, increased pay, and abolished all systems of punishment for delinquent workers.

Owen met resistance to this process at every step. Superintendents of different branches of the mill were suspicious, and after years of pitiless exploitation workers had learned to distrust employers. Only in 1807, after President Jefferson imposed an embargo on British cotton in a dispute over trade, and the consequent crisis in the English cotton industry, did Owen find a way to win his workers' confidence. The mills were shut down and there was nothing for the workers to do but oil the machinery, but Owen continued to pay out their wages. Four months later, when the mills reopened, morale was high. Productivity increased substantially, and, since profits also rose, even Owen's stockholders were happy.

Owen was now widely praised, and as his fame spread throughout Europe, he worked out a plan for a more humane capitalism and tried to convince other British capitalists and government leaders that his approach was better for stockholders as well as workers. But when he presented his plan to his business peers and to Britain's religious leaders, they listened politely and ignored his advice. Ever the optimist, Owen simply turned his attention to the New World.

Fortuitously, just as Owen was thinking of moving to America, the Rappites at their Harmony colony in Indiana had decided to move once again, this time back to Pennsylvania. At Harmony they had built a complete new village of some thousand members and they had again prospered. But hostile neighbors and the high incidence of malaria in southern Indiana were too much for them to bear. So they hired Richard Flowers, a prominent member of an English settlement in their vicinity, to find a buyer. For a fee of $5,000 he returned to England and sought out Owen. The timing was perfect. Owen agreed to buy the entire town of Harmony, including all its houses, factories, and mills, and 30,000 acres of land for $150,000. For their part, the Rappites, who had purchased new land on the Ohio River in Pennsylvania, happily built a steamboat and moved in detachments to create yet another colony.

"Out for big game" and with "boundless enthusiasm," as the historian T. D. Seymour Bassett told us, Owen arrived in New York on November 4, 1824. A great public relations man, he stepped off the ship talking "like a presidential candidate to everyone who would listen." For six months he sought out prominent and influential politicians, businessmen, educators, and clergymen. As a wealthy English manufacturer, Owen was allowed in early 1825 to speak twice to members of both Houses of Congress in the chamber of the House of Representatives. President James Monroe, the president-elect, John Quincy Adams, and the justices of the Supreme Court were also present, and later that year, Owen buttonholed the new president, Adams, and gained interviews with his busy Cabinet members. Much encouraged by the "polite expressions of interest and good will" accorded him, Owen misunderstood this "as signs of understanding and approval."

Meanwhile, in the spring of 1825, he closed on the deal to acquire the ready-made material for America's first experiment in secular cooperative association. As the Rappites departed, people who had heard of Owen's venture flocked to the settlement, now renamed New Harmony. Unfortunately, the recruits were a diverse lot who lacked both the ideological glue, the mutual trust, and the experience of working together that allowed New Harmony's previous owners to succeed. Most of Owen's recruits were pioneers from west of the Appalachians, many from nearby villages. These backwoodsmen, as Bassett wrote, "knew how to make a living under frontier conditions," but a speech or two from Robert Owen and a few direct conversations were not enough to teach such rugged individualists the principles of his new social system. On the other hand, the small group of Eastern recruits, while familiar with Owen's ideas, knew little about the reality of frontier living. Unaccustomed to the heavy manual labor required to keep such a settlement running efficiently, these city folk were not of much use in the day-to-day work of New Harmony's farms and factories.

Both groups started out filled with enthusiasm, but within six months the honeymoon had turned sour, and Owen made things worse by departing to proselytize elsewhere after the first month. In his absence the colony suffered from incoherence and quickly split into hostile factions. As the members fell into disarray, productive activity ground almost to a halt. Disagreements were apparent at the first committee elections, and as they developed, crops and stock were neglected while the members quarreled over dwindling supplies. By the time Owen returned five months later, the recruits were living on his capital. He attempted to set things straight, but it was too late. After writing five new constitutions in six months, New Harmony had split into three separate groups. Owen was forced to admit defeat.

Almost twenty years later, in the early 1840s, Albert Brisbane took up where Owen had left off and inspired a more robust movement. Brisbane was the son of a wealthy landowner in Batavia, New York. He had spent the years from 1828 to 1834 studying in Europe. As Bassett told us, Brisbane "sampled and rejected the theories of Hegel and the St. Simonians before he discovered, in 1832, what he had been looking for—Charles Fourier's complete system of social philosophy."

Back in America Brisbane spread Fourier's doctrines, which were a communitarian scheme of liberal reform. First, he Americanized Fourier's ideas by publishing a book of his own, in which, as Basset wrote, Fourierism became the social reform that "claimed to embrace and justify all the partial reforms of the day." In 1842 Brisbane converted Horace Greeley and inaugurated a paid personal column in Greeley's penny daily, the *New York Tribune*. With Greeley's strong backing in the *Tribune*, "associationism" (as Fourierism was commonly called) won the support of New England's leading intellectuals at Brook Farm, a well-known trancendentalist community, as well as the widespread interest and support of other liberal reformers in western New York, Pennsylvania, Ohio, and Wisconsin.

Brisbane's version of Fourier's writings was well adapted to the widespread spirit of reform that swept America in the decades before the Civil War. Between 1842 and 1845, the excitement he created led secular reformers, as well as Universalist and other liberal Christians and millenarian revivalists, to form several dozen Fourier "phalanxes," or colonies. But the phalanxes had deviated in two major ways from Fourier's theories. While Fourier advocated a strictly secular community, Brisbane promoted nondenominational Protestantism—which, in the American context, was a necessity. And while Fourier insisted that phalanxes required heavy initial capitalization, his American followers encouraged experimentation with what Fourier and Brisbane viewed as insufficient resources and preparation.

Brisbane condemned the rapid formation of these phalanxes as false starts and refused to participate in their organization. He worried that they lacked the capital, equipment, and members required by Fourier's system, and his fears were quickly realized. Inexperience and poor planning doomed nearly all the new colonies. Nor was economic insufficiency the only reason for failure. As the breakup of the Wisconsin Phalanx at Ceresco (now Ripon) demonstrated, a colony lacking the shared faith of a strong anti-individualist ideology could not withstand the pressure of mid-nineteenth-century capitalism, even if it was relatively successful. The Ceresco Phalanx was the only Fourier colony that increased in value during its short existence. Yet, the Wisconsin attempt was a social failure. As a member of Ceresco explained, "The love of money and the want of love for Association" proved too strong. When the property became valuable as a result of the members' hard work, they simply voted to sell it, take their profit, and move on.

V

Just about the time the utopian socialist movement in the United States was losing steam, Karl Marx wrote *The Communist Manifesto*. The social ideals that underlay this document were in large part an extension of utopian principles, but Marx's approach to socialism was different. While the religious utopians sought to escape capitalism's wanton individualism and to salvage the best of feudalism's communal social relations, Marx embraced capitalism's democratizing potential despite its dehumanizing aspects. And while the utopians shunned the larger society and attempted to create their own self-sufficient alternatives, Marx saw capitalism as a system that would create the prerequisites of a universally democratic society. Unlike the utopians, who tried to stop the historical clock, Marx saw capitalism as an essential stage in historical development. He sought to achieve socialism by transcending capitalism, not by avoiding it and escaping from society at large. In this sense, his socialism was materialist, while the utopians, who wanted to create their own little worlds outside of history, were simply idealist.

But Marx celebrated capitalism's dynamism with obviously mixed feelings. In the *Manifesto*, he wrote that during capitalism's rule of scarcely one hundred years it had "created more massive and colossal productive forces than have all preceding generations together." In just one century, he wrote, capitalism had subjugated nature, developed machinery, applied chemistry to industry and agriculture, created steam navigation, built railways, canals, and electric telegraphs, and cleared whole continents for cultivation. "What earlier century," Marx asked, "had even a presentiment that such productive forces slumbered in the lap of social labor?"

In *Capital* (his major work) Marx wrote that capitalism's "historic mission is the ruthless development of the productivity of human labor." But as greater productivity led to the growth of capital, constantly growing investment, and with it the expansion of the wage-earning class, the system would eventually reach a point where further increases of investment would "enable the entire nation to accomplish its total production in a shorter time." At that point, with a declining amount of labor needed to produce all of society's goods, the total number of gainfully employed workers would also diminish. Then, Marx believed, unemployment would eventually "put the majority of the population on the shelf" and this would cause a revolution.

Of course, Marx could not foresee the development of vastly expanded state-supported military production or the forced expansion of consumption that have combined to prevent unemployment on the scale that he envisioned. But in any case, he did understand that by constantly increasing productivity, capitalists were creating the basis for an equality of abundance—not just for the handfuls of people living in isolated utopian communities, but for the entire society.

None of this meant that capitalists were revolutionizing production for the common good. Though they were putting "an end to all feudal, patriarchal, idyllic relations" and "pitilessly [tearing] asunder the motley feudal ties that bound man to his 'natural superiors,'" they did so without providing any new bonds between people other than "naked self-interest [and] callous cash payment." In their rush to increase productivity, Marx wrote, capitalists were "drowning the most heavenly ecstacies of religious fervor, of chivalrous enthusiasm, of philistine sentimentalism in the icy water of egotistical calculation." And by converting "personal worth into exchange value" and eradicating the "numberless inalienable chartered freedoms" of pre-capitalist society, capitalists were setting up "that single unconscionable freedom—Free Trade."

All previous ruling classes, Marx wrote, strove to conserve the old modes of production in unaltered form. But capitalism could not exist without revolutionizing its instruments of production, and, thereby, the relations of production—and along with them all the social relations of society. Thus, Marx wrote in the *Manifesto*, the capitalist era is distinguished from all earlier ones in that it causes incessant disturbance of all traditional social relations and everlasting uncertainty. "All fixed, fast-frozen relations, with their train of ancient and venerable prejudices and opinions are swept away, all new-formed ones become antiquated before they can ossify. All that is solid melts into air, all that is holy is profaned." In this process, Marx saw capitalism stripping the halos from "every occupation hitherto honored and looked up to with reverent awe" and converting everyone, even "the physician, the lawyer, the priest, the man of science into its paid wage laborers."

Even so, this awesome process was to be humanity's salvation. For as capital increases, so in the same proportion does the modern working class. And by reducing everyone in every occupation and skill to dependency on wages, capitalism also creates and prepares a class that is capable of governing itself, and all of society, on a more humane basis. In capitalist society, people who depend on wages for their livelihood—"who must sell themselves piecemeal"—are like every other article of commerce in one respect: They are simply commodities. Therefore, they are "constantly exposed to all the vicissitudes of competition" and to all the fluctuations of the market. But they are a special kind of commodity—one that can act on its own behalf. So, Marx observed, as this new class develops, it begins to defend itself. Its members learn how to fight for their interests, to create their own rights, and to modify capitalism's ruthless tendencies. And because they gradually come to encompass all the knowledge and skills required to run society, working people also become capable of running society without the help of a ruling class.

In the early stages of industrialization, Marx wrote, workers resisted the process of proletarianization as individuals by slacking off. Then they resisted together as workers of a single factory and they broke machinery. Next they reacted as operatives in a single trade and formed trade unions. And over time, as industry developed and industrial cities were created, the working class not only increased in number, but also became concentrated in greater masses. This enabled workers to see the potential power in political action. From this process, trade union federations and labor parties emerged. And thus the workers, educated in organization and politics, were being forged into a potential ruling class—or so Marx asserted.

As this process implies, socialism becomes possible only when two conditions are met. First, capitalist development must reach the stage where the rational use of industry would make it possible to produce all the necessities of life for the nation's entire population. And second, working people must come together in a political movement that encompasses all the technical skills, organizational experience, and political knowledge required to manage and direct the life of the nation. According to Marx, capitalism is naturally and incessantly moving in this direction. And because of this, socialism is no longer just a good idea—a utopian wish—but is grounded in the possibilities provided by historical development.

But what exactly is socialism? Marx wrote about its possibility, but because he believed that the future belonged to those who would make it, he himself made few efforts to produce blueprints for the future. He did, however, suggest some general socialist principles inherent in his analysis of capitalist development. Socialism, he implied, required a fully developed civil society—a society of citizen associations that bring people together to participate in the process of making their own social lives and history. And he suggested that in socialism the state's coercive (police) power would be reduced to the minimum required for the administration of things that cannot be coordinated locally or by informal associations—such things as the establishment of uniform standards, the conservation and distribution of limited natural resources, and the protection of civil rights and liberties through a judicial system.

In short, for Marx socialism was to represent the fulfillment of the democratic promise inherent in capitalist development. Its specific nature would be determined by those involved in the political process of transcending market relations as the ruling principle of society. How that is done would depend on the culture of each country and the nature of each national movement. Living people make history, Marx wrote, but they do so within the parameters of their own experience. And while the will to make your own history is essential for any actor on the social scene, it is not enough. The experience of the utopians in America bears this out only too well. Many of them, no doubt, were unconcerned with changing the world. They wanted only to live their own lives in accord with their principles, and for that they should be admired. Still, trying to stop the tide of history was impossible and all of their efforts came to the same end. But Marx and his followers had a more ambitious goal, and the end remains unknown, as we'll see in the next chapters.

2
BIRTH PANGS:
SOCIALISM ENTERS
THE REAL WORLD

THE MODERN SOCIALIST MOVEMENT BEGAN its development in America during the post–Civil War decades. Inspired by
Karl Marx's writings and the first International Workingmen's party, the
early American movement consisted largely of immigrant German
skilled workers. Like the utopians of pre–Civil War years, these new socialists were acutely aware of their isolation from the mainstream of
American political life. But unlike their predecessors, they strove to assimilate themselves and their movement into the world around them. It
wasn't easy. In Europe, in the late 1850s, the modern socialist movement
was beginning, while in America the fitful process of creating an Americanized party lagged behind. Not until the turn of the new century did a
thoroughly American amalgam of populism, Christian socialism, and
trade unionism come together to form the Socialist Party of America.

I

When trade union leaders in Britain and on the Continent formed an international association to link up their national movements, Marx had already written the *Communist Manifesto*. But he was not among the

17

association's initiators. As his biographer Franz Mehring wrote, Marx, who estimated the importance of his intellectual work too highly to engage in "frivolous or hopeless organizational efforts," did not normally participate in such activities. Nonetheless, when a French trade unionist asked Marx to represent the German workers at the founding meeting of the new International, he agreed. He did so, he explained to Engels, because he saw evidence of a working-class revival, and, as he wrote to his friend Josef Weydemeyer, because "this time . . . there is the possibility of doing some real good."

That being so, Mehring wrote, Marx "considered it his primary duty to guide [the new organization] along the right lines." The initiators seemed to agree. They asked him to write the inaugural address for the International Workingmen's Association founding meeting in September 1864. Marx did so and wrote a speech that served as a general statement of the International's historic purpose—and that secured his intellectual leadership of the new movement.

Word of the new International soon reached American shores, and a wide spectrum of American radicals and reformers were exposed to Marx's ideas for the first time. As in Europe, so in America the International brought together veterans of nineteenth-century worker, liberal, and utopian movements, many of whom had their own—often longheld—visions of a more humane and egalitarian society. They accepted Marx's grandiose ideas about building a political movement for socialism, but most of the International's recruits came because they needed help defending themselves against the harsh reality of industrial capitalism. Some were motivated by the financial panic of 1857 and the massive unemployment and misery it had left in its wake. Others were inspired by the American Civil War, which, with its promise to end slavery in America, had become a rallying point for labor in Britain and on the Continent. Still others simply saw this as a way to realize a dream of forming a workers movement that would unite workers across national lines.

In the minds of the American radicals and socialists, of course, the Civil War was uppermost. Many of them saw it not simply as a fight against slavery, but also as a fulfillment of the promise of the American Revolution, and as a benefit to all mankind. As Harriet Beecher Stowe (author of the classic anti-slavery tract, *Uncle Tom's Cabin*), affirmed, this was a "war for the rights of the working class of society as against the usurpation of privileged aristocracies." That, she wrote, is why the War Between the States—"like a shaft of light on judgment day"—had divided people, both in Europe and America, "between right and left." On the right were the "privileged classes, nobles, princes, bankers and great manufacturers." On the left, were "the common working classes of Europe—all [who] toil and sweat, and are oppressed." European workers, especially those in Britain, had fought successfully to prevent their governments from aiding the Confederacy. They did so, Stowe wrote, "because they knew that our victory [against slavery] was to be their victory."

At the 1864 conference in London, delegates took special note of the American war. They approved a letter that Marx had drafted congratulating the American people on reelecting President Lincoln and affirming that slavery's abolition would benefit all working people. The delegates also condemned Russia's brutal suppression of the Polish patriots' struggle for independence and called on the leading European powers to help the Polish people liberate themselves from the tsar.

Initially, in Europe, the press treated the London meeting and the formation of the International as a joke. But, in his *History of Socialism in the United States,* Morris Hillquit wrote that this attitude changed as the new organization gained wide support among workers. Soon a frightened European bourgeoisie was exaggerating the International's strength and calling it a "great European menace," intent on instigating an immediate political revolution. Every labor struggle and political event in the years immediately following the London conference, Hillquit tells us, was portrayed by the press as part of a Communist conspiracy against the status quo.

In the United States, however, nothing like this happened. The International's American branch was all but ignored by those in power. After all, the American sections never reached beyond the outer margins of mainstream society. Native-born, or even English-speaking, members were rare. The first group to affiliate with the International's American branch was the Communist Club of New York, a small organization of recent German immigrants, most likely refugees from the failed 1848 revolution. These Communists became Section One of the American branch in 1869. In rapid succession seven more groups joined, but only one of them—a club of Irish radicals—had English as its first language. Four sections were German, one was French, and one Czech.

In the next few years, thirty-odd new sections were admitted to the International's American branch. Of these, Section 12, an organization of native-born Americans, was admitted in 1871. Its two most prominent members were Victoria Woodhull and her sister, Tennessee Claflin. Woodhull and Claflin were wealthy early feminists. They amazed Wall Street by founding their own stock brokerage firm—with the help of railroad magnate Cornelius Vanderbilt, who was infatuated with the vivacious Claflin. These "Bewitching Brokers of Wall Street," as they were called in the press, also published a newspaper, *Woodhull and Claflin's Weekly.* In it they published interviews with Marx and English translations of his writings, including the *Communist Manifesto*—and they scandalized America by advocating free love.

Woodhull, the more intellectual sister, was a strong advocate of women's rights. The first woman to testify in favor of women's suffrage before a congressional committee, she also supported proportional representation, the breakup of monopolies, low interest rates, environmental conservation, an income tax, public education, and the eight-hour workday. When the sisters joined the International, their *Weekly* became Section 12's official organ, and a major voice of the International. But because of their social views, it also became a major source of dissension, especially among several sections of socially conservative European immigrant workingmen.

Both in Europe and in the United States, the first International had a stormy, faction-riddled history. Friedrich Sorge, the leading figure of the American branch, complained that "reformers of every station and species, of every type and shade" signed up. These included money reformers, land reformers, language reformers, and tax reformers, most of whom joined the American-born sections in the hope of winning converts to their particular cause. These diversions were bad enough, but the most debilitating split was that between socialists and anarchists.

Like nineteenth-century reformers in general, anarchists came in many varieties. Most shared with socialists the belief that human society can reach its highest level of development in this world, or—in religious terms—that we can achieve the kingdom of god on earth. They also shared with socialists the goal of a classless society in which the coercive power of the state is eliminated. But, like some utopian socialists before them, the anarchists were implacably hostile to participation in capitalist institutions, especially the state. Believing that amelioration of capitalist oppressions only helped stabilize the hated system, anarchists shunned— in principle, if not always in practice—any advocacy of reform. For the same reason, they also generally opposed working within the mainstream of the trade union movement, preferring instead to organize their own separate, or dual, unions. And they viewed running candidates for office with special scorn—unless it was done simply to gain a platform for educating the public about the evils of capitalism.

These principles, and the dilemma in which it placed anarchists seeking broad support, were well articulated by Albert Parsons, a Chicago anarchist and—in 1886—one of the martyrs to his cause. While in jail awaiting execution for a crime he did not commit, Parsons explained, in an autobiography written as a last testament, the theory underlying the anarchists' call to arms. The state with its "men-made" laws, he wrote, were simply tools of capitalists, whose government "disinherits and enslaves the governed." Natural law, on the other hand, "is liberty." The laws that legalize capital stand and fall together with the state. They are twins, Parsons insisted, while "The liberty of labor makes the state not only unnecessary, but impossible." Thus, "When the people—the whole people—become the state—that is, participate equally in governing themselves—the state of necessity ceases to exist." Then what? *"Leaders, natural leaders, take the place of the overthrown rulers."*

Marx strongly opposed these views. In an interview in *Woodhull and Claflin's Weekly*, he argued that the anarchists' abstention from electoral activity and trade unions was elitist and anti-democratic. Workers spontaneously fought both to organize unions and for the right to vote, but anarchists arrogantly denigrated such activity. By thus divorcing themselves and their followers from the world of their supposed comrades, Marx argued, the anarchists were reverting to something like the utopian communitarians' self-imposed isolation. Furthermore, Marx charged that anarchists' hostility to "government" betrayed a simplistic understanding of the state. True, capitalists created the modern state, as well as the system of laws necessary for their own protection and success. But when capitalists overwhelmed feudal society they necessarily abolished hereditary rule and embraced the universal principles of equality under the law and individual freedom within the law for all citizens. Socialism would make possible the full attainment of these goals.

Indeed, Marx envisioned the universal premises concealed in the concept of the modern state as the basis of a socialist society in which the working class itself would become universal. In the *Manifesto,* for example, he had written that the "lower strata of the middle class—the small tradespeople, shopkeepers, handicraftsmen and peasants"—would all "sink gradually into the proletariat." They will suffer this fate partly by being "swamped in the competition with large capitalists, [and] partly [as] their specialized skills are rendered worthless by new means of production." Thus, "the proletariat is recruited from all classes of the population" as those in all walks of life become dependent on wages or salaries for their livelihood. The eventual result of this process is a universal class, not one in which skills would disappear, as Marx seems to suggest, but universal in the sense of encompassing all the skills and knowledge needed to run society. And this class is (or will be) the basis of a future classless society in which the state, which now exists to mediate class conflicts, will lose its coercive role and be transformed into decentralized associations of citizens charged with the administration of necessary functions.

II

By the time of the Hague Congress in 1873—only nine years after the International's founding—the party was deeply divided between anarchists and socialists. In Europe the disputes were constant and the anarchists strong, so to prevent the International from falling into the hands of its anarchist wing, Marx and his allies decided to relocate the General Council from London to New York. He rationalized this move by noting, accurately but disingenuously, that with half a million immigrants going to America yearly, the country was "preeminently becoming the land of the workers." The International, he said, must therefore "strike deep roots in this soil upon which the workers are supreme." The American branch of the International, however, was not in much better shape than the European. Two years after the move to America—irretrievably split into hostile factions and stagnating—the first International threw in the towel.

III

The following year, 1876, an American-based socialist movement had its shaky birth in Newark, New Jersey. This new grouping, the Socialist Labor Party, brought together veterans of the dead International, former socialist members of the National Labor Union, and various random radicals. Like the International, the new party was made up largely of recent immigrants. Indeed, only 10 percent of the SLP's members in its early years were American-born, according to SLP leader Morris Hillquit. In these circumstances, he explained, the SLP "realized the hopelessness of [trying] to effect radical social and economic changes in this country"— so, initially, they opted to become a primarily educational organization. Their first priority, Hillquit wrote, was to create a movement of native-born workers and citizens—and, thereby, to "Americanize" socialism. This remained the party's priority until the end of the century.

Yet despite the SLP's marginality, participation in American civic reality moved it fitfully toward the electoral arena. As in everything else, the membership was divided on how this should be done. American-born members, and some former followers of Marx's nemesis, Ferdinand Lassalle, advocated running their own token candidates as a strictly educational activity. Others objected that the party was too weak to make a respectable showing on its own and that few people would be educated by such an effort. Instead, they advocated either abstention from politics or cooperation with other reform parties in an "endeavor to infuse into the latter as much of the doctrine of socialism as possible."

Along these latter lines, the SLP's most noteworthy effort occurred in 1886 when the party supported Henry George's candidacy for mayor of New York City. George was the author of the wildly popular *Progress and Poverty*, a book that blamed the persistence of desperate poverty alongside increasing wealth on the private ownership of land and natural resources. As long as vacant land remained privately owned, George argued, only the wealthy would be able to pay the high rent required to engage in commerce or industry. Under such circumstances, the poor would have no choice but to sell their labor for whatever the capitalists or landlords were willing to pay, and poverty would continue to increase alongside the increase in wealth. To end this contradiction, George advocated a single, confiscatory tax on privately held unused land. This, he believed, would prevent speculation and encourage landowners to invest in development. In addition, he claimed, if unused land were free to all, even those with little or no capital could support themselves by subsistence farming or by small-scale artisan pursuits.

George's book struck a chord among working people, especially in New York. In 1886, the United Labor Party urged him to be its candidate for mayor. He was tempted, but wanted evidence of substantial support before he would agree to run. His condition was that the ULP secure 30,000 signatures on a petition pledging to support him. When the goal was easily surpassed, George accepted the ULP nomination.

The SLP had the usual sectarian disdain for radicals that shared only some of its principles, but they decided to support him because his campaign was a movement of labor against capital. They did so, however, without soft-pedaling their differences. During the campaign the party openly declared that it supported George "not on account of his single-tax theory, but in spite of it." And true to their intentions, they attempted to "infuse" George's campaign with their own ideas and program. George ignored them even while he championed pro-worker factory and labor legislation and a demand for greenback-style currency inflation. Still he campaigned largely on his single-tax proposal.

As the outsider in a three-way race George did amazingly well. He came in second, behind Democrat Abram S. Hewitt, a well-known philanthropist, and he easily surpassed Republican Theodore Roosevelt, then still a young unknown. With 68,000 votes, George trailed Hewitt by 22,000 and led Roosevelt by 8,000. For labor, the election appeared to be a great success, but it was George's victory, not the labor party's or the SLP's, and for George, one shot was enough. The next year he broke with the SLP, abandoned the ULP, and moved back to the Democratic Party.

For its part, the SLP benefited little from the experience of supporting George and turned to its alternative tactic, that of running its own candidate. In 1888 the party ran a purely "education campaign" with its own slate for governor of New York. The results were even worse. In a statewide race the party polled fewer than 3,000 votes, thereby confirming the fears of those in the party who opposed such ventures.

These tactical disagreements aside, the SLP, like the International, was almost equally divided between its political and anarchist wings. The party's fleeting success in the George campaign, however, followed by the disaster of its 1888 campaign two years later, weakened the party's anarchist wing in the East. Meanwhile, in Chicago, where the anarchists had greater strength, the 1886 Haymarket bombing and the subsequent execution of innocent anarchist leaders proved to be the anarchists' undoing.

The Chicago anarchists were initially adamant in their refusal to participate in any movements for reform. In this stance they were influenced by Johann Most, who, after his arrival in the United States from England in 1882, opposed participation in trade unions and agitation for shorter hours of work, higher wages, or better working conditions. Such things, Most and his followers believed, were mere sops to workers that only bound them more firmly to the capitalist system. His solution to the brutality of industrial capitalism was simple—direct action in the form of individual acts of terrorism. Anarchists saw this as a defense against the cruelty of capitalists. Not surprisingly, few working people agreed.

Anarchist leader Albert Parsons and his close associates, however, were more pragmatic than Most. They agreed that political action was futile, but they believed firmly in trade unions as an arena of struggle. Indeed, along with the later syndicalists, they viewed unions as the workers' instrument for the destruction of capitalism, and also as the social and organizational nucleus for the formation of a new society. And while they shared Most's theoretical aversion to immediate demands, they saw things differently when forced to choose between supporting reforms or suffering estrangement from the mass of working people. Thus, in his autobiography Parsons rationalized the Chicago anarchists' decision to support the struggle for the eight-hour day on the grounds that "it was a class movement against domination" and, therefore, "historical, and evolutionary, and necessary." The more pressing reason for choosing not "to stand aloof," however, was that they did not want to be "misunderstood by [their] fellow workers."

Having made the decision to participate in the eight-hour movement, Parsons wrote, "we gave it all the aid and comfort in our power." And, indeed, Parsons's and his associates' consistent agitation for the eight-hour day gained them substantial support among Chicago unions. By 1886, when the movement for an eight-hour day was at its peak, the Chicago anarchists had become the dominant force within the city's Central Labor Union, which included Chicago's seven largest locals among its twenty-two member unions.

Within the CLU, however, anarchists not only advocated reforms, but also put forward their ideas about armed resistance to capitalism. In October 1885, for example, August Spies (along with Parsons, one of Chicago's two leading anarchists) had urged the Central Labor Union in his Germanic English, to "call upon the wage-earning class to arm itself in order to be able to put forth against their exploiters such an argument which alone can be effective: Violence." And when Spies wrote a circular calling for support of a meeting to protest a deadly police attack the day before on a group of strikers at the McCormick works, he called on the workers to "arm" themselves and "rise in [their] might."

On the evening of May 4, 1886, the protest meeting was held at the Haymarket—a popular meeting site on the city's West Side. Despite the inflammatory rhetoric of Spies's flyers, the rally was entirely peaceful. Albert Parsons brought his wife and two young children to hear his speech. The mayor came to observe, and after concluding that "nothing had occurred yet or looked likely to occur to require interference," he departed at ten o'clock, along with most of the audience, and instructed the police chief to let the meeting proceed.

Instead, as soon as the mayor was gone, the police began to break up the meeting. But as they moved in someone threw a dynamite bomb into their ranks. The explosion killed one officer outright and fatally wounded six more. The police immediately opened fire, killing an unknown number of workers and wounding almost two hundred others. The bomber was never identified, but the police and city administration saw an opportunity to destroy the local anarchist movement. Parsons, Spies, and six of their comrades were charged with provoking the attack.

The eight anarchists were tried for murder in an atmosphere of hysteria created by the city's leading newspapers. At the trial, the judge's handpicked jury openly expressed hostility to the radicals. And while no prosecution witnesses could link the defendants to the bombing, and a police captain was caught lying on the stand, all eight of the anarchists were convicted. Seven of them were sentenced to death and four were executed before a new Illinois governor, Peter J. Altgeld, pardoned the rest in an unprecedented and politically costly act of decency.

The Haymarket defendants were clearly innocent, but their rhetoric and their refusal to participate in the electoral arena, despite the growing importance of the state as an arena of social action, fatally limited their ability to have a modifying influence on the raw power exercised by government on behalf of capital. The prosecutors, of course, used this rhetoric in the trial to inflame public opinion against them. In any case, the trial and executions were a blow to the anarchists from which they never recovered.

Socialists, of course, had long argued against the anarchists' ideas. As Schlomo Aveneri pointed out in *The Social and Political Thought of Karl Marx*, Marx charged that both the tactics and ideology of Michael Bakunin and other anarchists led in a totalitarian direction. Fearing the impact of their methods and theory on a future society, Marx argued that a revolutionary movement based on terror, intimidation, and blackmail would ultimately produce a society based on these same methods. In other words, far from the ends justifying the means, the means would more likely determine the ends.

In any case, the anarchists' rhetoric, even though not acted upon, contributed to the hysteria created by the Haymarket bombing—and to making the anarchists pariahs in the eyes of trade unionists and the general public. "While the anarchists disclaimed responsibility for the particular act of throwing the fatal bomb," Hillquit wrote in his history of American socialism, the deed "was in accord with the methods of violence countenanced by them." As a result, he continued, "whatever support organized labor had [previously] given to the movement was now rapidly withdrawn."

But while the Haymarket affair may be the watershed event in anarchism's trajectory as a popular movement in America, the event was not the underlying cause of the movement's ultimate decline. Anarchism, after all, was a cry for freedom more in tune with small-scale competitive capitalism and the idea of the open frontier, than a movement that could effectively influence the course of a society dominated by quasi-monopoly corporations and government bureaucracy.

In a developed capitalist society such as ours, freedom can be achieved only through participation in organizations that working people have developed to limit and control the power of unrestrained capital. That means trade unions and intelligent participation in the electoral arena. Even so, when the left fails to create viable movements that offer a place in which to act on the left's own behalf, anarchist ideas and groups have had a lingering appeal, especially to newly radicalized young people. In the 1880s, however, Haymarket did clear the path for the propaganda of socialism, or so Hillquit claimed. And as the anarchists were shunned by labor, the SLP, shorn of its anarchist wing, quickly took advantage of the opportunity to increase its appeal among workingmen. New sections of the party were organized, extensive lecture tours were arranged, and new party newspapers, mostly in German, were established.

IV

But there were still divisions in the SLP that prevented it from participating in a broader movement. Daniel DeLeon, the party's leader, was an uncompromising divisive sectarian who believed in dual unionism. Morris Hillquit, on the other hand, sought to broaden the movement and believed strongly in working within the mainstream unions. It was he, rather than DeLeon, who would lead many of his fellow SLPers into the promised land.

Hillquit was an immigrant and the son of progressive German-speaking Jews. Born Moishe Hillkowitz in Riga, Latvia, he came to America in his late teens, in 1869, probably to escape being drafted into the tsar's army. His parents were factory owners in Latvia and were among the first generation of Eastern European Jews whose contacts with Western ideas induced them to reject the traditions of the ghetto. They made sure that Moishe was well-educated. And, according to Hillquit's biographer, Norma Fain Pratt, they instilled in him the ambition to become a lawyer or an academic, in the hope of assimilating into the broader gentile community.

Hillquit's earliest encounters in New York were with the young Russian-Jewish radicals on New York's Lower East Side, among whom anarchism was still prevalent. He rejected their ideas, later explaining that while anarchism "made a special appeal to the Russian mind, largely because of the seemingly hopeless political condition of [czarist] Russia," such ideas were inappropriate for the New World. Instead, seeking "realistic and practical programs," he joined the SLP in 1887, a year after he came to America, and stayed there until 1899. Then he split with SLP leader DeLeon over the issue of dual unionism and—claiming the mantle of authenticity—formed a separate Socialist Labor Party that would later merge with others to realize his dream.

V

An earlier offshoot from the SLP had been led by Victor Berger of Milwaukee. Like most early socialists, Berger had joined the party soon after he arrived in America, but he quit just about when Hillquit joined. Berger was also a German-speaking immigrant whose parents were assimilated Jews. He received a classical education in Vienna and Budapest, but in 1878, at the age of eighteen, he left the university in Budapest and came to America to escape the draft. A year later, his parents and siblings followed and settled in Bridgeport, Connecticut, where the elder Berger took up farming and later became a moderately successful manufacturer. Victor, however, struck out on his own and in 1881 found his way to Milwaukee, a stronghold of socialists who had come from Germany to America in two waves. The first wave came after the revolution of 1848 collapsed. Many of this group were utopian socialists. The second wave came after Chancellor Bismarck enacted a series of anti-socialist laws in Germany in 1878. These Germans tended to be followers of Marx and believers in "scientific" socialism.

Berger taught school in Milwaukee for eleven years, nine of them in the public schools. He was primarily a German teacher, but he also taught history, political science, and the physical sciences. The more active he became in local politics, however, the less fulfilled he felt as a teacher. In 1892, with widened horizons, he quit teaching to become editor and publisher of a weekly German newspaper, the *Wisconsin Vorwaerts*. The paper, which prospered under his guidance, soon became one of the most important socialist dailies in America. And Berger emerged as a leader of the Milwaukee socialists.

Unlike most socialists of his day, Berger believed strongly in cooperation with other reformers in order to create an effective political force, and in 1883 he quit the party. As editor of the newspaper he reached a relatively wide public and became the dominant force in the city's *Socialistischen Verein (Socialist Union)*. Under his leadership the *Socialistischen Verein* worked closely with the Milwaukee Federated Trades Council and the Peoples (Populist) Party. Yet Berger maintained cordial relations with the SLP despite his disagreements with it and frequently published reports of party activities in the *Vorwaerts*.

Berger participated in the Populist Party until his impatience with its emphasis on the free coinage of silver—and its fusion with the Democrats in support of William Jennings Bryan's presidential candidacy—became too great for him to bear. The break with the Populists left Berger—and the *Socialistischen Verein*—momentarily adrift. But in early 1897 he found new allies and formed a diverse Social Democratic coalition.

Outside of Wisconsin the Social Democrats' scattered ranks were held together largely by publications such as J. A. Wayland's *The Coming Nation* and later by the *Appeal to Reason*—which began publishing in Girard, Kansas, in 1895 and soon had many times more readers than any previous (or subsequent) American socialist publication. Various utopian socialist colonies, such as the Ruskin Cooperative Colony of Tennessee, also affiliated with this new movement. And, perhaps most important, Eugene Victor Debs announced, in January 1897, that he had become a socialist and that he, along with the remnants of the American Railway Union, were joining the Social Democrats.

VI

Debs's conversion to socialism symbolized the movement's Americanization. A genuine popular hero, Debs had gained national stature by organizing the American Railway Union and by his role in the 1894 Pullman strike. As Elizabeth Sanders pointed out in *Roots of Reform,* he represented a merger of populism and socialism and was seen by millions of Americans, socialist and non-socialist alike, as the personification of everything good that America stood for. Not surprisingly, therefore, in the years following his conversion the movement he led came to be known as Debsian socialism.

Debs was the son of a well-to-do merchant and grew up in Terre Haute, Indiana, at a time when class lines in that small city were still fluid—at least for native-born Americans of Northern European ancestry. At fourteen he quit school and went to work on the locally owned railroad, where he quickly became a locomotive fireman, then one of the highest skilled and best-paying jobs on the road. But his luck was short-lived. In 1874, the depression that had begun the previous year claimed his job, and a year of fruitless traveling in search of work followed. Unable to find anything acceptable, Debs came back to Terre Haute, where his father had arranged for him to be taken on as an accounting clerk for a family friend, Herman Hulman, the city's largest wholesale grocer.

Debs enjoyed his work at Hulman's and was well liked by his employer, but the romance of the railroad still claimed his heart. So, early the next year, when the founder of the then-two-year-old Brotherhood of Railway Firemen called Debs and nine other railroad men together to organize a Terre Haute Firemen's lodge, Debs signed up and quickly became one of its leaders. Spending his days working at Hulman's, Debs now gave his nights to the Brotherhood. It was the beginning of his commitment to labor, the first step on the path he was to follow the rest of his life.

Elected recording secretary in his first year, Debs was continually re-elected for eight years, and then, in 1883, was chosen to be the lodge's top officer—its "master workman." By 1879 he had also become associate editor of the *Locomotive Firemen's Magazine,* published in Terre Haute, and soon thereafter he was elected editor—a post he retained until he quit the Brotherhood to organize the American Railway Union in 1893.

Like most of the men in the Brotherhood, Debs at first identified the workers' interests completely with that of the railroad owners. In his first editorial for the *Firemen's Magazine*, for example, he wrote that firemen were duty-bound "to give the railway corporations a class of sober and industrious men" who would serve "the direct interest of their employers." Firemen, he argued, should be "men who will save fuel and oil, and protect the machinery and other property entrusted to their care." In other words, he concluded, "our highest aim" should be to "give our superior officers trained and intelligent labor."

As this view suggests, Debs did not start out as a rebel, but very much as a man of his time and place. His initial belief in the social harmony that he saw in the Terre Haute of his youth was based on the American ideals of democracy and equality—and his commitment to these ideals played a large part in his powerful appeal to working people in all ranks of life. But not even Terre Haute was idyllic. Like every other city, it had its rich and its poor, its capitalists and its workers, as well as a middle class of artisans and small businessmen.

Still, as Nick Salvatore explained in *Eugene V. Debs, Citizen and Socialist,* the industrial and social structure of the city in 1877 encouraged the belief in social harmony. With few exceptions, Salvatore pointed out, no industry in Terre Haute averaged more than thirty employees per shop, and most shops employed less than twenty. Even the locally owned Vandalia Railroad, where Debs had his first job, maintained a personalized work atmosphere. Despite its 1,300 employees, William McKeen—the owner of the line—hired his workers' friends and family members to fill vacancies whenever he could. And the company's top managers personally interviewed applicants for new positions. Then, too, the city's relatively homogenous ethnic composition reinforced a sense of community. Fully 85 percent of Terre Haute's 26,000 inhabitants in 1877 were American-born—an exceptionally high percentage for industrial towns of the period—and the largest percentage of immigrants were from Germany, Ireland, or England.

The great railroad strikes in the summer of 1877, however, challenged Debs's belief in "good citizenship" and social harmony. Especially on the large railroads, such as the Pennsylvania, that summer's strikes and riots involved engineers, firemen, and brakemen, as well as yard and track workers, all of them desperate to restore the wages that had been cut several times over four years of depression. As Robert V. Bruce wrote in *1877: Year of Violence*, discontent had been rumbling up and down the lines of the Eastern roads for months when a spontaneous strike in Martinsburg, West Virginia, set off a conflagration that sent waves of arson, rioting, and looting to Pittsburgh, Buffalo, Baltimore, Chicago, and many smaller cities and towns. During these riots tens of thousands of railroad and factory workers poured out of their shops to attack company property, the police, and anyone or anything else that threatened to stifle the expression of their anger.

In Pittsburgh, where almost the entire city supported the workers, 104 locomotives, 2,154 railroad cars, several roundhouses and sheds, the depot, and other railroad property were burned to the ground. So, too, were the city's grain elevator and other related buildings. When the elevator was under attack, an official of the company implored the strikers to spare it since it was not railroad property. But a striker yelled out: "It's owned by a damned monopoly—let it burn." And it did. The *Pittsburgh*

Leader quoted a striker as saying that even if "so-called law and order" should beat them down, "we would at least have our revenge on the men who have coined our sweat and muscle into millions for themselves while leaving [us] to starve." And a militiaman reported that among the strikers he could find but a single spirit and purpose, namely "that they were justified in resorting to any means to break the power of the corporations."

Nor was that purpose unique to the workers. Local militias, called out to control the strikers, sympathized with them and sometimes joined them instead. Before the National Guard restored order, millions of dollars worth of railroad property had been destroyed, and many workers killed.

In Terre Haute, the situation was substantially different. The local lodges of firemen and brakemen had voted to strike, but only if a request they had made for a 15 percent wage increase was not met within twenty-four hours. McKeen failed to respond, and the Vandalia line was shut down, but the process was entirely peaceful. McKeen simply canceled all trains originating in Terre Haute, except mail trains, and told the men that before agreeing to a settlement he would wait to see what the major Eastern lines settled for. The workers responded meekly, affirming their belief that he would do all he could to comply with their wishes. Expressing "full faith" in McKeen's "honor and integrity," they blamed the major Eastern lines for the wage cuts, not their hometown owner. As one strike leader argued, they were not warring with McKeen or the other local businessmen (with whom they still shared a strong sense of community) but with "that gigantic Eastern monopoly, the Pennsylvania road."

Ultimately, however, McKeen, in Salvatore's words, "demonstrated the limits of harmony and community as applied to working people" and called in the U.S. Army. The men peaceably relinquished their control of the depot and that was the end of the strike in Terre Haute.

In all this, Debs stood by and remained silent. Still within traditional bounds, he believed firmly in the ideal that government, as a neutral force, would balance the interests of capitalists and workers fairly. The experience of the strike helped to change that view. It initiated a process of growing class consciousness that was to flower over the next several years. While Debs was not yet prepared to join any reform groups, he was ready to act on his democratic beliefs. Thus, for example, in 1880, when Terre Haute's Occidental Literary Society (of which he was then president) refused to sponsor a talk by the suffragist Susan B. Anthony, he found her a hall and personally sponsored her talk.

In politics, despite being closely in accord with the demands of the Greenback-Labor Party, Debs remained a loyal Democrat. In 1879, he ran as a Democrat for Terre Haute city clerk and won handily. His strongest support came from two of the city's labor wards and from its one heavily black ward. But he was also strongly supported by voters in the city's mostly upper-class ward. Reelected easily in 1881, Debs ran for and was elected to the Indiana state assembly as a Democrat in 1884.

By then, Salvatore said, Debs had come to a fuller acceptance of his role as a labor spokesman in the political arena. And his experience as a workers' representative in the state legislature led him to oppose the ever-growing power of corporations—especially their control of the legislative process. Debs experienced this control personally when a pro-worker bill that he sponsored fell victim to corporate lobbyists. After passing unanimously in the assembly, the bill was eviscerated in the senate when the railroad lobby "reached" a sufficient number of state senators and induced them to do the railroad's bidding. In the end, the outraged Debs refused to vote for the watered-down version of his own bill. Disillusioned, he declined to run for reelection to the assembly in 1886.

Debs's growing class consciousness also brought him into increasing conflict with the railway unions. Divided into brotherhoods of locomotive engineers, locomotive firemen, railway conductors, railway trainmen, and telegraphers, the brotherhoods showed little or no concern for the unskilled workers in the industry and were more likely to undercut each other than to cooperate. Finally, after years of agitating and organizing to overcome what he had come to call the "caste mentality" of the brotherhoods, Debs concluded that they could not be changed. A new union, one encompassing all who worked in the industry was, he believed, the only hope for bringing about labor unity. In 1893, therefore, in an effort to abolish craft divisions and to unify all railroad workers, Debs set out to organize the American Railway Union.

VII

The ARU was born just as the United States entered another deep depression. Its organizers faced rampant unemployment, aggressive cutbacks in wages, and increasingly harsh treatment of railroad workers by employers. Under these conditions, the odds seemed to weigh heavily against the new union's success. But in large part because of Debs's messianic charisma, and especially after the dramatic success of an ARU strike against the infamous James J. Hill's Great Northern Railroad in early 1894, the ARU grew rapidly. A third wage cut in less than eight months, and the workers' discovery of Great Northern's plan to fire all ARU members, had brought on the strike. And a remarkable unity of the men in all crafts, and at all levels of skill, won it. As Debs told Hill when the strike began: "The grievance [of the wage cuts] is a universal grievance and all the men are united in this action. It will be to no avail to attempt to divide us into factions." If wages were not restored to pre-depression levels, Debs warned, Great Northern would "no longer have the services of the men."

In an industry marked by a traditional hierarchy of craft organizations that resembled medieval guilds more than modern unions, Debs's call for unity of action and purpose was unprecedented. But membership solidarity proved not to be an empty threat. Almost to a man, railroad workers throughout the West eagerly supported the strike. This was the decisive factor in what Debs later called the "only clear-cut victory of any consequence ever won by a railroad union in the United States."

After the Great Northern strike was won, aggrieved workers on many railroads flocked to join the ARU. For a while they signed up at the rate of some 2,000 a day, and the union soon had 150,000 members, 60,000 more than the combined total of the old railway brotherhoods. Debs, of course, was elated by this dramatic growth. But, as Salvatore noted, he also feared "that the energy and confidence of the new and untested members might force [another] strike before the union could solidify itself." And that fear was management's hope. Having concluded that Debs and his ARU must be destroyed, the railroad corporations longed for the opportunity a rash misstep might provide.

Implicitly, the battle lines had been drawn, but the forces on each side would prove to be fatally unequal. The fledgling union had few resources except those brought to it by remnants of the once-powerful Knights of Labor. And it had little support beyond its ranks. Samuel Gompers, fearing the ARU as a threat to his nascent craft–based American Federation of Labor, could be counted on only for weak—and insincere—words of encouragement. And the railway brotherhoods, fearing major defections from their ranks, were all but openly hostile.

The giant railroad corporations, on the other hand, were united against the threat of an organized workforce. They could also count on powerful allies in other industries and on the aggressive support of their close friends in the federal government.

Big capital—avidly awaiting the opportunity to nip this new workers' movement in the bud—did not have long to wait. Only a month or so after the victory over the Great Northern line, the workers at George Pullman's paternalistic model town, just outside of Chicago, unwittingly provided the excuse to smash Debs and his upstart union.

The immediate cause of the Pullman strike in the spring of 1894 was yet another severe wage cut by yet another major company. Wages at Pullman had been reduced steadily for almost a year, for some workers by as much as 50 percent. Yet the rent that workers paid for their company-owned homes remained unchanged, as did prices in the company-owned stores. Faced with this latest cut in pay, a committee of desperate workers petitioned a Pullman vice president for relief. He listened and assured the committee members that they would suffer no reprisals for their initiative. The very next day the company fired three of them. As word of this raced through the plant, the entire workforce dropped their tools and walked out.

Debs, who had watched the situation unfold, was sympathetic to the Pullman strikers. Determined to help, he had sent his friend George W. Howard, grand chief of the Brotherhood of Railway Conductors, to help them organize. But while Debs and Howard did what they could to help the strikers, they also did their best to distance the ARU from any official connection with the strike. Instead, as they had also done during the Great Northern strike, they sought wide community support for the workers. Howard, for example, requested aid from the Civic Federation of Chicago, a middle-class citizens group that disliked Pullman's paternalism. After an investigation of conditions led by Jane Addams of Hull House, the Civic Federation attempted to draw Pullman into arbitration. When Pullman refused the federation's entreaties, it supported the workers with food and other provisions.

Despite the *Chicago Tribune's* feral hostility to the Pullman workers (shared by most of the city's other leading newspapers), the strikers enjoyed broad public sympathy. Chicago's mayor, John P. Hopkins—himself a former Pullman paymaster who had been fired for displaying too much sympathy for the workers—donated $1,500 to relieve their suffering. Of course, Chicago's labor union locals supported the strikers wholeheartedly.

This help from a wide spectrum of Chicago radicals and liberals enabled the strikers to hold out while the company adamantly refused arbitration. Then, about a month into the strike, the ARU held its first annual convention. As Debs mingled with the delegates he cautioned against direct involvement in the strike. "Money, supplies, organizers, speakers— all this and more Debs gladly supported, but he did not want to commit the union in any official capacity," Salvatore wrote. As a result of the ARU's early successes, however, the delegates were euphoric and feeling invincible. Rejecting Debs's cautions, they voted overwhelmingly to initiate and support a nationwide boycott of all trains carrying Pullman's sleeping cars. Confronted with this threat from the ARU, Pullman once again refused arbitration, whereupon the union ordered the national boycott to begin.

In city after city, Almont Lindsey wrote in *The Pullman Strike*, workers walked off their jobs when the railroads' General Managers Association ostentatiously refused to detach Pullman's cars from their trains. The brotherhoods opposed the strike, but the boycott was remarkably effective. It paralyzed the major Western lines and seriously interfered with railroad traffic in other parts of the country.

This, however, was the event that the railroad owners had hoped and planned for. They had appointed John Egan, a former manager of the

Chicago and Great Western Railroad, as full-time coordinator for management's strategy, and now they welcomed the opportunity to smash the ARU. For its part, the union understood the general managers' game. It accused them of purposely delaying trains and of putting Pullman cars on trains that normally did not carry them, so that workers would refuse to move them and the railroads could cry interference with the mail. For his part, knowing that this would hasten federal intervention, Egan happily portrayed the situation as ominous and happily admitted that the railroads had been "fought to a standstill."

In fact, management maximized the disruption of their own operations in order to create a public climate favorable to federal intervention. As Lindsey related, Egan insisted that federal troops at Illinois's Fort Sheridan should be called out as there was "no other recourse left." The union had beaten the railroad companies, but they couldn't beat the government, he insisted. With these troops, he explained, "the strike would collapse like a punctured balloon." As the prospect of federal intervention increased, the managers, almost jubilantly, announced that the railroads were "out of" this fight. Now, the railroads said, the battle was "between the United States Government and the American Railway Union, and we shall leave them to fight it out."

The government, of course, was ready to step in. An ally of the railroads, Richard Olney, a Democrat, had been a corporation lawyer for thirty-five years before he became the U.S. attorney general for President Grover Cleveland. He not only had close personal and professional ties to many railroad executives, but he was also a member of the board of directors of numerous rail lines, including the Chicago, Burlington, and Quincy. When the railroads claimed that by stopping trains, the ARU was interfering with the U.S. mails, he became their point man in directing the forces of the federal government against the railroad workers.

His strategy was simple. Despite assurances from Chicago's mayor and Illinois governor John P. Altgeld that local and state forces were sufficient to keep the peace, Olney drew up an injunction against the union, and then used a minor disturbance at Blue Island, a town adjoining Chicago, as an excuse to wire President Cleveland asking that federal troops be sent to Chicago. Cleveland readily obliged. Federal troops were sent and provoked the first seriously violent disturbances. This manufactured incident was then used as an excuse to smash the strike. Then Olney proceeded to railroad Debs and several other ARU members to jail for violating his injunction.

VIII

By the following year, when Debs left the Woodstock jail, he had experienced a political sea change. As he related in an article published in the *New York Comrade* in 1902, victory in the Pullman strike, like that in the Great Northern strike earlier the same year, had been "clear and complete. "The railroad corporations" he said, "were paralyzed and helpless." But at this juncture "there was delivered, from wholly unexpected quarters, a swift succession of blows that blinded me for an instant and then opened wide my eyes." This, he wrote, was his "first practical lesson in socialism."

The role of the government in destroying his union and in marginalizing him within the organized labor movement had convinced Debs that union activity alone was inadequate. "All great strikes," he wrote later, "prove that the government is under the control of corporate capital." Pullman, therefore, focused his attention on the class nature of the American government and on the need to contest directly for government office. But where to get involved? All of his adult life he had been a Democrat. But Cleveland was a Democratic president, and Olney a Democratic Attorney General—and they had betrayed both the Pullman workers and the ARU to the railroad corporations.

First, Debs turned tentatively to the Populists. In his earlier years, he had thought the party's appeal was too limited, especially among workers. He had begun to change this view by early 1894, even before the Pullman strike. At the last meeting of the Brotherhood of Locomotive Fireman that he attended, Debs had revealed a desire for labor "to unify at the polls and vote for an independent people's party." Noting the growing dominance of the "money monopoly, the land monopoly and the rest of them" over the major parties, he argued that neutrality or aversion to politics would be fatal for organized labor. In the aftermath of the Pullman strike, with thousands of ARU members unemployed and blacklisted, Debs's resolve strengthened. He left jail determined to help these men, and in the 1896 presidential election the Populist cause became his means of doing so.

Debs may even have considered running for the Populist presidential nomination. Certainly that's what Henry Demarest Lloyd wanted him to do. But before the Peoples Party convened to nominate its own candidate, the Democrats had nominated William Jennings Bryan and adopted his inflationary platform calling for the free coinage of silver. Lloyd, author of *Wealth versus Commonwealth* and the Populist's leading intellectual, opposed Bryan because he thought that the Western state Silverites had abandoned the anti-monopoly thrust of populism. Within the Populist party Lloyd had built a strong movement for Debs's nomination, and as the Populist convention assembled it looked as if Debs had a shot at being chosen. But at the last minute Debs withdrew his name, and the Populists, with no viable alternative, joined the Democrats and also nominated Bryan.

In the election, Debs campaigned enthusiastically for Bryan, who lost badly to Republican William McKinley after an unprecedentedly vicious campaign of corporate propaganda, accompanied by widespread threats that plants would close if Bryan were elected. Deeply disappointed, Debs acknowledged populism's demise, and a year later announced his conversion to socialism.

Debs embraced socialism, he said, because he was for humanity. "Money," the scramble for which characterizes capitalism and controls the major parties, he said, "constitutes no proper basis of civilization." Insisting that the time had come to "regenerate society," he announced that he intended to begin by bringing the issue of socialism versus capitalism into the arena of public discourse.

But what did socialism mean to Debs? In practice, at this stage in his life, Debs's concept was closely akin to that of the utopian colonizers, es-

pecially those at the Oneida colony, which was officially nondenominational, but whose members were mostly Christian universalists. Debs
himself had never joined any church, but he was deeply influenced by
the evangelical movements of the mid-nineteenth century, and he frequently relied on biblical references and Christian allusions in his defense
of labor. As editor of the *Locomotive Firemen's Magazine*, for example, he
had written in 1893 that every blow struck by a union for the emancipation of labor "has the endorsement of Christ," and that labor is, "rever-
ently speaking, in alliance with Christ to oppose pomp and splendor."
(Salvatore wrote that these were "apt sentiments for one seeking the
Kingdom of God on earth, but that many firemen found them offensive
and even sacrilegious.") Later, in a speech to prospective members of a
new socialist party, Debs asked, "What is socialism?" and answered:
"Merely Christianity in action. It recognizes the equality in men."

Debs was now committed to two disparate paths. Based on his understanding that capitalism could most effectively be fought on the level of
national power, he shared with Victor Berger a commitment to electoral
politics on that scale. At the same time, however, he felt a strong obligation to the now unemployed and blacklisted members of the ARU. On
their behalf, though on a much larger scale than the old utopians, Debs
adopted a "grand co-operative scheme." The idea was to settle ARU veterans in a Western state, capture the state government through electoral
means, and then call for the "laborless thousands" to join them so that
they might "enjoy 'life, liberty and the pursuit of happiness'" in their
own domain. From this frontier base, Debs said, the new utopians would
"rapidly overleap boundary lines" and occupy other states "in all directions until the old barbaric system" was destroyed and the republic in fact
became "the land of the free and happy people."

Debs brought these intentions with him when he brought what was
left of the ARU into the Brotherhood of the Cooperative Commonwealth, a utopian socialist organization that had been called into being
by Wayland and his magazine, *The Coming Nation,* and by Berger and his
more traditional socialist organization in Wisconsin. In June of 1897,
these groups merged into the short-lived Social Democracy of America.

This, however was an unstable coalition. From the beginning it was sharply divided between Berger's electoral wing and Wayland's colonizers. After a year of raising funds to purchase land for their project, the colonizers announced that they were negotiating to buy 560 acres of land in Cripple Creek, Colorado, for the sum of $200,000. At their first national convention, in June 1898, however, Berger forced a showdown. He insisted that colonization was unrealistic and called for an exclusive focus on political and educational activity at the local and national levels. After a debate that lasted into the small hours of the morning, the colonizers won by a vote of 53–37. The two groups then went their separate ways. Eventually the colonizers founded two small colonies in the state of Washington, which quietly withered on the vine. Meanwhile, forced to chose one side or the other, Debs joined Berger and the minority. Together, they then founded yet another new organization, named the Social Democratic Party of America, and both were elected to its executive board.

This new party was finally on track to form a socialist organization capable of uniting a broad range of traditional radicals. It benefited, less than a year later, from Hillquit's split of the Socialist Labor Party. The SLP, as we've seen, had suffered from a constant stream of schisms and splits in its brief history, especially since 1891, when Daniel DeLeon, a Curacao-born lawyer and a domineering presence, took control of the party. DeLeon was a quintessential sectarian whose personality and policies drove away many of the more mainstream-oriented party members. Abraham Cahan, the future editor of the New York *Jewish Daily Forward*, and Meyer London, a lawyer and the future Socialist congressman from New York's Lower East Side, for example, departed in 1895. Finally, in 1899, Morris Hillquit, attempted to overthrow DeLeon. He helped elect a new national executive committee and seized the party's headquarters in New York. But the courts awarded the party name and its newspaper, *The People*, to DeLeon. In the end Hillquit took almost half of the party's 7,000 members with him, thereby creating two parties, each claiming the mantle of authenticity.

In 1895, Hillquit had opposed DeLeon's formation of the Socialist Trade and Labor Alliance as a dual union that would only split an already

weak American working class into two hostile camps. And he had seen
DeLeon's emphasis on the ST&LA's revolutionary role as a denigration
of electoral activity. Along with such socialist labor leaders as J. Mahlon
Barnes of the Cigarmakers Union and Max Hayes of the Typographical
Union, Hillquit advocated working within the craft–dominated Ameri-
can Federation of Labor. Always intent on Americanizing socialism,
Hillquit's ideas closely paralleled Victor Berger's. Now Hillquit sought
out Debs and Berger and proposed a merger with the SDPA.

In 1900, as the candidate of the SDPA, Eugene V. Debs ran for president for the first time. Supported by Hillquit's SLP, and by many former
Greenbackers, Populists, and Christian socialists, the new—and still
poorly-organized—coalition produced only 100,000 votes. But its
prospects were brighter than the vote totals indicated. The groups had
come together around Debs's candidacy at a propitious moment in the
development of American capitalism. Now they sought finally to achieve
a socialist party attuned to American conditions.

The process took another half year of internecine squabbling, but finally, in 1901, the SDPA and Hillquit's SLP, joined by many smaller
groups, met at Indianapolis for the largest and most representative
national gathering that socialists had yet held in America. The convention included men and women who had been active in all phases of socialist and liberal reform movements of the previous half century. Of
the 124 delegates, four out of five were native-born, three were African-
American, and one came from Puerto Rico. This party, which broadly
reflected the nation, came together to prevent, or limit, corporate domination of the nation's economic and political life. It included farmers
(Oklahoma would become the most heavily socialist state), workers
(primarily the more skilled trade unionists), and professionals (especially
Protestant clergymen, lawyers, and journalists). As Morris Hillquit commented, socialism had come into its own. No longer would it be "an ex-
otic plant in this country."

3

LIMITS OF GROWTH:
PRINCIPLES TRANSCEND PARTY

I

IN THE LATE NINETEENTH CENTURY, with the transconti-
nental railroads completed, the Indians either pacified or exterminated, and a truly nationwide market created, the continental United
States achieved its present character. No longer obsessed with the taming
and extension of their internal empire, businessmen and their politicians
began aggressively to seek markets and investment opportunities abroad.
With an eye on Spain's crumbling empire, they took a first step in 1898
by provoking a war with that nation and taking Puerto Rico, Cuba, and
the Philippines as their own colonies. By the turn of the century, then,
the United States was emerging as a world-class imperial power.

These developments marked a major step in the maturing of American capitalism. They were reflected also in the coming of age of social
and political movements representing the interests of workers and farmers, among which was the creation of the Socialist Party. Even when socialism burst onto the political landscape as a bona fide American
movement, however, its greatest strength did not reside in numbers. Indeed, socialism was a relatively minor player in the panoply of farmers,
workers, and middle-class businessmen and professionals who formed
the social base of the Populist and Progressive movements of the late
nineteenth and early twentieth centuries.

Still, the new party did grow rapidly. By 1912, its defense of working
people and its democratic vision permeated all ranks of society and pro-

45

vided much of the yeast for the intellectual ferment of the time. From this mix of social forces and ideologies, the Socialists emerged as the most enduring organized group. To many of those who had not followed the arcane course of the sectarian left, the popularity of this new movement came as a shocking surprise.

Within ten years of the party's founding, more than 100,000 members were paying dues each month, and there probably were an equal number of sporadic adherents. By 1912, when Debs received 900,000 votes for president, Victor Berger had been elected to Congress from Milwaukee, seventy-four municipalities throughout the country had elected Socialist mayors, and 340 cities and towns had elected more than 1,200 lesser Socialist officials. In the American Federation of Labor, too—despite president Samuel Gompers's hostility and the influence of the Catholic Church's anti-Socialist Militia of Christ—one-third of the federation's international affiliates had elected Socialist presidents. Still, in the years before the United States entered the first World War, Socialists elected only two men to the House of Representatives.

Agrarian progressives had done much better. They had elected hundreds to Congress and they had played a major role in initiating reform legislation. Yet the farmers movements were, on the whole, a rearguard defense of their former status, while the Socialists' ideas and programs corresponded to the developmental path of corporate capitalism. As the living embodiment of socialist principles, the party far surpassed farmers in influencing the corporate transformation of property and market relations during the Progressive Era. That was the movement's greatest strength and the cause of its wide appeal.

II

After its formation in 1901, the Socialist Party also helped create a more coherent, though still rudimentary, practical worldview among socialists. Before then, socialism was a movement of many mutually exclusive, frequently hostile parties, alliances, and clubs. After 1901, for the better part of two decades, socialism was pretty much defined by what the Socialist

Party of America said and did. True, Socialist Party members were of many minds on many issues. Yet, diverse as its various factions and tendencies were, the party held them together in one decentralized organization. And that organization's form and activities defined socialism's public meaning. Three things kept the party unified despite its diversity: its members' implicitly shared vision of a more humane, egalitarian post-capitalist society, its aura of social progress, and its belief in the possibility of ultimate success within the framework of American democratic institutions.

And Socialists had taken the lead in proposing progressive reforms, most of which were aimed at improving working conditions and the social well-being of working people. The demand for an eight-hour workday at prevailing union wages for government work; public health and safety inspection; compulsory health, life, and unemployment insurance; workmen's compensation; and legal protection of labor's right to organize were fundamental. Other demands, for reforms such as a progressive income tax, prohibition of child labor, and education about birth control had a more universal character. Still others were aimed at democratizing the economy—nationalization of industries organized on a national scale, such as railroads, telephone, shipping, and municipal ownership of ice plants, electric power plants, and public transit.

Few of these reforms would be won until the 1930s, when the Great Depression produced Franklin Roosevelt's New Deal—and with it the Social Security Act, the Wagner Labor Relations Act, and several other reforms initially proposed and fought for by Socialists. Some, like environmental protection and health and safety legislation, would not be adopted until Richard Nixon was president. But Socialists introduced many of these ideas and fought for these reforms. And while their numbers remained relatively small, the party and its vision of a better society gained wide enough appeal by 1912 to lead Ralph Easley, executive director of the National Civic Federation (NCF), to warn against "the menace of Socialism"—not only among workers, but also in "colleges, churches and newspapers." The spread of the Intercollegiate Socialist Society, and other party "front groups," especially alarmed Easley. When the National Association for the Advancement of Colored People was organized in 1909, for example, he warned President William Howard Taft that this movement was primarily "a scheme to further Socialist propaganda." Two-thirds of its founders, he wrote, were "avowed Socialists." Their theory, he claimed, was that "the ten million citizens who are being deprived of their constitutional liberties in this free land would be willing to join any party or movement to stand for their rights."

In short, in 1912, socialism appeared to be on a trajectory of steady growth and influence and was causing alarm among corporate and financial leaders. But the threat was an illusion. These were years of rapid changes in the nature of American society. The transformation from a highly competitive system of industrialization to one dominated by huge corporations and banks provided the grounds for the Socialists' rapid rise. Their agitation, along with the growth of the trade union movement and agrarian radicalism, induced changes in both major parties and was to assist in the humanization of American capitalism. Thus, by 1912, social reform and accommodation of trade unionism had become hot topics in the internal discussions of Republicans as well as Democrats. This in turn, led many on the left to see participation in one or the other of the major parties as a viable path to reform. When Woodrow Wilson took office in 1913 and began to promote progressive changes, some Socialists concluded that more could be achieved within the framework of the Democratic Party. W. E. B. DuBois, one of the NAACP's founders and the editor of its journal *Crisis*, had reached that conclusion in 1912, when he quit the Socialist Party to vote for Wilson.

III

As noted, the Socialist Party was far from monolithic. In the traditional lexicon of politics, it contained right, left, and center groupings. In part these differences were hereditary—legacies of the diverse paths taken to socialism by those of different occupational, geographical, or ideological backgrounds. Some differences were substantive, others were primarily stylistic. Those labeled right-wing tended to be from the larger towns and cities of the country's long-settled industrial regions—New England, New York, and the cities of the Midwest—and they tended to be active in unions, most of them affiliated with the AFL. Milwaukee was the bastion of the party's right wing, at least as party members and most historians have seen it.. And Victor Berger, who led the Milwaukee movement, has come down to us as that wing's symbolic leader.

Berger's approach to politics flowed from his understanding that there was no immediate prospect for a transition to socialism in the United States—or, for that matter, in any other part of the world. That led him to take the long view, and to seek alliances with other reformers. Among other things, he was a leader of the Milwaukee local of the International Typographical Union and editor of the Milwaukee Federated Trades Council's official publication. This approach led his detractors to call Berger a "sewer socialist"—a reference to the Milwaukee local's promise to build a sewage system designed to last fifty years. In fact, the sewer was built, and it was only a part of the local reforms and stable electoral organizations that Berger championed—all of which helped to make him the party's most successful politician.

Both his emphasis on reform and his close working relationship with local AFL affiliates were anathema to many of the party's left-wingers, especially those clustered in the small towns South and Southwest and in the hard-rock mining and lumber camps of the frontier. The westerners were mostly young, single, and rootless—miners, lumberjacks, and itinerant workers who lived in conditions still characteristic of nineteenth-century raw competitive industry. They were affected by the new era of corporate capitalism, but they existed on its margins, and as a result had little need for stable union organizations or long-term strategies. Like radical Christians of the old century, their vision tended to be millenarian. In the frontier South—Oklahoma and Texas in particular—radical tenant farmers made up the core of left-wing strength. In the West, the left found its ideological home in the Industrial Workers of the World. That union, organized in 1905 in the hope of creating a major center of industrial unionism, fought heroic battles— occasionally with brilliant success—but organized only episodically and disdained the contracts with employers that were the basis of the more stable unions of the AFL.

While the left tended to be apocalyptic, Berger's approach was developmental. Based on his understanding of Marx's writings (he was one of the few American socialists who actually read Marx), he saw that the emergence of giant corporations in the United States had brought about a profound change in the nature of our society. Indeed, he said, while capitalism had "already become a menace to civilization," it had nevertheless "stepped into a new phase," the duration of which was "unlimited according to our present light." And while he saw socialism as the next epoch of civilization, into which the world was evolving, he understood that this would be a long-term process. Neither feudalism nor capitalism had arisen or disappeared at a given date, he wrote, nor would socialism replace capitalism "at one stroke." The period of transition, Berger often repeated, would require two conditions in each country: the winning of a majority of the population to the side of the Socialist Party and a concentration of industry sufficient to make it "ripe for collective production."

With revolution not on the short-run agenda, Berger insisted that the socialists' task was to educate workers about the principles of socialism and the possibility of a more humane society in the future, while struggling in the present for a program that would improve working people's lot, "economically, morally and physically." Because working people greatly "outnumbered the capitalist class," Berger believed that ultimately they had the "fate of every country in the world in [their] hands"—especially if the party could come to terms with the farmers.

Along with all followers of Marx in the days before the Russian Revolution, Berger was unable to imagine the possibility of socialism in an undeveloped country. Thus he argued strongly against those socialists who were constantly speaking of revolution, which he interpreted to mean a "catastrophe." And while he understood Marx's comment that "force is the midwife at the birth of every new epoch," he found in this "no cause for rejoicing." Looking for "another way out," Berger found it in the ballot, backed up by an armed people. Of course, he wrote, there was a danger that the capitalist class would attempt to negate a future working-class electoral victory. But if the people were fully armed, a peaceful transition would be assured. "An armed people," Berger frequently insisted, "is always a free people."

If Berger epitomized the so-called right wing of the party, William D. (Big Bill) Haywood represented the self-proclaimed left. A one-time secretary-treasurer of the Western Federation of Miners, and later general organizer of the IWW, Haywood, like Debs, came to socialism through his experience as an industrial unionist. Unlike Debs, however, Haywood had little experience of political activity and never developed any regard for its educational value. Haywood's idea of socialism, and how it would come about, was even more vague than Berger's or Debs's. Fighting labor's immediate battles and organizing the unorganized determined his attitude toward political action. While he urged "every workingman to use his ballot at every opportunity"—and was himself a candidate for governor of Colorado in 1906—the value of elections in his eyes was simply to win administrative control of local governments, in order to "use the powers of the police to protect the strikers."

In any case, Haywood's constituency consisted in large part of disfranchised nonferrous metal miners in the remote camps of the mountain states, lumber workers of northern Louisiana and the Northwest, migratory agricultural workers, and recently immigrated industrial workers. While Debs's roots were among workers in the more settled industries, Haywood's constituents were more marginalized. The demands of his followers, therefore, were narrower, and his hostility to reform flowed largely from a belief that few reforms could effect the conditions under which they lived. Nor did Haywood share with Berger or the other party leaders the view that capitalism might survive for a considerable time. Believing that a revolution could occur any moment, he saw no need for a long-term strategy.

All of this separated Haywood from the mainstream of the party. Still, his beliefs were within its boundaries, and he was extremely popular, especially in the West and Southwest. A powerful speaker who loved to emphasize his differences with the Eastern party leaders, especially lawyers like Morris Hillquit, whom Haywood loved to twit at speeches in New York City, the heartland of Hillquit's influence. In one well-publicized debate with Hillquit at Cooper Union, Haywood could not resist proposing industrial "sabotage" as a labor tactic, and he announced that he was "not a law-abiding citizen." A few months later he boasted that he believed in sabotage, "that much misunderstood word."

This rhetoric delighted Haywood and many of his followers, but it had little or nothing to do with the way he ran his union. During strikes, Haywood rarely, if ever, advocated the use of violence. His leadership in the Lawrence, Massachusetts, textile strike in 1912—the IWW's greatest victory—was marked by the quiet discipline he instilled in strikers. He followed a policy of nonviolence there and wherever else it was possible. In Akron, Ohio, in a strike of rubber workers in 1913, for example, he told the workers that their "greatest weapon" was keeping their hands in their pockets. "Let there be no violence," he said, "not the destruction of one cent's worth of property, not one cross word."

By 1912, because of his leadership of the Lawrence strike, Haywood had reached the height of his popularity within the party. But, by then, the IWW's dual unionism—its policy of organizing dual unions—had also become an increasing problem for many of the Socialist leaders of unions affiliated with the AFL. Because the party officially absented itself from union affairs, however, it would have been difficult to attack Haywood on the basis of his attempts to raid the Western Federation of Miners or the United Mine Workers. Instead, Haywood's propensity to advocate "sabotage" was seized upon as a way to reduce his presence. This was done by amending the party constitution to outlaw the advocacy of sabotage, and then by a referendum recalling Haywood from his position on the party's executive committee.

After his recall in 1913, Haywood ceased being active in party affairs, though those who shared his views continued to exercise some influence in Minnesota, Washington, and scattered other areas throughout the West. Former Populists and tenant farmers in Texas, Oklahoma, Alabama, Louisiana, and Missouri also tended to support Haywood and the left, but this was as much because of their distrust of easterners—and what they considered to be an overly bureaucratic national office—as it was over differences of policy. The Texas Socialists, led by Tom Hickey, editor of the Halletsville *Rebel,* a weekly newspaper with more than

26,000 subscribers, voted overwhelmingly to oppose Haywood's recall. Hickey also supported IWW-style unionism and led a faction of "Red" decentralizers. But, unlike Haywood—and unlike the more traditional urban Christian socialists—his paper preached a fundamentalist "Bible socialism," while promoting racial segregation, virulent Anglophobia, and anti-Catholicism, all of which were anathema to Haywood and the IWW.

IV

By the end of its first decade, the Socialist Party had won a substantial following among workers all over the United States. In the electoral arena, 1911 was an especially good year. In seventy-four cities and towns Socialists elected mayors, while in seven states the party elected a total of nineteen state assemblymen, thirteen of them in Wisconsin. In the smaller cities and towns, the vast majority of Socialists elected as mayors, as well as the many hundreds of lesser officeholders, were workers and trade unionists—railroad conductors and brakemen, machinists, teamsters, cigar makers, tinners, woodworkers, miners, and day laborers. In the larger cities, however, party candidates for the top offices tended to be professionals or ministers. In Los Angeles, a lawyer and former minister, Job Harriman, was the unsuccessful candidate for mayor, while in three other mid-sized cities ministers ran and won. In Berkeley, California, the Rev. J. Stitt Wilson was elected; in Butte, Montana, the Rev. Lewis J. Duncan won the first of his two terms; and in Schenectady, New York, the Rev. George R. Lunn began his long career as a public official.

Lunn was New York State's first Socialist mayor. He swept into office in the industrial city of Schenectady along with eight of the city's thirteen aldermen, several district supervisors, and the state's first Socialist assemblyman. A Christian Socialist and the founder and pastor of Schenectady's United People's Church, Lunn had fought municipal graft long before he joined the Socialist Party. He was endowed with what historian Kenneth E. Hendrickson called "an unbridled faith that the gospel in action could solve man's problems." From his days at Princeton University

and Union Theological Seminary, until hired to the pulpit of Schenectady's most prestigious Presbyterian congregation, Lunn had been resolved to fight for a better social order. He intended, he said, "to preach
the gospel of life and also to have a hand in doing real things." But doing
real things, especially his agitation for lower trolley fares, got him in trouble with some of the wealthy Presbyterian congregants. The idea of
lower fares particularly offended the manager of the Schenectady Railway System. This man's vociferous displeasure led to Lunn's resignation
as pastor of First Presbyterian.

After resigning, Lunn planned to leave Schenectady. But 1,500 former
parishioners petitioned him to stay and start a People's Church. He accepted the challenge and began preaching in a downtown theater. A
short time later he merged his church with Schenectady's First Congre-
gational Church to form the United People's Church. The merger provided financial support and once more gave him an appropriate building
in which to preach on Sunday mornings. Meanwhile, at night, he continued to preach at the theater.

In May of 1910, Lunn launched *The Citizen,* a weekly newspaper in
which he campaigned against graft, corruption, and government inefficiency. In addition, he debated the merits of socialism with prominent
Progressives, and offered to take on all comers. By then, Lunn, a former
Republican who had supported Bryan in 1900, had joined the Socialist
Party. He did not do so with the hope of immediate political success. He
did so because he believed firmly that while socialism was "growing," neither of the great parties held out "promise for the [solution of] problems
that confront us." In September 1911, after visiting Milwaukee to study
the administrative techniques of that city's newly elected Socialist government, Lunn accepted the Schenectady local's nomination for mayor.

Like Milwaukee, Schenectady was a working-class town. Twenty-six
thousand men and women, more than a third of the city's population of
72,000, worked for General Electric or American Locomotive, the city's
two major employers. The workers at each plant, many of them skilled
machinists (and members of the Machinists' union, which was soon to
elect a Socialist as its own president) were the party's strongest supporters.
The party local of 250 was relatively large and well-organized, especially in

the two wards of mostly skilled Irish-American workers, which gave Lunn his most solid support. But in November he also did well in the city's middle-class and professional ward. Only in the wards of unskilled immigrant workers did Lunn and the other Socialist candidates do poorly.

After the election Lunn and the party local clashed for the first time. For six weeks the new mayor failed to appoint his cabinet. The press speculated that conflicts between the new mayor and his party were causing the delay, and, indeed, Lunn and the local were butting heads on the question of appointments. Lunn insisted that men of "demonstrated ability" would be appointed regardless of party affiliation. The local, backed by the state office, insisted that Socialists alone could be appointed, and that the local had to approve the nominations.

Finally, an agreement was reached, but within it were the seeds of future discord. Lunn's major appointments were all good party members. As commissioner of public works, Lunn imported Charles A. Mullen, a well-known paving expert from Milwaukee. As commissioner of charities, he brought Walter E. Kruesi back to Schenectady from Boston. To head the board of education he appointed Charles P. Steinmetz, General Electric's chief scientist, whose method of calculating alternating current had revolutionized the field of electrical engineering. As city clerk, he appointed Hawley B. Van Vechten, a party hack. And, in a bow to the New York City leaders, he appointed Morris Hillquit as special counsel to the city. But to the annoyance of local party members, Lunn also appointed two Democrats, one as city engineer, the other as corporation counsel. Finally, as his personal secretary, Lunn appointed a militant young Socialist, Walter Lippmann, to his first job since graduating from Harvard University.

Lippmann, who was attracted to power as a moth is to flame, was soon to abandon socialism, first for progressivism and later for more conservative pursuits as a journalist. He lasted in Schenectady for only four months, during which he became increasingly critical of the Lunn administration, and upon leaving he wrote a long letter to the manager of the Socialist Party's national office outlining his differences with the party. It is a strange letter, indeed, since it appears on the surface to be a critique of Lunn—and of municipal socialism in general—from the left, and yet it clearly provided Lippmann with a rationale for abandoning socialism altogether.

Some of Lippmann's criticisms of the party, if not of Lunn, were well taken. For example, Lippmann noted, correctly, that the majority of those who voted the Socialists into office were neither party members nor true believers, but simply supporters of Socialist-espoused reforms. In that situation, Lippmann asked, "If an administration is elected by non-socialist votes, does it owe any allegiance to the wishes of its non-socialist supporters?" He answered that "Socialists should not, even if they could, go beyond the actual will of the constituency." This was a principled position, but it was at odds with the attitude of many party members and leaders—and, for that matter, of politicians of all stripes. Once in office, most politicians, for a variety of reasons, frequently ignore the wishes and interests of their constituents. Lunn did not.

Lippmann also criticized the Socialists' tendency to condemn progressive reformers as phonies when they adopted demands first put forward by the party. "The general attitude of the party press," he wrote, "is that all reformers are either fools, crooks, or hypocrites." But Lippmann insisted that in the realm of what Socialists call immediate demands, "it is sheer nonsense to pretend that we alone are capable or willing to carry them into effect." Indeed, he asserted, there is probably not a reform in the party's program that "progressivism is not capable of accepting."

If Socialists had no monopoly on immediate demands, if their program was simply progressivism presented as socialism, what then should a Socialist administration do? Here, Lippmann got himself into rhetorical trouble. He started by saying that the difficulty in Schenectady was in the budget, which was made on the principle that "taxes must not be increased." This was a political necessity, he conceded, because an increase in taxes would lose the support of the majority of non-socialists who voted Lunn into office. Lunn knew this. In fact, Lippmann wrote, the administration boasted that it had not raised taxes. Yet, Lippmann argued that raising taxes on business enterprises is "a clean-cut issue between Socialism and anti-Socialism, for it is quite clearly the business of a Socialist administration to cut into the returns of property." In other words, he insisted, to be a real socialist it is necessary to "take as much as possible"—through taxation—"for social purposes."

On this issue, Lippmann argued, Socialists must distinguish themselves from the Progressives, who had already adopted most of the Socialists' immediate demands. And, since Progressives held "the balance of power in America," the Socialists needed to find popular reforms that Progressives could not co-opt. To survive, they needed "a practical program for the next few years that would really affect the balance of power, that would really cut into profit."

Such a program was "difficult to formulate," Lippmann admitted, but he gave it a try: "Take the municipal ownership and operation of subways," he wrote. "That in itself is an immediate reform that will find no great opposition among the Progressives." Municipal ownership would be "an installment of Socialism" only if it were to be "conducted on Socialist principles." The difference was this: Progressives wanted to use the profits from the operation of mass transit to reduce taxes, whereas Socialists should use the profits "socially, by raising wages, reducing fares and improving service."

In fact, however—as Lunn had said in his inaugural address—Socialists were severely limited in what they could do when in control of a municipality. Even if charter restrictions permitted (which they rarely did), Socialists could not substantially raise commercial property taxes or put through reforms that would seriously impinge upon business interests, lest industry be driven from the city. In practice, a Socialist administration could press for public ownership of utilities and transportation facilities; increase social, recreational, and cultural services; and adopt a friendly attitude toward labor, especially during strikes. But, as Lippmann suggested, some, or all, of these things were done by reformers such as Tom Johnson and Newton D. Baker in Cleveland, Samuel Jones in Toledo, and John Peuroy Mitchell in New York—and even by some business groups under city manager charters. There was nothing here that Progressives have been unable to accept. (Indeed, public transit, which in the next decades generally ran at a loss, was widely municipalized by Progressives who paid union-scale wages and kept fares low for many years.)

In any case, Lippmann's point was that by putting principled demands of this sort forward, Socialists would lose the non-socialist votes that were putting them in office. Like many left-wingers, even Debs, he saw this as a good thing, because the resulting smaller vote would then be a measure of the true believers in socialism. "Of course," Lippmann wrote, this also meant "that we shall win less elections, and come into power more slowly." Indeed, for the foreseeable future, Socialists would have "to stand by and let the progressives look like the saviors of humanity." Some, he added revealingly, might find this "too great a strain on their ambitions." If so, their only alternative would be to "join the Progressives."

In other words, to "make anything of political action," Lippmann insisted, Socialists must "keep themselves clearly distinguished from the progressives," concentrate on that which is theirs alone, and "leave [to] the progressives what is theirs."

That idea made some sense to Debs because he operated on a national scale, where his chances of getting elected were nil, and where broad universal principles could be credibly considered, even if not immediately acted upon. And it might make sense in a parliamentary system, where narrowly ideological minority parties can gain a few seats and function effectively inside parliament, either as part of a governing coalition or by using their influence as a balance of power. In the American political system, however, especially at the local level, social principles are not easily expressed in systemic terms, but can be reflected in attitudes and proposals about specific, even parochial, problems and by the behavior of public officials in critical instances.

Lippmann, however, suggested that the Socialists forego compromise and be martyrs to their cause. They had a choice, he wrote, "between the effort to pile up a real Socialist constituency and the sham effort to pile up a vote." He told the party officials that they should campaign "without bait" and use "votes [simply] as an index of converts." Their agitation, he argued, should be outside the electoral arena—"year in and year out without the immediate desire for office," while elections should be used "only when the social forces are organized and ready."

That, of course, could take generations, if not forever, especially because the campaigns for electoral office were the most potent means that Socialists—and, indeed, all politically principled people—had to gain adherents and organize them on a sustained basis. In any case, Lippmann used this argument disingenuously to justify his leaving the Socialists and joining Theodore Roosevelt's Progressive Party in 1912.

V

But what about the Socialists? Were their demands and actions indistinguishable from the Progressives'? And, if on some issues they were, was that a reason to relinquish these demands to their rivals?

There are several ways to look at this. First, consider the actions of the Lunn administration that inspired Lippmann's letter. In February 1912 Lunn hired boilermakers from the American Locomotive company—on strike and out of work—to cut and store 2,000 tons of ice from the Mohawk River for distribution to the city's poor. He planned to give the ice to those who could not afford to pay and to sell it at cost to those who could. Not surprisingly, the city's ice dealers objected. They took the city to court and secured an injunction forbidding it to sell the ice, or even to give it away. This did not stop Lunn. He and some associates, acting as individuals, bought ice wholesale in the nearby city of Troy and distributed it—until the Schenectady ice dealers got their local banks to cut off the Troy suppliers' credit. Still, Lunn somehow managed to keep the distribution going for a year.

Similarly, the city bought coal wholesale and distributed it through grocery stores for fifty cents a ton below the retail price. This time it was the coal dealers who went to court and got an injunction. Once again, Lunn foiled them by incorporating as George R. Lunn and Associates, and then continuing to sell discount coal until the end of his first term. In addition, Lunn set up a city grocery store at which groceries were sold at cost or less, and he established a municipal lodging house and farm as well as a municipal employment bureau.

All of Lunn's actions were in keeping, not only with socialist principles, but also with the actions of other Socialist-run municipalities. In Milwaukee, for example, when Victor Berger was an alderman-at-large, he fought to increase the minimum wage for city workers, regardless of politics, race, or color, to build hospitals for low-income workers, and to create new parks and city-sponsored concerts. He also fought for and got home rule, so that the city might operate utilities and the transit system. As Berger put it, even if Progressives might do the same, with each demand won with Progressive support, the Socialists should go on to the next demand. The basic idea, he said, was to change the way the public thought about the purpose of government and how it could serve them. Only thus, he said, could the party build its popular following while it moved on toward socialism. And if socialist proposals were copied by Progressives, so much the better for all.

That is the more salient point, for it was often as a result of Socialist initiatives that Progressives espoused reforms that benefited working people. Without Socialists either opposing or joining their ranks in the electoral arena, it is doubtful that Progressives would as readily have adopted many of the Progressive Era reforms. Berger, as well as Lunn, understood that for a party of the left to gain widespread support it must enter the public arena and make real changes in people's lives. These require the kinds of compromises that make legislation possible. A party that remains pure, as Lippmann advised, may be morally admirable, but it is unlikely to make life better for its constituents, or, if elected, to hold office for more than one term.

Furthermore, as the *International Socialist Review* argued in 1913, socialist reforms were all a part of the process of capitalism's development. "The clearest thinkers among the capitalists and their politicians," the *Review* wrote, realized that if American manufacturers were "to compete with Germany in the world market," they must have "the same sort of help from the government in conserving the labor supply that the German employers get." This provided "no ground for anxiety on the part of Socialists." Child labor laws and other pro-labor reforms—this left-wing monthly concluded—helped rationalize capitalism and at the same time ameliorated some of its harshness. The Progressive reforms, so far as they go, were "a good thing for 'all the people.'"

VI

In the end, by suggesting that Socialists should contest elections "only when the social forces are organized and ready," Lippmann aligned himself with the anarchists and syndicalists. They also forswore electoral politics, in their case because they saw it as an impermissible acknowledgment of the state's legitimacy. Lippmann, of course, did not share the anarchist view of the state as nothing more than a capitalist tool. He understood that the state was a place of contestation between classes. Workers, African-Americans, and women also understood this. That's why they made the late nineteenth century and much of the twentieth into arenas of struggle over their right to participate fully in the electoral system. Working people, in other words, wanted to participate in elections in order to protect their interests and to have a say in the development of our nation. That's what democratic politics is ultimately all about. Abstaining from this process, which Lippmann told the Socialists to do, would not only have cut the party off from access to the people most likely to be interested in its views, but also would have removed it from the scene as an historical actor.

In a formal democracy, political movements win legitimacy and popular support by contesting in the electoral arena. Outside of that arena, a movement is only a pressure group for a particular interest or issue. It can lobby the people and parties in office, and sometimes win victories. But those who go that route have little or no interest in gaining support for universal governing principles, and even if they do, those in office whom they lobby have their own principles, priorities, and class loyalties. They may be induced to make concessions on particular demands, but they do so in the framework of their own ideology. Socialists who wish to advance their principles within civil society do not have a choice. Choosing the outsider's route, which Lippmann suggested, is to leave the game—or, at best, to stand on the sidelines as ultimately feckless kibitzers.

VII

In one regard, however, Lippmann was right on target. As he implied, the tendency of the party to remain organizationally pure would have proven fatal in the long run even if all other circumstances had remained favorable. This became clear in Schenectady when Lunn was reelected in 1915 (after having lost to a Democratic-Republican fusion candidate in 1913). As he had clearly stated in his first inaugural address in 1912, Lunn understood that no Socialist administration could establish all the principles of socialism overnight. "We know that we cannot abolish the capitalist system in Schenectady," he said. But "we can and will demonstrate to all the spirit of Socialism and the application of socialist principles insofar as possible with the handicap of laws framed to establish and sustain capitalism." Working within this framework implied the necessity of making compromises, as well as the necessity of working with non-socialists. This, in turn caused difficulties, even in his first term, with the Schenectady local's more sectarian members.

Lunn's reelection in 1915 was not so much a party as a personal victory. The only other Socialists elected that year were Steinmetz, as head of the board of education (he had been elected president of the Common Council in 1913 when Lunn lost to Democratic-Republican fusion), and the aldermen of the two strongest working-class wards. Several days after Lunn resumed office in January 1916, a new dispute within the party local arose over his appointment of several Republicans and Democrats to city jobs. Once again, the state organizer came up from New York City, this time for two days of inconclusive talks. Then Lunn was summoned down to New York, where talks continued. Finally, the state party demanded the removal of at least one of his appointees. Lunn refused, the party suspended the Schenectady local and, in effect, Lunn was expelled from the party. That pretty much destroyed the Schenectady local. Under Lunn it had grown to 750 members. After he left, it dropped again to about 250. However, Lunn continued running for mayor and was reelected twice as a Democrat, after which he was elected as the Democratic lieutenant governor of New York.

The New York party's treatment of Lunn, unfortunately, was no aberration. Overall, many Socialists were expelled once they reached office and had to deal with political compromise. Many times narrowly practical reasons prevailed, as in Ashtabula, where a councilman was expelled for voting "dry" when the local was "wet." But sometimes there were matters of principle involved, as when H. K. Davis, a Nevada state assemblyman, was expelled for voting against women's suffrage. In Edmunds, Washington, Socialist school board members who refused to appoint a Socialist as principal of the local high school were summarily expelled. And, although this was not typical, many Socialist locals throughout the country viewed the practical activity of elected Socialists with extreme suspicion.

Socialists were expelled from the party, or hounded to the point of resigning, for many reasons. In Ashtabula, Ohio, W. E. Boynton, the Socialist president of the city council, resigned from the party after he had been attacked by his local's "reds" for voting in favor of a commission charter that included proportional representation, and, therefore, was in full accord with official party policy. In Los Angeles, the city council's lone Socialist was expelled from the party after voting for a Democrat as council president. In Duluth, Minnesota, Socialist state Senator Richard Jones was expelled from his local, dominated by an IWW-oriented Finnish branch, apparently simply because he had managed to get himself elected. And in Pittsburg, Kansas, when two local members accepted Trades and Labor Council support of their campaign for city council, they were brought up on charges of diluting socialist principles in the "quest for mere election."

VIII

The history of third parties in the late nineteenth century—and the changes made in the electoral process during the Progressive Era—may account for some of the Socialists' tendency toward semi-paranoid distrust of their elected representatives. The last four decades of the century—from the end of the Civil War to the presidential election of 1896—saw the rise and fall of the Union Labor Party, the Greenback party, and the Populist party. Each had its day in the sun, but none lasted as long as the Socialist Party, which was the only sustained third party of any significance in the twentieth century. That fact is a tribute to the power of its ideas, but the party's hostility to progressives, both Republican and Democratic, for "stealing" and then diluting Socialist ideas, which Lippmann noted, may well have had its source in the fate of the Populists in 1896, when Bryan ran as a Democrat.

In 1914, one state party—North Dakota's—directly confronted the problem of party loyalty and the third-party bugaboo. North Dakota's Socialists were well-organized—second only to Oklahoma among agricultural states. They had elected several important local officials, as well as one state assemblyman, and had come close to electing a few others. The party's platform, which included state rural credit programs, state-owned grain mills and elevators, state hail insurance, and insurance against plant and animal disease, had a high level of support from the state's farmers. And its call for unemployment insurance for the state's workers was popular with North Dakota union members.

But, as Robert Morlan wrote in *Political Prairie Fire, the Nonpartisan League, 1915–1922*, after many years of campaigning on these issues, party leaders were "acutely aware" that their program "was in much greater favor than was the party." The great majority of the state's farmers "heartily endorsed the proposals," party leaders believed, "but they were too much afraid of the name" to join, or even to vote for Socialist candidates.

Acting on this insight, the party state committee launched an experiment. It set up an organization department to which non-Socialists who favored the program could belong without having to accept a red party card and hired Arthur C. Townley as its organizer. Townley was a former farmer who had been known as the "flax king of North Dakota" before a devastating winter snowstorm destroyed most of his crop and speculators had made the remainder almost worthless.

Townley was a brilliant and indefatigable organizer. Supplied by the party with a Model T Ford and loads of Socialist literature, he criss-crossed the state holding meetings arranged by headquarters, selling literature, and taking pledges from farmers to vote and work for candidates who favored the state program and to pay a dollar a month to support the work. If farmers were short at the time, Townley took post-dated checks, payable after the harvest.

Success was instantaneous. Farmers signed up in such great numbers that within three months Townley had to hire four other organizers. But for the party, the success soon became too great. Some party members considered the program dishonest. The more doctrinaire members objected that the new members were not sufficiently schooled in socialist principles. And, more importantly, the leaders also worried that at the rate farmers were joining this auxiliary, "the tail would soon be wagging the dog." More concerned about the purity of their ideas than in testing them in a more popular forum, the delegates at the January 1915 state convention voted to discontinue the effort.

Townley, who in 1914 had run for the state assembly on the Socialist ticket, was more than disappointed. Convinced that the party was as hopelessly conservative as the major parties in its methods and its aversion to new ideas, he quit. Then he and A. E. Bowen, a one-time Socialist candidate for governor, went on alone. Not a man of small ambition, Townley began by going to farmers not to ask them to elect him to office, but to help him form an organization, the Nonpartisan League, that would capture the entire state government. His platform was similar to the Socialists': state ownership of terminal elevators, flour mills, packing houses, and cold storage plants; state inspection of grain and grain dockage; exemption of farm improvements from taxation (an old Henry George idea); state hail insurance on an acreage tax basis; and rural credit banks operated at cost.

The first day, Townley and Bowen visited nine farmers and signed them all up. They agreed to vote only for the candidates who pledged to support the Nonpartisan League platform, regardless of party label, and to pay $2.50 per year (later raised to $16) in dues. Within weeks they needed help in signing up all the farmers eager to join. A group of new recruits bought three new Model Ts for Townley and he then hired several young Socialist farmers as additional organizers.

Constantly stressing the need for tight organization, Townley believed that dues payments were essential, not only to finance the league, but also because a farmer who put money into an organization "would stick with it if only to get a return on his investment." Equally important, Townley knew that this organization could be held together only if information and intellectual stimulation continuously reached the members through their own publication. So subscriptions to the radical *Pearsons Magazine* and, before the end of the first year, to the league's new weekly newspaper, *Nonpartisan Leader*, were included in the dues payments. The *Leader*, edited by yet another Socialist, H. E. Behrens, played a vital role in the league's success. Soon, with 30,000 subscribers, it became the most widely circulated North Dakota publication.

The new direct primary laws (the first of which had been passed in Mississippi in 1902) made it possible for the first time for party nominations in many states to be taken from cliques of party professionals and placed in the hands of organized voters. The Nonpartisan League intended to do just that by running its own nominees in each district's majority party primary, and also in the majority party's contests for statewide office. The league's mission, in other words, was to unite all farmers in an organization "that will stand apart from every political party, every political machine and free from every political boss and put men in office [who] will legislate in [their] interest."

For the first several months, Townley's organizing was done quietly, farmer to farmer, with as little publicity as possible. Indeed, when he went to the Fargo postmaster in the fall of 1915 and asked for permission to mail 18,000 copies of the *Leader*, the postmaster said that he couldn't do so until he had 18,000 paid subscribers. When Townley said that's what he had, the postmaster was incredulous. "I've never heard of your paper or your organization," he said. Townley replied, "You're right. I've been organizing farmers, not postmasters."

In February 1916—less than two years after Townley had quit the Socialist Party—the league's first precinct meetings were held. The members were called together to select delegates to a state convention where individual candidates were to be chosen to run in the primary election of each legislative district—and statewide for the state's top offices. Naturally, in a Republican majority district, the league's designee would run in the Republican primary and in a Democratic majority district its designee would run as a Democrat.

These first precinct meetings were genuine grassroots affairs. An astounding 26,000 farmers, almost the entire signed-up membership, attended the meetings. And, because there weren't enough headquarters officials to be present at more than a handful of these gatherings, local farmers ran most of them themselves. Members simply gathered at their precinct, elected a chairman and secretary, and got down to the business of electing delegates to the convention. Dozens of precincts had a 100 percent turnout, none had less than 90 percent. Not surprisingly, the great majority of delegates chosen at the precinct meetings were nominal Republicans, but a fair number of Democrats were also selected, along with two Socialists. Those chosen then gathered in Fargo in late March for a convention that formally nominated candidates for statewide office and for the legislature.

In the June primary, every league-endorsed statewide nominee won his party's nomination. Lynn J. Frazier, a farmer and political unknown, led the Republican ticket and became that party's candidate for governor. William Langer, a future U.S. senator, was nominated for attorney general. P. M. Casey, the lone Democrat on the league's list, was nominated for state treasurer. League nominees for the state assembly and senate did almost as well. Of ninety-eight nominees for house seats, eighty-seven won, and of twenty-two nominated for the state senate, seventeen won.

The election in November produced an even greater victory. Woodrow Wilson surprised the pundits and carried the normally Republican state of North Dakota by 1,735 votes, but Frazier, running on the Republican line, out-polled Wilson and carried large numbers of Democratic precincts. In one precinct with only five registered Republicans, Wilson beat his Republican opponent, Charles Evans Hughes, 44–6, but Frazier carried the precinct 50–0. In legislative races the league did almost as well. In the house, the league elected sixty-eight of the ninety-seven Republicans and thirteen of the sixteen Democrats. In the senate, where only twenty-five of forty-nine members were up for election in 1916, the league elected eighteen of the candidates it endorsed, fourteen as Republicans, four as Democrats.

The Nonpartisan League now controlled the entire state government, except for the senate, half of which consisted of holdovers. That was good enough to get some of the league's program enacted, but a new constitution was required for the state or its political subdivisions to establish publicly owned elevators, flour mills, and other businesses, to pay for state hail insurance through taxation, and to make other democratizing changes. A draft constitution drawn up by the league passed its first test, in the assembly, by a vote of 81–28, but it was defeated in the senate, 29–20. Two years later, however, league members had replaced most of the twenty-four senatorial holdovers from 1916, and the new constitution was enacted. From these victories, the league went on to elect the state's sole U.S. representative and its two U.S. senators. It was to keep control of the state for decades.

Early on, the striking success in North Dakota had brought forth a flood of requests from many parts of the country, and even from Canada, about the league's program and organizing methods. Farmers and workers in adjoining states, especially Minnesota and South Dakota, were eager to follow suit. Shortly after the opening of the 1917 legislative session, therefore, the league moved its headquarters to the more centrally located St. Paul, Minnesota, and changed its name to the National Nonpartisan League. It was now poised to spread rapidly. But even as the Nonpartisan–dominated North Dakota legislature assembled for its first jubilant meeting, the dark clouds of World War I were gathering. Only three months later, as President Wilson led the country into war—five months after being reelected as the man that had "kept us out of war"— a period of unprecedented turmoil began.

IX

At its emergency convention in St. Louis on April 7, 1917, one day after the U.S. Senate declared war on Germany, the Socialist Party condemned the declaration as "a crime against the people of the United States." Reiterating its allegiance to the principle of international working-class solidarity, the party pledged active opposition to the war and called on workers of all nations to oppose what it characterized as a fight between capitalist interests over colonial markets. The delegates at St. Louis pledged that Socialists would "not willingly give a single life or a single dollar" in support of capitalism. Instead, the party promised "continuous, active and public opposition" to conscription and "vigorous resistance" to censorship of the press and restrictions of free speech and the right to strike.

Initially—as the only party firmly opposed to American participation—this stance produced a new spurt of growth for the party. In the 1917 municipal elections, held shortly after the April declaration of war, Socialists got record high votes in dozens of major cities. In New York City, party leader Morris Hillquit got 21.5 percent of the vote for mayor and the party elected ten state assemblymen, seven alderman, and a municipal judge. In Chicago, the Socialists got 34 percent of the vote in judicial elections—and it carried nineteen of the twenty-nine towns in the rest of Cook County. In Ohio, the party received more than 30 percent of the vote in seven cities and two towns. Socialists also elected mayors in sixteen small cities and towns, from Camas, Washington, to Garret, Pennsylvania.

Even a year later, in Wisconsin, Socialist leader Victor Berger got 26 percent of the vote in a statewide April election for the U.S. Senate, and then, in November, was reelected to Congress from Milwaukee. The party's entire county ticket also won, and Wisconsin Socialists increased their numbers in the state assembly from thirteen to twenty-two. Similarly, in Minneapolis in 1918, the Socialist delegation on the city council jumped from three to seven. Socialist Mayor Thomas Van Lear, however, was narrowly defeated in a two-way race, though his vote increased from the previous three-way election.

The Socialists' 1917 success inspired the party's daily *New York Call* to proclaim: "The great victories that we are winning and that we are going to win are the most significant political events of the century . . . it is not a political revolution. It is *the* political revolution." Indeed, support for the party seemed to be growing so rapidly that this view is almost understandable. In Wisconsin, for example, the Progressive Republican *Plymouth Review* commented, "Probably no party ever gained more rapidly in strength than the Socialist party is at the present time." The paper, a strong supporter of Republican Senator Robert A. LaFollette, concluded that "a war-sick world" was turning to the Socialists. "Thousands assemble to hear Socialist speakers in places where ordinarily a few hundred are considered large assemblages." If a new local election were held, the *Review* believed, the Socialists could "carry Sheboygan county by three-to-one against the two old parties together."

In Akron, Ohio, C. L. Knight's conservative *Beacon-Journal* agreed: "Were an election to come now a mighty tide of Socialism would inundate the Middle West" and "maybe all other sections of the country." This was so, Knight wrote, because the United States had never embarked on a more unpopular war. The "vast majority of the people . . . had never been convinced that the war was necessary either to sustain our honor or protect or interests." So, the *Beacon -Journal* concluded, "people vote the Socialist ticket as a means of protest."

In North Dakota, Nonpartisan League members were also largely against the war. In January 1917, one of the new legislature's first official acts had been to petition President Wilson to maintain neutrality. Calling the drive toward war the result of propaganda on the part of munitions and armor-plate makers, the legislature had suggested that Congress give the president authority in the event of war to seize and operate all manufacturing plants, shipyards, armor-plate mills, and flour mills, "so that citizens of wealth may be enabled and compelled to contribute to the common welfare and need of their country on the same terms as the enlisted soldiers and sailors who give their lives and their all." But once war had been declared, the league formally endorsed American participation while persisting in its demands for a statement of war aims and peace terms. No person should profit from the war, league speakers insisted as they called for conscription of wealth as well as men.

But despite electoral gains and the popularity of their views, the antiwar forces were no match, even in the short run, for the federal government and local chambers of commerce. The commercial press, too, whipped up pro-war propaganda and encouraged the suppression of dissent. By the end of the war, under constant harassment from federal agents, dozens of Socialist newspapers—the party's primary method of building and leading its membership—had been banned from the mails and driven out of business. And as the federal government prosecuted some 2,000 Socialists for sedition, and privately organized vigilantes terrorized all who failed to display sufficient patriotic fervor, the party's public support faded. By the time the war ended, 3,500 of its 5,000 pre-war locals had disappeared, never to be heard from again.

In North Dakota, the league, because it controlled the state government, survived more or less unscathed. But its efforts to expand into other states were not so lucky. This was true even in Minnesota, where anti-war sentiment was strong and the league had 50,000 members. In 1917, Socialists in Minnesota had held dozens of mass meetings to protest the war. In New Ulm, 7,500 farmers and townspeople had gathered to hear Minneapolis Mayor Thomas Van Lear denounce conscription at a meeting jointly presided over by the local college president and the mayor. Two weeks later 6,000 gathered in Glencoe to protest the sending of American troops to France, and 4,500 of them signed petitions against sending troops overseas.

These meetings and others addressed by many less prominent Socialist speakers led to many arrests and inspired local chambers of commerce to organize "loyalty" meetings throughout the state. Among those arrested was J. O. Bentall, a farmer, a former editor of the *Christian Socialist,* and a one-time Socialist candidate for governor. In a letter from jail Bentall described a meeting at Hutchinson, which, he said, attracted 10,000 farmers. "I never saw anything like it," he wrote. The farmers were "full of enthusiasm and eagerness," but "in the middle of my speech, the local postmaster rushed up and struck me in my face." He was "promptly reduced to quiet by some big farmers," and Bentall talked for another hour and a half. "People are falling over each other these days to hear about socialism," he wrote. "The farmers are most radical and fearless. . . . Eight thousand attended a meeting at Dale, including two sheriffs, three judges, and several U.S. deputy marshals and a number of plainclothesmen . . . I never talk against the war, all I do is talk peace."

But talking peace instead of opposing war was too fine a distinction to provide protection for Socialists or other pacifists. The Minnesota League found this out in 1918, when it made its first electoral effort. That year, delegates to the precinct caucuses had selected a statewide ticket and had nominated candidates in forty-eight of Minnesota's sixty-seven senatorial districts. (In the remaining urban and mining districts, where farmers were few and far between, the league pledged to support labor-endorsed congressional and legislative candidates.) The majority of the candidates selected were Republicans, but many Democrats and a few Socialists and Prohibitionists were also chosen.

As its candidate for governor, the league endorsed Charles A. Lindbergh, a farmer and former five-term congressman (and the father of the aviator who would later be the first person to fly solo across the Atlantic Ocean). Lindbergh was a Republican who had strongly opposed American participation in the European war. He had been a strong supporter of the league since its inception, and while he now supported the war effort, he shared the league's criticisms of the administration.

After choosing its slate for the state's primary election, 7,000 league members and trade unionists held a joint two-day rally in St. Paul. Governor J. A. Burnquist, as the state's chief executive, was invited to deliver a welcome address. Instead, he wrote a scathing attack on both the league, which he said was pro-German, and on organized labor, which he called a "criminal element," because it was in the midst of a prolonged strike against St. Paul's municipal railway.

That set the tone for the campaign, which began before a crowd so huge that the meeting had to be moved to the city fairgrounds. Speaking about the war's origin, Lindbergh acknowledged that Americans sincerely believed it to be a war to make democracy secure throughout the world. This aim, he said, must constantly be kept to the fore. This meeting was no anomaly. Throughout the campaign, in places that he was allowed to speak, huge crowds greeted Lindbergh as a hero. At his largest meeting, toward the end of the campaign, 14,000 people came from as much as seventy miles away to hear and cheer him.

In his acceptance speech Lindbergh had attacked those fostering distrust of fellow citizens by shouts of "pro-Germanism." These people were seriously harming the nation's well-being, he said. And, calling on the government to "put into practice at home those principles for which we have sent our boys abroad," he argued that it would avail little to win a war for democracy abroad while the traditional rights and privileges of the people at home were abrogated. Disloyalty was a problem, he agreed. But the truly disloyal were those "seeking to perpetuate themselves in special privilege and in office" by falsely raising the cry of loyalty. "The battles for industrial democracy," he concluded, "are still to be fought at home."

Meanwhile, Governor Burnquist announced that he would not be campaigning this year because he didn't believe that this was "a time to go into politics." That enabled him to avoid all the issues in the campaign, as well as the debates. Instead he held a steady stream of so-called "loyalty" meetings throughout the state. At Burnquist's first big loyalty meeting, in Minneapolis, the governor warned local authorities that if they could not—or would not—stop "anti-American" meetings, "every resource at our command will be used to punish offenders and prevent such meetings from being held." And if "bloodshed and loss of life" result, the supporters of "these un-American demonstrations," by their presence would be responsible. Chambers of commerce and other vigilante groups got the message. Where they could they closed every store in town and barricaded streets to keep Lindbergh from speaking. In Red Wing, the Home Guard was called out to disperse a league parade as it approached the city. In other towns parades were met with firehoses, ripe tomatoes, and yellow paint, and cars were overturned and vandalized.

Stoned, rotten-egged, hanged in effigy, Lindbergh did not flinch. As the campaign progressed he was clearly leading in popular support. But, as Robert Morlan wrote in *Political Prairie Fire,* "Towns and even whole counties were barred to this candidate for the Republican nomination for governor, and he was constantly followed by detectives." In the major city of Duluth, Lindbergh was locked out of the hall where he was scheduled to speak. A local newspaper explained that the city had "entertained too many returned soldiers, bearing the wounds of battle to be willing to act as a host to a friend of the Kaiser."

In the end, Burnquist was renominated with 199,325 votes to Lindbergh's 150,626. The league had lost this wartime battle, but it had laid the groundwork for the emergence of the Minnesota Farmer-Labor Party, which went on to dominate Minnesota politics for many years. During the campaign, the *Minneapolis Journal*, a staunch Burnquist supporter, had chided the league for promoting a class combination that not even the dreaded Bolsheviks had attempted—"that of the capitalist farmer and the industrial worker." But Arthur Townley had intended this from the beginning. In North Dakota the effort had little visible effect because there was so little industry, but in Minnesota urban labor was an important force, and the unions strongly supported the league. At Lindbergh's closing campaign rally, Arthur Townley had emphasized this point: "Farmers of Minnesota, is there any hatred in your hearts toward organized labor?" The building shook as the men roared back "No."

"Those of you who pledge your allegiance to the workers of the city will stand." Thousands of Minnesota farmers jumped to their feet and the applause was tumultuous.

"Workers of the city, if you likewise pledge your allegiance to the farmers of Minnesota, please stand." In an instant, Morlan wrote, the rest of the auditorium was on its feet, while hats sailed in the air amid deafening cheers.

This was an alliance that some of the self-styled Marxists in the Socialist Party would denounce. But, as Marx himself had written, classes were not fixed political entities, but were formed when different groups came together to protect themselves against a common enemy. And that is what happened in Minnesota in 1918. Interestingly, too, as Elizabeth Sanders pointed out in *Roots of Reform*, farmers, America's quintessential rugged individualists, were the ones who called for government hail insurance and ownership of things like grain elevators and flour mills—businesses that, in the new era of large-scale corporate capitalism were strangling the operation of the farmers' traditional free market. Labor, on the other hand, did not call for public ownership of business, but for an eight-hour day, prohibition of industrial child labor, a minimum wage law for women in industry, workmen's compensation for injuries, freedom from injunctions against strikes, and government programs like unemployment insurance and Social Security. Farmers in North Dakota and Minnesota supported these demands because they would strengthen labor's rights in their struggles against the common enemy, and because the positive government programs would protect working people's welfare, all of which was for the common good.

Both the farmers' and the workers' demands were, of course, consistent with socialist principles as developed and enunciated by the old Socialist Party. The new political strategy, initiated by Townley and some other North Dakota Socialists, had greatly expanded the social and political constituency for these demands.

X

By early 1919, after the government's brutal attacks on the Socialist Party during the war, which included the banning of all major Socialist publications from the mails and the House's refusal to seat Victor Berger following his reelection to Congress in 1918, it was difficult to sustain faith in the party's unimpeded growth. That situation was vastly exacerbated by the growing split in the party brought on by the new apocalyptic followers of the Russian Revolution, and then by the Bolsheviks' founding of the Third (Communist) International, with its demand for immediate insurrections and subordination to the Communist Party in Moscow.

As far as socialism was concerned, the greatest damage done by these events was a growing confusion about its meaning and nature, especially as the Russian Revolution created a euphoric turning toward its great achievement and the promise it seemed to many to hold for a real-world transformation of society.

But what did that revolution mean? Did it advance or retard the development of socialist ideas and principles? Could a viable American left be built on the shoulders of Leninism? To answer these question, we must turn to Russia and the developments there in the 1920s.

4

GOOD INTENTIONS:
THE RUSSIAN REVOLUTION
AS AN ACT OF WAR

I

ON NOVEMBER 7, 1917, the Bolsheviks (the majority faction of the Russian Social Democratic Labor Party) seized power in Petrograd and established what the journalist John Reed called "the most marvelous [adventure] mankind ever embarked upon." In the months before and after the Bolsheviks' victory, Reed had observed and studied these developments firsthand. The initial phase of the revolution, he wrote, was a brief period of feckless rule by a vacillating Provisional Government, led by the Mensheviks (the minority faction of the RSDLP). For eight months, the Mensheviks alternately encouraged and resisted breaking up the great estates and distributing land to the peasants. They failed to turn factories over to the workers. And they did not allow the soviets (councils) of worker, soldier, and peasant deputies to "assume the task of local administration in every village, town, city, district and province." When the Mensheviks faltered, and a state of near chaos ensued, Lenin stepped in, led the Bolsheviks to power, and attempted initially to put through these reforms.

In his classic story of the Revolution, *Ten Days that Shook the World*, Reed described these events with an optimism typical of the euphoria that gripped the left throughout the world in the early years of Communist rule in Russia. In the United States, three months after the revolution, the Socialist Party's national executive committee rejoiced that the Bolsheviks now threatened "the thrones of Europe" and had made the "whole capitalist structure tremble." Almost every Socialist leader expressed similarly positive views. Eugene Debs had early praised the Bolsheviks, and in 1919—while in prison for a speech he made opposing the war—he wrote in the magazine *The Class Struggle* that "from the crown of my head to the soles of my feet, I am a Bolshevik, and proud of it." Morris Hillquit, in June 1918, saw Russia as standing "in the vanguard of democracy, in the vanguard of social progress, all through from top to bottom, of the people themselves, of the working class, the peasants." Not to be outdone, Victor Berger wrote on the revolution's first anniversary that "The Russian people love the Soviets. They are the Soviets. Here is a government of the people and for the people in actual fact. Here is political and industrial democracy."

Even some of the Socialists who had supported U.S. involvement in the war showed enthusiasm for the Russian Revolution. Max Hayes of the Typographical Union wrote in his newspaper, the *Cleveland Citizen*, that the Soviets were "the most extreme democratic government that has yet been inaugurated." A few months later at the 1919 emergency convention of the Socialist Party—where those who formed the Communist Party, the Communist Labor Party, and the Proletarian Party all broke ranks with the Socialists—Dan Hogan of Arkansas took it for granted that Socialists of all stripes gave "unqualified support to Soviet Russia."

II

Despite the best intentions of the Bolsheviks, a potential for democracy, much less socialism, did not exist in tsarist Russia. Lenin and his comrades understood this full well. But Lenin was also aware that Marx and Engels had speculated in 1880 that the tsarist state's weakness might allow socialists to seize power in Russia and act as a catalyst for proletarian revolution in the more developed West. In 1917, Lenin seized upon this hope and, with some difficulty, managed to convince his fellow Bolsheviks that they could ignite the spark that would set off an uprising in the West. (*Iskra*, the name of Lenin's pre-revolutionary newspaper, means "spark" in Russian.) And when the spark set off revolution in the West, Lenin wrote, leadership of the world socialist movement would pass again to the German Social Democrats, where it belonged. Only thus, Lenin and his comrades believed, could their revolution survive. Firm in this belief, the Bolsheviks took the fatal step and seized power in Petrograd and Moscow.

By doing this, as Moshe Lewin conceded in *Russia/USSR/Russia*, Lenin opened himself to the charge of acting prematurely, and thereby of creating a "catastrophe." But, Lewin argued, such a critique ignored the historical situation in which the Bolsheviks found themselves in late 1917. Coup or no coup, whether they had acted or not, Russia was already a catastrophe. With millions of soldiers poorly supplied, hungry, and in humiliating retreat, with millions of peasants starving and increasingly isolated in the countryside, and with industry in a state of near collapse, the tsarist state had fallen of its own dead weight in February 1917. A few months later, with Russia still in the same condition and with the Social-Democratic provisional government unwilling to act decisively, the government fell again, also with barely a struggle. Lenin's initiative had enabled him to pull off the coup, but like Charlie Chaplin's little tramp in *Modern Times,* he found himself at the head of the mob waving a red flag almost by chance.

Lewin wrote that even when the Bolsheviks were preparing to contest for power, during the eight months of Menshevik rule, Lenin believed that the most realistic scenario for Russia's development was to replicate a "version of the bourgeois democratic revolution that had brought or was pushing the [more] developed countries into a democratic era." Without this stage of development, Lenin understood, there was no path to a socialist future.

During the months of the provisional government the Bolsheviks had become a legal party. They had operated within the short-lived multi-party system and, functioning as "a democratic political party under strong authoritarian leadership," they had done well. In a few short months, the party had grown from some 17,000 members to perhaps 250,000. However, the provisional government's inability to establish a viable political democracy seemed to Lenin to close off the possibility of creating a Western-style political system, which left the Bolsheviks with two choices. They could stand by and helplessly observe continued chaos and degeneration, or they could seize power themselves and attempt to create a stable society.

Once they seized power, however, the Bolsheviks had to defend their new regime against stunned tsarist and capitalist forces. These White Russians (as the tsarist forces were called)—aided fitfully by the Western powers—fought desperately in a civil war against the Bolsheviks. In 1921, when the war finally ended, the further devastation it had caused left Russia in even more primitive shape than it had been in 1917.

Meanwhile, Communist efforts to spread the revolution to the West had failed to generate successful uprisings. Only in Hungary, under Bela Kun, did Communists come to power. But their regime, established in 1919, survived for only a year. In Germany, which was at the heart of Lenin's dreams, a revolution attempted when the war finally ended failed completely. Elsewhere even less was accomplished. By 1921, Russia and the Communists stood naked and alone, without hope of aid from more developed countries.

Inside Russia, because of the widespread ruin of industry during the civil war, agriculture and the peasantry, Lewin tells us, "loomed larger in Russian society than ever before in modern times." Even at the height of its pre-war industrial development, Russia had been an overwhelmingly peasant country. Now, with the civil war–induced "ruralization of a rural country," the peasants retreated into an age-old shell, characteristic of "much more primitive times." This experience completely reversed the sketchy beginnings of a capitalist market economy that the pre-revolutionary peasantry had undergone before the World War. As these capitalist beginnings broke down, the peasants transformed themselves into "a family-oriented ocean of microfundia"—a nation of inward-looking subsistence farms that calculated production in terms of "mouths to feed," rather than efficiency and market opportunities.

In other words, according to Lewin, when the Bolsheviks finally got the chance to lead the country toward its declared goals, they faced conditions not seen since the nineteenth century. Not only had thousands of the more politically advanced party members and workers been killed in the civil war, but the democratic components of the revolutionary regime—the trade unions, the workers' committees, the soviets—had been weakened, atrophied, or exterminated. These institutions had given the revolution its democratic promise. Now they were gone. The civil war, and the seemingly endless series of crises in its aftermath, had also transformed the inner life of the party. In pre-revolutionary Russia the Communists could work openly only after the first revolution in February brought the provisional government to power. Before that Bolsheviks could not participate directly in the narrowly restricted civil society. To protect themselves, and to work efficiently as illegal entities, they had already developed the habit of operating as a military-style hierarchy. The ordeal of the civil war reinforced this extensive use of coercive measures and made them seem natural.

At first, after the war, the Bolsheviks staffed their new state agencies largely with revolutionaries and workers, but that only masked the "ever-deepening trend toward a pervasive authoritarianism." As the need for experienced administrators became apparent, the old tsarist bureaucrats and commissars became mainstays of the system, and the revolutionary masses were eased out as meaningful actors and partners in the new regime. More ominously, Lewin wrote, the coercive measures that the Bolsheviks devised initially for the struggle against the bourgeoisie—labor conscription and forced labor—"soon began to be applied to other groups and, finally, to the principal backers of the regime itself."

During the civil war, of course, military needs were all-consuming. As the war dragged on—and as social support faltered, including, in its later stages, the support of industrial workers—constant vigilance became necessary. Under these conditions of profound anxiety, the party changed from a relatively democratic political organization—one in which policy was vigorously debated and voted on by its members—into an increasingly militarized and bureaucratized arm of the state. Orders from on high now were followed without question. And in order to handle the crises that kept popping up everywhere, cadres (active party members) were frequently dispatched on involuntary organizing missions by the state bureaucrats. At first, these were seen as temporary expedients, but soon these practices became permanent features of the Soviet state.

In this situation, Lewin wrote, Lenin became obsessed with the necessity of proving that "the new masters know how to run things" to the peasants' advantage. "Either we pass the exam of competition with the private sectors," he told the eleventh party congress in 1922, "or there will be a *proval* [downfall]." But the Bolsheviks knew little or nothing about running things. To pass the exam, he said, required learning from the primary source of necessary knowledge—from the despised capitalists, international and local, from "the lowly employees in a commercial firm," or even from the "White guardsmen" who had fought the civil war against the Bolsheviks. The point, Lenin insisted, was not to lose the peasants. They had become the Bolsheviks' most important social base, and they could not assimilate or adapt to rapid change. So, if necessary, the party should "proceed infinitely slower in working toward its goals" than its members had anticipated.

In line with these beliefs, Lenin had announced the New Economic Policy at the party's tenth congress in 1921. The essence of NEP was tolerance of small-scale capitalist enterprise, combined with a regulated market to serve as a link between nationalized industry and peasant farms. For Lenin, this was not a new idea. As early as 1918 he had considered adopting a form of "state capitalism," a variation of NEP in which state-owned industries would operate on market principles. He reiterated this idea at the eleventh congress, in 1922—the last he would attend. Clearly, Lewin said, Lenin favored the market-driven path, as long as the capitalist forces could be kept under the party's political control. But he also feared that if the party got too involved in administering everything it would become depoliticized and grow into a rigid bureaucracy. To avoid this, he wanted party members to concentrate primarily on political leadership, while leaving the administration of industry to professional bureaucrats and to the cooperative organizations that had sprung up under the NEP.

But Lenin was already fatally ill when he proposed this, and party bureaucrats were increasingly happy with the power given them by "administering everything." Furthermore, NEP had real limitations. Its pace of development was not rapid enough for Russia to keep pace with the West, much less to catch up. NEP's assigned task was modest—to restore Russia's industry back to its 1913 level. So even if it achieved its aim of accelerating industrial development, Russia would keep falling further behind other countries. As the Russian economy chugged sluggishly toward attaining its pre-war level, the West, already far in the lead, was inexorably increasing the gap. Then, too, NEP's widespread popularity threatened to lead to a rival, pro-capitalist political force, one that might threaten Bolshevik power if it were not sharply curtailed.

When Stalin consolidated his power in 1928, therefore, the Soviet Union was at a real crossroads. With NEP not adequately meeting Russia's needs, something drastic needed to be done. But, as Lewin wrote, while "good leadership would have responded to the complexity of the situation with an appropriately formulated, thoughtful strategy," instead the Soviet Union got industrialization as an "'onslaught,' a civil war cavalry charge, a quasi-military operation, in which military terms themselves became the language of the day." Of course, what Lenin feared took place. The path of individual capitalist development under party control and supervision was abandoned. As the party bureaucrats assumed direct control of almost all legal economic activity, the top party and state bureaucracies all but merged and together took the place of a capitalist class in Russia's industrialization.

Even in the democratizing capitalist West, the initial period of rapid industrialization had often been brutal and corrupt, but this concentration of economic and state power in the same hands was a formula for social disaster. In the Soviet Union, now totally depoliticized and with a population devoid of the civil rights and liberties that had been fought for and won by working people in the capitalist countries, industrialization was inevitably more oppressive. The early years of the revolution had been hard enough on the general population, but at least the party's leaders had still been guided by humane principles and had vigorously debated social policy. Stalin, however, put an end to that. Taking full advantage of his unchallengable power, he ruthlessly utilized the statist traditions of Russia's tsarist past to pursue the growth of heavy industry.

Much of this push was made possible by importing foreign technology, but this could only be paid for with exports of agricultural products, mostly grain. To increase the grain exports that made industrialization possible, Stalin collectivized agriculture. This was an excruciating, often vicious, process that nevertheless accelerated development at an extremely rapid rate. In the twelve years that followed Stalin's consolidation of his personal power—from 1928 until Germany invaded in 1941—his forced march created some 8,000 huge and—in Lewin's words—"presumably modern" industrial enterprises.

Lewin estimated that during these years industry developed at an average annual rate of more than 16 percent, although at tremendous social cost. All of this was done under the rubric of "five-year plans." The "plans," however, were simply acts of will that had little to do with planning. Stalin gave them a socialist gloss, but the principles that had inspired the revolutionaries and galvanized its supporters were absent, or, rather, they were transformed into little more than camouflage for statist methods of management and nationalist goals of development.

III

Lenin understood the need not to alienate the peasants; Stalin used them as a substitute for capital. He said openly that they had to pay a "tribute" of grain to finance his grandiose industrial plans. In a letter to his most trusted aide, Vyacheslav Molotov, in 1930, Stalin wrote that "we must push grain exports *furiously*" or "risk being without our new iron and steel machine-building factories." Most historians attribute Stalin's drive to convert the basic productive units of the countryside from small individual farms to giant collectives (*kolkhozy*) to this imperative. But the resistance of the peasants to this move, and the massive investment in repressive forces needed to collect the surplus grain, were so great that collectivization may actually have impeded this process. In any case, the resources for industrialization came largely from the peasants, who starved to death in incalculable numbers in order to make this process of primitive capital accumulation possible.

Meanwhile, under the five-year plans, Soviet industry no longer worked for profit or for consumers. Instead, it worked "for the plan," which meant that it worked as the expression of Stalin's obsession with accelerating basic industrial development. The first five-year plan took two years to write. The final version called for an increase in production of 180 percent, a wildly optimistic figure that was soon discarded for even higher targets. Many party members questioned the new goals, but Stalin, noting that the Soviet Union was "fifty to a hundred years behind the advanced countries," disagreed. "On the contrary," he said, "we must increase [the tempo]." In 1931—ten years before Germany invaded—he warned about the danger that the country faced from the Nazis and from the expanding Japanese empire. If the country did not "make good the distance in ten years," he warned, "we shall go under."

But Stalin was like Lenin in one respect. In the process of trying to close the gap between the Soviets and the West, he also became an enemy of his own bureaucrats. In Stalin's case, however, it was not because he favored a more politicized party, but rather because the logic of bureaucracy clashed with his need for rapid change. Completely dependent on bureaucrats to carry out his plans, he was constantly frustrated by their sticky sluggishness. To speed them up, he resorted to ruthless terror, but that, too, had contradictory results. While it sometimes sped up action on particular problems, it also served to smother initiative. Instead of cutting corners to get things done, most bureaucrats were too fearful of attracting attention to themselves to take individual initiatives. So they hewed closer and closer to the rules, hoping they would not be noticed.

In any case, bureaucrats naturally worked by the numbers. They did not like surprises, much less constant new demands. As Lewin pointed

out, "A bureaucracy that is allowed to operate independently of economic criteria and results, and that lacks a concept of cost, looks for criteria and reference points that are, in its view, natural and manageable."
Thus quantitative targets and specifications became the rigid parameters
of usually unworkable plans.

IV

Gennady Andreev-Khomiakov, who had wide experience at the Soviet
Union's grassroots level, recounted in his memoir, *Bitter Waters, Life and
Work in Stalin's Russia*, how the five-year plans actually worked in the lumber industry. As a youth, in 1927, Andreev had been convicted as "an
enemy of the people." After eight years in various labor camps he was re-
leased, but forbidden to settle in Moscow or forty other large Soviet cities.
Being an ex-convict made him anathema to most employers, especially in
the terror years of the mid-1930s, so Andreev found it necessary to travel
widely in the Soviet hinterland, looking for work. First, after futilely seeking employment at dozens of factories and institutions, he got lucky and
was hired by an unusually courageous factory director who desperately
needed an experienced and literate bookkeeper (a skill Andreev had
learned in the camps)—and who was not afraid to take on a former political prisoner. For a year and a half, until the factory was shut down, Andreev worked contentedly in a small county seat in southeastern Russia.

Out of work again, he moved to a nearby university town and regional center. He wanted to attend the university part-time, but he could
not afford to study without income from a job, and he couldn't get hired
anywhere. Making the rounds of "hundreds of institutions and enterprises," he encountered the same story everywhere. First, he would ask
whether the enterprise needed an accountant, and since skilled workers
were in short supply, the answer was usually yes. But when he offered his
services, he would be asked for his documents, and the "inevitable question" followed: Where had he been employed before his previous factory
had shut down? Then, when he showed his prison release paper, his in-

terviewer "would read it as if he was holding a bomb that was about to explode." No prospective employer refused him outright—it was illegal to deny anyone employment because of a past conviction. But neither did anyone hire him.

Finally, Andreev got a job at the All-Union Regional Fish Trust, which urgently needed an accountant and hired him on the spot, no questions asked. He worked there for several months and was promoted to head bookkeeper. Then one day the oversight was discovered. The trust's director panicked, and, once again, Andreev was out on the street. But— thinking himself invulnerable—the director had fired him illegally. Andreev, who at this point had nothing to lose, sued. He lost his case in a local court, where the judge was also the fish-trust director's friend, but then went to Moscow, where the director was unknown, and appealed directly to the chief counsel for labor conflicts of the central committee of his trade union. The chief counsel took one look at his papers, said the firing was illegal and issued an order to the fish trust to reinstate him. Andreev, however, knew he had no future there. And the trust was glad to let him go. Once again, he was on his way.

Several days before these last events, he had written to his old factory director—now in charge of a lumber mill in a small town northwest of Moscow—asking for a job. The director telegraphed back: "Come at once. I will pay your way." Thinking, he said, that in all the Soviet Union he could apparently work for only one man, he went to the station and bought a ticket.

On the new job, he and the director hit it off once again. The two were a perfect match. The director, a highly competent party member and a man of untiring initiative, was barely literate. Andreev, much better educated, was able to negotiate the bureaucratic intricacies of the plan. Within months, as the director's most trusted assistant, he had been made head of the mill's planning department.

As a prisoner in the camps Andreev had experienced widespread cheating and deception. But he assumed that this was an abnormal condition, unique to prison life. Under "normal conditions," he assumed, such things could not exist. At the lumber factory, where on the surface everything worked according to the plan, he expected that there would be no room for "scheming." All the lumber produced would be accounted for, and lumber would be shipped only with the correct requisitions from Moscow. Reality, however, was completely different. No matter how strictly the plans were drawn up, they could neither anticipate nor coordinate everything. So factories, in order to operate outside the plan when necessary, routinely requested more supplies than they needed, and, when possible, they produced more goods than required. According to the plan at Andreev's mill, 67 percent of the logs were to be converted into usable lumber. But the manager contrived to make it 70 percent. The difference became a reserve that could be exchanged for goods not in the plan or not delivered when needed. One time, for example, the factory found itself with only enough saws for two or three weeks. The technical director had ordered saws according to the plan months before, but none had arrived—and none were likely to. When the technical director told the plant director that he was concerned, the plant director exploded. "How could you rely on an order?" he fumed. "This is not your first day on the job, [you know that] you have to wait a year for Moscow."

The director thereupon picked up the phone, called the plant's off-the-books (and illegal) purchasing agent in Moscow, and asked him to find saws. To motivate him, he sent a 300-ruble advance. After a week, the agent wired that he had found 150 brand new saws, which he could get in exchange for two train cars of lumber. The director agreed and the agent submitted a bill of 800 rubles for his services. Of course, Andreev explains, the saws that the agent acquired undoubtedly should have been shipped to another factory, which now would not receive its planned allocation. In turn, the other factory would also have to turn *na levo* (to the left, as the alternative economy was called) for its saws. But this did not bother the director. "Don't be a fool; just be careful," he told Andreev. "If you rely on the plan, you will sit idle. And even though we got them by questionable means, we now have saws and can calmly await the saws allocated to us by the plan."

The heart of the problem was that every enterprise had to go through the bureaucracy in Moscow for its equipment and supplies. As Stephen

Kotkin related in *Magnetic Mountain: Stalinism as a Culture*, Sergo Ordzhonikidze, a Poliburo member and people's commissar for heavy industry, lamented in 1930 that if things continued as they were, the "paper flow
. . . will drown us." But the efforts to combat the flood of paper with decrees and investigations only led to the further proliferation of officials,
and thus, as Lewin noted, to more paper. This situation led one economist
to suggest in 1932 that prices for industrial goods should reflect supply and
demand, and that firms should deal directly with each other, instead of
having to go through Moscow. Surprisingly, Ordzhonikidze ordered the introduction of just such procedures for the iron and steel industry. However
his order was abruptly canceled before it took effect.

Overall, the system was unworkable without cheating, and even with
cheating few enterprises made their plan targets. At Andreev's mill, however, thanks to the director's constant conniving, things worked well and
the plan was exceeded. His superiors up the line of command undoubtedly knew that he bent the rules, but they overlooked it and even encouraged him with the gift of a used Model A Ford. But there was a catch: To
succeed you had to cheat, and cheating was illegal. That meant that you
constantly had to look over your shoulder. If you had enemies in the
wrong places, no matter how well the plant performed you could suddenly become a candidate for the gulag. This being the case, the incentive was negative. Many more-timid directors preferred simply to play it
safe and perform badly.

The plans institutionalized inefficiency in other ways. For example,
each enterprise was allocated a fixed number of workers for its various departments. But in many departments the workload varied according to the
season or the bureaucratic schedule. So, if enough workers were provided
for the busy periods, some—or many—had nothing to do during slack periods. If a director of a department laid off these surplus workers during
slack times, however, getting them back later was all but impossible. So
factories hoarded workers as well as product, leading to the old Soviet joke
that "we pretend to work and they pretend to pay us." During the years of
forced industrialization, therefore, while shortages of labor were endemic,
large numbers of "employed" workers sat around with nothing to do.

In the lumber mills, constant shortages of logs were also a major problem. Before the revolution, Andreev said, this was not so. Indeed, the industry worked reasonably well until the civil war, when "lumbering stopped almost entirely." Under NEP, lumbering revived quickly, mostly in the form of *artels* (cooperatives). An All-Russian Cooperative Timber Union brought together the majority of these *artels*, along with many small privately owned firms. The union also leased state sawmills, repaired them, and worked alongside the state lumber trusts to increase production. By 1928, however, when Stalin ended NEP, the industry had barely been brought back to 1913 levels. Then, under the five-year plans, massive new construction sharply increased the demand for lumber.

As the collectivization of agriculture and the "subjection of forest villagers to *dekulakizatsiia* (the elimination of well-to-do peasants' farms and other enterprises)" went forward, the cooperative *artels* and the All-Russian Cooperative Timber Union were eliminated. A tidal wave of workers and small entrepreneurs then left the forests and production fell even farther behind demand. This new severe labor shortage, Andreev said, "could not be surmounted by normal methods." Instead, a system of forced labor replaced the traditional loggers. Lumber for export now became the responsibility of the NKVD-MVD (a branch of the secret police), which used prisoners for the work. In addition, "specially resettled" kulaks were sent into the forests to create a labor force. As early as 1929, Andreev said, some 500,000 prisoners were at work felling trees, alongside about a million kulaks and their families. The prisoners were not enthusiastic workers, and the kulaks, "whose labor was even less productive," were worse. Some managed to survive, but many others fled or died under the exceedingly harsh conditions.

As the system emerged under the "plan," the NKVD-MVD became responsible for the prison labor needed to produce lumber used to help finance the purchase of modern industrial equipment from abroad. (This was known as "squeezing credits from the forests," just as exacting grain for export "squeezed credits" from the farmers.) Production of logs for domestic use was the responsibility of the various territorial divisions of the People's Commissariat of Forestry. But the People's Commissariat faced an acute shortage both of workers and carting facilities in the forests and regularly fell far short of its plan. This forced the government to allow many builders and enterprises to conduct their own lumbering operations, with their own means.

Most branches of industry that did their own construction fell into this category. Called "self-providers," they were usually allocated the worst timber reserves, situated far from flotable rivers or from roads. In addition, their needs for labor were subordinated to the People's Commissariats. So, with one goal in mind—to provide themselves with lumber at any cost—the self-providers paid little attention to the rules. They lured workers away from the People's Commissariat by illegally paying them two to three times the official wage scale. In turn, to keep their workers from leaving, the People's Commissariat provided them with food and manufactured goods outside the plan. So it went, greatly raising the cost of labor above that mandated. As Lewin observed, practices like this and many other peculiarly "uneconomic" methods of operating came about because the quantity of production, rather than its cost or profitability, was the bottom line.

It was a system motivated by the will to catch up with the more highly industrialized capitalist countries, and disregard for market considerations facilitated growth. But as the system came to be "hooked on waste," it built up huge constituencies that thrived on inefficiency and that eventually found themselves incapable of making the changes needed to create a fully modern economy.

V

Nothing better illustrates the extent to which sheer willpower drove Soviet industrialization than the construction of Stalin's greatest project— the giant steel mill and city of Magnitogorsk.

Magnitogorsk was created almost overnight out of nothing but a barren mountain of exceedingly rich iron ore, located on the desolate, wind-swept steppes of western Siberia. The site had no railroad, no electricity, a road that in good weather was more like a dirt path and in bad more like a quagmire, and few, if any, fulltime inhabitants. It was as unlikely a place for what would be the Soviets' most important single factory as one can imagine. Yet, in less than a decade, Magnitogorsk grew into a city of 200,000, centered around one of the largest steel plants in the world.

No one in the Soviet Union had ever built anything even remotely like this plant, much less an entire modern city from scratch. And no one could have imagined the scale on which the city would eventually be built when the State Institute for the Design of Metallurgical Factories (Gipromez) began its work on the project in February 1926. Not only did the country lack the modern machinery and infrastructure required for the task, but it also lacked engineers and architects with the necessary skills. "Although all known experts in contemporary technology were in Gipromez," the official history of the organization noted, it still lacked the experienced specialists required for the whole range of tasks involved in creating a modern steel mill.

Faced with the predicament of having to create a Socialist steel mill and city, but not knowing how, Gipromez turned to those who presumably did. In 1927, it hired the Henry Freyn Company of Chicago, which, in 1906, had designed the U.S. Steel plant at Gary, Indiana. The Gary works and city, named after U.S. Steel Chairman Elbert H. Gary, was the largest steel plant in the world. When Stalin was told about it, according to Sergo Ordzhonikidze, he immediately decided to build just such a plant in the Soviet Union. And Freyn's role in the Gary project made it the logical choice to be hired for the job.

Designing the new complex was a daunting effort. Many people, even among the country's leaders, were awed by the difficulties to be overcome. Two years dragged by while Freyn worked on plans at the Gipromez main office in Leningrad, and skepticism about the project's viability grew apace. Finally, Freyn produced a 700-page volume of charts, graphs, and tables. Yet, as Stephen Kotkin told us in *Magnetic Mountain,* these plans were a long way from the thousands of blueprints that would be needed to guide the actual construction. Indeed, they appeared "to have been published less as a guide to building a plant than as reassurance against mounting doubts that a plant would in fact be built."

In any case, no designer could have kept pace with the constant changes projected by the country's leaders. In the years from the inception of the project in 1926 to the Freyn plan's publication in 1929, the political leaders ratcheted up the proposed capacity of the plant until it had little or no resemblance to the project the company had been hired to design. Originally, the annual capacity of the plant was set at 650,000 tons of pig iron. By the summer of 1929, the capacity was raised on paper to 850,000 tons. Almost immediately, Kotkin related, it was raised to 1.1 million tons, and then again to 1.6 million tons. Then, in the first five-year plan, the target became 10 million tons, and in 1930, even that was revised upward to 17 million tons.

In the end, for reasons that Kotkin said were unclear, Freyn was let go and Arthur McKee and Company of Cleveland, Ohio, specialists in the construction of blast furnaces and oil refineries, was hired. McKee was famous for designing and building the most advanced and largest blast furnace to be found in the pages of leading capitalist technical journals. That was just what Stalin wanted, so McKee was given a contract for $2.5 million in gold rubles to design the entire plant, including all auxiliary shops, the iron-ore mine, a dam, and an electric power station. The company agreed to train Soviet engineers on site and in Cleveland. It was also in charge of directing work on the site until the factory and mine were put in operation.

Meanwhile, some work had gone haltingly forward, though at every turn the builders met with what anywhere else might have been insurmountable problems. For example, construction of a rail link from Kartaly, 145 kilometers away—and the nearest junction to the site—had begun in 1926, then stopped until 1929 with only 40 kilometers of track laid. Finally, the line was completed with the help of the Red Army. But it had been built without the ballast needed to keep the rails from spreading, so trains could only crawl across it without derailing. The rail connections from Kartaly to Moscow were not much better. The first freight shipped from Moscow was said to have taken seventy days to arrive at Magnitostroi.

As Kotkin wrote, on-site leadership was one of the first problems to arise. The initial director, Sergei Zelentsov, went blind and had to be replaced. His immediate successor turned out to be incompetent and also had to be replaced. His successor Vadim Smolianinov (who had worked with Lenin in the early days of the revolution), was sent to Cleveland as part of the Soviet delegation. He was replaced by his deputy, Chingiz Ildrym. Ildrym, who had participated in the storming of the Winter Palace in 1917 and then was the first commissar of the navy in Azerbaijan, knew absolutely nothing about metallurgy. Even so, when his successor, who had been his deputy, was also sent to Cleveland, Ildrym stepped in again and served as de facto director.

According to Soviet witnesses, when the American team arrived at the site in the early summer of 1930 "there was not a single well-built settlement [and] no roads." Dumbfounded, the Americans "couldn't fathom how it was going to be possible to work without skilled workers, without complete sets of tools, without machines or construction materials." Even more disorienting, Kotkin wrote, was the Soviet approach to management. Much time and energy were spent on long-winded speeches to the effect that "only we Bolsheviks could undertake such tasks." Sadly, this was all too true. The intrigue and bluster of overlapping agencies and authority made the all-but-impossible circumstances even worse and institutionalized a state of "permanent crisis."

Lack of experience in building a steel plant was the greatest problem. Kotkin gave this example: One of the largest trusts assigned to build the steel plant in Magnitogorsk was Tekstilstroi, a firm that specialized in building textile mills. Upon reassignment to Magnitogorsk, it was simply renamed Stalstroi (steel construct). For those few people with experience in steel-making, this was a shock. As the chief of open hearth construction wrote, "The fundamental thing that sharply struck us was that among those who were at the site, there was no clue as to what a steel plant was." Of course, Kotkin commented, this was part of the plan: "In building a steel plant, everyone would learn—and quickly." In the seemingly mad rush to industrialize, not only were factories being created, but also an industrial working class.

VI

The first party of settlers arrived at Magnetic Mountain in March 1929, on horseback. They came to build some barracks and a small bakery, organize a workers' cooperative, and recruit more people. By mid-summer the rail line had been completed and the first train had arrived, carrying banners that read: "The Steel Horse Breathes Life into the Magnitogorsk giant" and "Long Live the Bolshevik Party." If many of the several thousand people on hand had never seen a train before, Kotkin wrote, "the train had perhaps never before seen such a wild and isolated place." True, for the steel plant, there was a mountain of rich ore, clay for bricks, and water for power. For a city, however, Magnitostroi lacked just about everything. There were almost no trees and no coal. There were few nearby agricultural centers to supply food and almost no good pasture land for livestock. And the severe climate, long winters with bitterly cold winds sweeping down from the Arctic, followed by unbearably hot, dry summers, made it almost uninhabitable. For the necessities of life, Magnitostroi was completely dependent on long-distance rail.

Even so, in the three and a half short years that followed, the twenty-five or so people who had arrived in March of 1929 grew to a city of 200,000. And, while people came and went pretty much as they pleased in those first years, a permanent urban population soon formed.

How did they come? Let me count the ways.

First, in keeping with Bolshevik practice, people were "mobilized," which is to say ordered, to relocate. Party members and skilled workers were the priority, but not even party officials knew what this new assignment was all about. One official sent to the site in 1931 recalled how a deputy in the Central Committee Organization Department broke the news about the mobilization of his group: "Comrades, you're going to Magnitka. And do you know what Magnitka is?" he asked. "No, we haven't a clue," was the answer. Well, "unfortunately, neither do we, but you're going to Magnitka all the same."

Go to Magnitka they did. In mid-1930, Kotkin related, "the office of the Magnitostroi trust, housed in the cozy quarters of the grandest building in Sverdlovsk," was suddenly ordered to move. Not surprisingly, many of the specialists were distraught about moving from the oblast (regional) center, where there were theaters, cinemas, and other cultural activities, "to the bare, wild steppe." A member of that original group later recalled that the order to move was usually greeted as "a personal tragedy." It was "very difficult," he said, "to forsake the comfort of one's own apartment in the busy and well-known city" to settle "in the middle of some deserted mountain."

For those sent from Moscow, the move was even worse. Like many specialists they were housed in one of Magnitogorsk's few habitable places, the relatively comfortable Central Hotel. But they were not happy. At night they would gather to discuss "whose assignment ended when." A favorite trick of these people was to put in for a short "vacation" and simply not return. Everyone had the same thought, recalled a local party official: "What was the quickest way out of Magnitka?"

Nor was mobilization always effective in the still fluid days of the early 1930s. Many more people were "mobilized" than arrived. The Moscow Komsomol (Communist Youth League), for example, ordered hundreds of young Communists to go to Magnitogorsk in 1930, but only twenty appeared at the site, including three girls legally too young to work eight-hour days. Some of those mobilized were foreigners. A handful of highly qualified specialists came on individual contracts with Amtorg (the American trading organization). Most, however, were either political refugees who had fled to the Soviet Union from Europe, only to be arrested when they crossed the border, or foreigners who had come to the Soviet Union on tourist visas. These mobilizations by command brought some badly needed specialists, or at least educated people, to the site. But, overall, mobilization contributed only a very small percentage of the city's rapidly growing population.

Ordinary citizens were not mobilized; they came as the result of "recruitment" by the Central Labor Commissariat. This voluntary system was the only way that ordinary citizens were supposed to be brought to the construction site; however, it required more than a bit of official pressure. Many recruits came from collective farms, which were offered raw materials and machines in exchange for workers. Others, especially white-collar employees, members of artisanal cooperatives, laborers, and uncollectivized "poor" peasants, were also targeted. Still, the central government's efforts to recruit workers fell short of the need. So Magnitostroi created its own recruitment arm. It sent agents into villages to promote the wonders of the "world-historical giant" being built at the foot of Magnetic Mountain. If that didn't entice recruits, the agents offered free rail transportation, work clothes, and a bread card on arrival, and even the promise of an extra full month's pay for recruits who stayed for five months. As further inducement, cash advances were sometimes offered.

These efforts were supported by a press campaign urging people to go to Magnitogorsk. Documentary films and newsreel footage about the great construction were shown in factories and movie houses. Worker-correspondents visited other factories and construction sites to stump for recruits—and to hand out train tickets on the spot. Other construction sites were especially good sources for recruitment, particularly if they had short-term projects nearing completion. In the enthusiasm of the moment, "entire work gangs would sometimes declare their desire to participate in the building of socialism at Magnetic Mountain," Kotkin wrote. Victor Kalmykov, for example, was one of hundreds who went to Magnitostroi after they had finished the preliminary foundation work at the Stalingrad tractor factory site in 1930.

Of course, given the endemic shortage of competent workers, recruiting did not always go smoothly. Many managers of factories and other construction sites, also short of workers, did their best to frustrate the recruiters. Collective farm chairmen also resisted the loss of their members by concealing recruitment announcements or by lying to the workers about the inducements being offered to lure them to Magnitostroi. Nevertheless, despite the tug of war for workers, 56,000 recruits arrived at the site in 1931.

But recruitment that year accounted for only 48 percent of those arriving at Magnitostroi. In 1932 the share dropped to 29 percent, and it went down again to 24 percent in 1933. In short, despite relentless efforts to recruit workers, only about a third of those arriving over the three years had come as a result of such efforts. Worse, many recruits did not stay. For several years people were coming and going by the tens of thousands, the number of workers arriving in Magnitostroi barely exceeding the number leaving. To combat the leakage, workers were lectured and cajoled about their moral obligation to the project, and local authorities declared mandatory registration for anyone leaving the site. In a more successful effort, many workers were given small plots of land on which to grow their own potatoes and other vegetables.

Despite these efforts leakage remained a major problem. In desperation, in December 1932, Sovnarkom reintroduced the tsarist system of internal passports. (The immediate cause of this "passportization" may well have been the fear that famine conditions in the countryside would drive peasants en masse into the cities in search of food. But, Kotkin wrote, the Bolshevik leadership was also trying to bring some order to its construction sites.) The reintroduction of passports, launched in Magnitogorsk in February 1933, was a step into the semi-feudal past, but it was announced with much fanfare as a another major step toward socialism.

Meanwhile, the central authorities had already made another move that would help solve Magnitostroi's labor shortage. In the late summer of 1930, the party central committee had adopted a resolution calling for the "liquidation of the kulaks as a class." The main purpose of this "reform" was to increase the production of surplus grain for export. As Stalin explained—after Minister of Trade Anastas Mikoyan reported that he was then exporting 18,000 to 27,000 tons of grain a day—that was not enough. In a letter to Vyacheslav Molotov, his right-hand man, Stalin wrote that "The quota for daily shipments should now be raised to 54–81 tons at a minimum. Otherwise we risk being left without our new iron and steel and machine building factories. . . . In short, we must push grain exports *furiously.*"

Displacing the kulaks removed enemies of collectivization from the countryside and may have reduced rural consumption, but it also created a new source of workers for various projects. Those accused of being kulaks, kulak "henchmen," or "ideological" kulaks had their property confiscated and were forbidden to join collective farms. Many were simply shot, but most were sent to camps or were exiled to Siberia and other regions to mine gold or fell trees. The next year, a far larger wave of dekulakization was ordered, and soon tightly packed boxcars carrying "dekulakized peasants" began to arrive at Magnitostroi. These candidate members of the new Soviet working class continued to be sent in great numbers. In the month of June 1931 alone, the kulak population at Magnetic Mountain increased by 50,000.

One Soviet eyewitness, quoted by Kotkin, recalled the scene:

> [They] began to drive the special settlers to Magnitogorsk. An extraordinary plenipotentiary arrived . . . . "Here's how you can help me [he said] . In three days there will be no fewer than 25,000 people. We need barracks by that time." . . . They herded in not 25,000 but 40,000. It was raining, children were crying, as you walked by, you didn't want to look.

Of course, the barracks were not built in three days, or even three months. Instead, the 40,000 men, women, and children lived in tents. During the winter, thousands died.

VII

Kulaks were not the only ones in the tents, which for several years remained the primary means of housing the majority of new arrivals at Magnitostroi. Other housing was being built, but not as rapidly as the population was growing. In March 1931 Magnitogorsk's population had reached 83,000, but there were only 160,000 square meters of living space, roughly 1.9 square meters per person. A year later the population had grown to 196,000, and living space had grown to 359,000 square meters, or 1.8 square meters per person. One and eight-tenths square meters is about six feet by six feet, an unimaginably small space for a home. This figure, of course, fell far short of the state's own assessment of the population's needs. Still, not until the 1940s did the per-capita amount of living space in Magnitogorsk exceed four square meters (about 180 square feet).

Under any circumstances the flood of people arriving at this remote barren spot would have taxed the resources—if not the imagination—of those responsible for housing them. But matters were made worse by the fact that the builders of the steel works were also responsible for housing. Completing the factory, not building homes, was their priority. And given the difficulty of their primary task, they constantly had to be prodded to allocate material and labor to building homes. In 1931, for example, 8 million rubles were allocated for housing construction but only 1.5 million were spent for that purpose. The rest was diverted to the factory and related projects. The next year, to speed things up, the government established a separate construction agency and provided it with its own money, materials, and workers.

Even then, things went slowly. Tents were gradually displaced by barracks, which for many years remained the main form of housing. ("Virtually everyone who lived in Magnitogorsk spent some time, often several years, in barracks," Kotkin wrote.) These were better than tents—at least they had wooden floors and provided better protection against the winter winds. But they were still primitive constructions without running water or inside toilets. The first barracks were divided into four sections, each of which was a gigantic room filled with metal cots. A public area, or "red corner," served as a rudimentary recreation room and library. Usually there were separate women's barracks, though sometimes a women's section was partitioned off from the men in the same structure. Some barracks had tiny jerry-built rooms, but more commonly even whole families lived in open space. For a bit of privacy, they enclosed their area with sheets or blankets.

At first, barracks were built to hold no more than one hundred people, but twice that many were routinely packed inside. Two workers frequently shared a cot—one slept while the other worked. As barracks grew larger, the overcrowding kept pace. In 1931 one barracks was said to house 800 people. That same year, *Komsomolskaya Pravda* described the barracks as "suffocating, filthy and infested with parasites." They were filled with people lying on bare boards with their arms under their heads for pillows. There was "hardly any space between beds. Every corner [was] packed with people."

There were, of course, no bathing or washing facilities in the barracks. To bathe, one went to a public bathhouse, of which there were but thirty in the entire city. Small public laundries were attached to some of these, but they required work clothes to be left for several days, and few workers had two sets of clothes. In 1934, when Magnitogorsk's population was close to 200,000, the bathhouses had a total capacity of 16,000. Six of the thirty were in mud huts, which were described at the time as "dirty, raw, and with absolutely no elementary comforts." But even for the mud-hut baths, queues were always long. By 1939, the thirty baths had been consolidated into eight, more modern ones. That year they served 1.36 million people. On average, each resident took about seven baths a year.

Since everyone was expected to eat in communal dining areas, barracks at first had no cooking facilities. Later, small stoves were supplied, but these were always crowded with pots—and with tenants fighting to get cooking space so they could avoid the dining rooms.

Both the tents and the barracks were considered to be temporary housing. Solid brick apartment blocks were to replace them in the new "socialist" city. But the Soviets had no more experience in designing housing than in designing steel mills. So they looked to the West for help. In Germany they found their man, Ernst May, an architect who in 1929 had won acclaim at the International Congress of Modern Architecture for his workers' housing settlement in Frankfurt. The latest in capitalist design, May's buildings minimized cost and time by using standardized prefabricated components, right down to the kitchens and the furniture. In the first year of construction in Frankfurt, 2,200 units had been built against a plan for 1,200. In the second year 3,000 were built. This intrigued Soviet leaders, who invited May to come to the USSR not just to plan large housing developments, but to create whole cities.

In Frankfurt, as chief architect, May exercised wide powers. Now, he thought, he would have even greater latitude. Accompanied by most of his Frankfurt staff, he arrived in the Soviet Union in 1930, with—he believed—"a free hand to solve the problems of the contemporary city." From the beginning, however, things did not go well. First, May took a year to draw up a plan, which he had to abandon when he got to Magnitogorsk and saw that his linear city could not fit into the local topography. Then he discovered that three months before his arrival—but just in time for the ballyhoo of the Sixteenth Party Congress—local Magnitogorsk authorities, acting on their own, had laid the cornerstone for a first apartment building.

May did not last long. By the time of his departure in 1932, only one of his superblocks was under construction. Although it later came under heavy criticism, it followed official guidelines that called for a "socialist city" with "maximum socialization of everyday life." This meant, according to an official governmental report, that "life in every superblock will be the same. . . . There will be no reason to go to a different one." To solve the problem of residents getting confused about where they lived, the report proposed to "paint each superblock a different color."

May's design was based on his idea of equality, and in line with government ideas about socialization. It consisted of parallel rows of five-story equidistant apartment buildings positioned to allow each resident generous access to light and air. The buildings were divided into single-room sleeping "cells," joined by a corridor. There were no kitchens, not even communal ones, because the city planned an extensive network of dining halls. And even though the buildings had space for toilets, there were none to install, and, in any case, no sewage system in the city. Instead, when the buildings opened for occupancy, there were only outhouses across the street. In the wintertime at forty degrees below zero, people had to climb down and run across the street to go to the toilet.

When the potential tenants saw what was being built, they called a protest meeting. They "pleaded," I. Ivich, a Soviet historian, wrote, "that what was being designed by May was not at all what a Soviet worker needed." May's buildings provided equal air and light to all tenants, but the rows of narrow linear buildings provided no protection against snow and the fierce, bone-chilling winter winds. The workers wanted enclosed courtyard buildings that would provide some protection against such severe weather. But instead of the design being changed, construction went ahead as planned and the protesters got "booted from the trade union" for "engaging in the discrediting of German specialists."

In 1933, after May had departed, Politbureau member Griorgii Ordzhonikidze came to Magnitogorsk to inspect its progress. The chief of city construction tried to steer him away from May's "socialist city," as the single superblock was initially called, but, to his dismay, Ordzhonikidze insisted on seeing it. As he approached, Ivich wrote, "the scent of the outhouses whacked him in the nose." Infuriated, Kotkin wrote, he issued an avalanche of impatient decrees calling for improvements in living conditions. He also changed the name from "socialist city" to "urban district." Lecturing local officials, he said "You have named some manure a 'socialist city.' . . . This is a direct insult to socialism."

Tents, barracks, and eventually brick apartment blocks were the work of the Soviet state. All of these, even the apartment blocks, promoted a primitive form of communalism, either of necessity (given the low level of resources) or of ideology (given the absence of positive concepts of socialism). Kotkin called this a clash between traditional family-centered living patterns and the Soviet collectivist social vision, and he attributed, at least in part, the fourth major form of Magnitogorsk housing to the workers' desire for family living. These were the mud huts, primitive but sturdy traditional peasant structures carved out of the local hillsides.

Until 1936, about a quarter of the Magnitogorsk population lived in huts that they had created themselves. They were comparatively dry, warm, and clean, and they provided the privacy that was impossible to find in tents or barracks. They were strewn all over the city, but a concentration of them near the mine was popularly known as "Shanghai," the Chinese city synonymous with dark, trash-littered narrow streets—and with all the other evils of an early-twentieth-century capitalist city. The mud huts were not popular with local authorities, but given the housing shortage they had to be tolerated. Even so, partly because they were an unwelcome reminder of Russia's rural poverty and primitive agricultural ways, and partly because they provided for family living at a time when the early Bolshevik cry for the "abolition of the family as the basic cell of society" was still the order of the day, the huts were scheduled to be torn down in 1936. Ironically, this command was given just before the family was rehabilitated as a result of sharply declining birthrates. In any case, the uproar against this order was so great that it had to be amended. As a compromise, it was decided that only abandoned mud huts would be destroyed. When someone moved out, a hut was deemed to be abandoned, and no new permits for living in mud huts were issued, so they gradually diminished in number.

A final form of housing was the prison labor camps. There were two types of these, the Special Labor Settlement, which held dekulakized peasants, and the Corrective Labor Colony, which housed ordinary criminals. Established in 1931 and initially enclosed in barbed wire, the Special Labor Camps held some 30,000 "class enemies," brought to Magnitogorsk against their wills and forced to live under extremely harsh conditions. Nevertheless, these class enemies proved to be more docile and productive than the ordinary criminals. Within a few years they had some of the best household garden plots in the city and were raising their own livestock. In 1936, when their citizenship was officially restored by the new Soviet constitution, the barbed wire came down. Even earlier, in a 1933 speech, Ordzhonikidze had joked that the kulaks' settlement was better maintained and far more orderly than the free part of the city.

The Corrective Labor Colony evolved in the opposite direction. At first, it was an open settlement averaging about 10,000 people, but many tried to escape and others kept on stealing or committing other crimes. So in late 1932 the camp was enclosed in barbed wire and divided into sectors with varying degrees of restrictions. By 1936, armed guards were being used to escort Corrective Labor Colony inmates to Magnitostroi's work sites, just as they did in the lumber camps. Ten years later, in 1946, prison labor was still widely used. At the secret Soviet nuclear facility known as Arzamas–16, for example, one nuclear scientist, Lev Altshuler, wrote of seeing "the inevitable companions of that period—the 'zones' [prison camps] populated by representatives of all regions of the country, all the nationalities." On the bus trip to Arzamas he was struck by the columns of prisoners passing through the settlement on their way to work in the morning and returning to the zones in the evening. "Lermontov's lines," he wrote, "came to mind, about 'a land of slaves, a land of masters.'"

Of course, not everyone at Magnitogorsk lived like workers or prisoners. In 1930, when American specialists working for McKee were scheduled to arrive, Moscow ordered the top leadership at the site to provide living conditions approximating those to which the Americans were accustomed. The order was carried out to the letter. This new American town, initially known as Amerikanka, was built at the only wooded area anywhere near the mill. It consisted of individual homes and a few larger multioccupancy, two-story stucco bungalows. The bungalows had separate sleeping quarters, a common living room, a kitchen with a wood-burning stove, indoor toilets, and bathrooms with water heaters. The authorities also provided volleyball and tennis courts.

At first, Kotkin wrote, only foreigners were quartered in Amerikanka. But soon Iakov Gugel, the local party secretary, was given a home. He was followed by the GPU (secret police) chief. That opened the gates, and, in the words of one of the American specialists, "From then on it was a stampede." The free-for-all included incidents of squatting in unfinished structures and forced evictions. This continued until Gugel proclaimed that as far as Soviet citizens were concerned, only the higher-ups would be allowed in, whereupon he "installed himself in the best house in the American village and completely furnished it with fine furnishings." This old Bolshevik and civil war veteran also maintained a retinue of servants, two cars, the finest local team of horses, and the best carriage and sleigh.

Finally, when the American and foreign specialists left and only Soviet officials remained, the name of the village was changed to Berezka, or "birch tree." And, given their relationship to the lord of the new manor, the lucky recipients of these homes—the construction chiefs of the various steel mill shops—were appropriately, if informally, known as "appanage princes" (principal vassals who received grants from the sovereign).

So much for equality and the workers' state.

VIII

The dictatorship of the proletariat was the official basis of the Soviet state. This meant, Stalin liked to say, that the workers owned all property collectively and that the leaders were their servants. But, of course, servants are ordered around by owners, who can fire them at will. In the Soviet Union the opposite was true. The "servants" had all the prerogatives that owners have in capitalism and that lords had in feudalism—and more. More importantly, the very concept of owner and servant was foreign to socialist tradition before 1917, just as traditional socialist principles were increasingly foreign to Soviet leaders after Stalin consolidated his power.

5

PLAYING CATCH-UP
BUT LOSING GROUND

I

W HAT, THEN, WAS THE SOVIET UNION? To most Americans Soviet
reality defined socialism. For many years, however, people on the
sectarian left debated how to characterize the Soviet Union. American socialists of various stripes called it a deformed workers state, or state socialism, or even state capitalism. On the other hand, Communists—and
also "free market" ideologues and the corporate media—agreed that the
Soviet Union was socialism incarnate. Ostensibly objective academics
were willing to take Stalin at his word. Indeed, even so fine an historian as
Stephen Kotkin insisted that the Soviet Union was socialist because that's
what Soviet leaders said it was, that's what Soviet citizens were told, and,
consequently, that's what they thought they were sacrificing to achieve.

Kotkin's argument is complicated somewhat because he conflates two
issues: First, whether the revolution could ever have been socialist in anything but name (and in the hearts, if not the minds, of Lenin and his followers). Second, whether Stalin's accession to power in the late 1920s
constituted a "reversal" of Lenin's course. Kotkin is on stronger ground on
the second issue. Stalin did carry out the early Bolshevik goal of rapid industrialization, but he did so in a manner that Lenin did not sanction and
that he might well have opposed. In any case, even if we accept Kotkin's argument about the second issue, he merely begs the question about the first.

I am not concerned with the second issue here—although I believe
that Stalin's regime, while certainly not a total reversal of Lenin's, did

represent a significant change of course. However, the first issue—whether the Soviet Union was socialist—is of vital concern to anyone attempting to understand what socialism meant in the decades leading up to the revolution, or what it might mean in the future. Thus Kotkin's insistence that the Soviet Union was a socialist country could make sense only if he meant that the Soviet experience fundamentally redefined socialism. Such a redefinition, however, would so profoundly alter socialism's historical record as to render it meaningless. And it would make any analysis of socialist tradition (and of Marx's thought) invalid.

Starkly stated, my view is that the Russian Revolution and all that followed stood socialism on its head. That is certainly what Marx and his pre-1917 followers would have thought, had they lived to see the revolution in action. And it is what non-Marxist Oscar Wilde had argued in 1893, in his pamphlet *The Soul of Man under Socialism*: "If Socialism is Authoritarian; if there are Governments armed with economic power as they are now with political power; if, in a word, we have Industrial Tyrannies, then the last state of man will be worse than the first."

The Bolsheviks did not—could not—create socialism as they and their comrades in Europe and America understood it. Instead they cobbled together a unique society, one with a nationalistic command economy, a tsarist political structure, and a ruler who had a medieval mentality. This reality was hidden behind an official egalitarian ideology that was used to legitimize the regime, both in its own eyes and in the eyes of many leftists throughout the world. Grafting post-capitalist ideas of social equality onto a retrograde political culture confused friend and foe alike. The confusion persisted because many of the old Bolsheviks who had fought for the revolution and served the regime devotedly were motivated by pre-revolutionary ideals. They, of course, paid a terrible price for this. Many ended up as Stalin's victims. Some, like Grigorii Ordzhonikidze, committed suicide when they could no longer hope to humanize the regime and despaired of opposing it.

Marx, of course, envisioned socialism as something entirely different from Soviet reality. His socialism grew out of capitalism's greatest achievements and was to be built by transcending its material, social, and political accomplishments. The Bolsheviks, on the other hand, had more in common with the early utopians' relationship to capitalism. They simply wanted to eradicate it—to eliminate all forms of individually owned property—although as the successor to a pre-capitalist, semi-feudal society, the Bolsheviks did not have much capitalism to eradicate. The irony is that the Bolshevik imperative, especially under Stalin, was "to catch up and surpass," which in practice meant to copy, capitalism. In the main, that is what the Bolsheviks attempted. In other words, it makes sense to see the Soviet experience not as having created the material, social, and political basis for socialism, but as having created the material, social, and political basis for the corrupt and primitive form of capitalism that Russia now enjoys.

In the early 1990s, Vladimir Glebov, a Soviet philosophy professor, argued along these lines during an interview for Adam Hochschild's *The Unquiet Ghost*. Glebov is the son of Lev Kamenev, the Soviets' first head of state, who fell victim to Stalin's executioner in 1936. Four years old at the time, Glebov was the only family member to survive the dictator's wrath. Yet despite this experience, or—as Hochschild suggested—maybe because of it, he grew up to be a student of Marx and then, in the early 1990s, a critic of those who imagined that Russia could slip easily into the contemporary capitalist mainstream. In his interview, he chided colleagues who believed that the moment private property was introduced in Russia the country would achieve an "American standard of living."

"They don't understand," Glebov told Hochschild, that when private ownership is introduced, Russia will not take a place as an equal beside today's capitalist nations. Instead, it would "become like England and America of the nineteenth century." It took the United States two centuries "to reach the modern level," Glebov said, and, he suggested, it would also take Russia a long time to get there. Speaking ten years ago, Glebov observed that by adopting capitalism, Russia was "rushing headlong into the nineteenth century, with its poorhouses out of Dickens, its riots by the unemployed and the hungry." Ten years later, we could see the capitalist past flourishing in what is now the former Soviet Union. That, indeed, is Bolshevism's legacy.

II

For Marx, "the full and free development of every individual" was the basis of a socialized society, and capitalist development was the context in which the working class would acquire the democratic principles and the knowledge required to create such a society. Only a highly developed, technologically advanced capitalism could produce the required conditions. Even that would be insufficient unless working people had also matured politically as a result of their struggles in the workplace and, especially, in the political arena.

In Russia, because few of these things had occurred under the tsars, none of the prerequisites existed for such a revolutionary transcendence. All that was possible for the socialists was the seizure of state power, not as a result of the strength and general adoption of their ideas, but because of the corruption and weakness of the tsarist empire (and, after the February revolution, the vacillation of the tsar's liberal successors). The Bolsheviks had only two things going for them: the opportunity to seize the reins of a riderless state and the will to do so. The first condition stared them in the face. The second was created by the belief—or hope—that the revolution would spread to the West and thereby provide them with some of socialism's prerequisites. As we've seen, that's how Lenin himself saw things in 1917.

In contrast to Marx's scenario of socialists incorporating and building upon capitalism's most advanced material and social achievements, however, the Bolsheviks, and especially Stalin, utilized tsarist feudal traditions to replicate, and enhance, some of capitalism's more draconian practices. As Andreev and Kotkin amply demonstrated, the Bolsheviks were obsessed with creating a society that was better than capitalism, but their definition of an alternative was almost entirely worse. The most they could say about the institutions they were creating was that they were "not capitalist." True, the Bolsheviks were the first rulers to institute what we would now call a welfare state. The Soviet state guaranteed everyone a job, low-cost housing, and bread, and it provided free medical care and education. But, except possibly for the education, none of this could be, or was, the equal of that supplied to most citizens of developed capitalist systems. In fact, most of the Soviet state-provided welfare was considerably inferior to the living standards created by advanced capitalism. This was true even after the Soviet Union had achieved the goal of becoming an urban, industrialized nation. That should have been no surprise, given Russia's backwardness when the revolution was made in 1917.

Even so, as Kotkin wrote, Bolshevik leaders saw Magnitogorsk not simply as a desperate way of catching up, but as an example of a quintessentially "socialist city of the future." As one propagandist proclaimed, Magnitogorsk was the Soviets' model for development. He boasted that this was not just a giant industrial center, but was also "a future center for the Sovietization of the southern Urals." This new city, he predicted, would deeply inculcate "the new socialist way of life."

But like its steel mill, which was modeled on U.S. Steel's Gary works, the city of Magnitogorsk followed in the footsteps of U.S. Steel's Indiana city. It, too, was created simply to house the mill's workers. Both cities were, and are, one-industry towns attached to a factory, from which they have derived their purpose and form. Whether capitalist or "socialist," relatively modern or frontier crude, such cities cannot be the locus of a higher civilization. Like Magnitogorsk, Gary became, and remained, a troubled place. Long before the steel mills cut back their production and workforce, leaders of Gary were desperately trying to diversify the city's industry. Seventy years later they are still trying. So far they have succeeded only in attracting riverboat gambling. Magnitogorsk, too, has suffered in its own way from being the creature of its aging mills and stifling pollution. It, however, has been spared the gambling boats.

In other words, far from producing a "new socialist way of life," Magnitogorsk re-created an arcane capitalist model of industrialization. Like most of the Soviet Union's new industrial cities, Magnitogorsk was little more than a place for the state to settle the factory's workers. Tragically, this was unavoidable. Given the limited resources available and the founders' lack of know-how, the city could only be an afterthought. This is illustrated, Kotkin wrote, in all of the dozens of pamphlets written about Magnitogorsk in the 1930s, none of which was ever devoted exclusively to the city itself. Indeed, "if it was mentioned at all," discussion of the city occurred only in the last chapter of every pamphlet—after descriptions of all the industrial shops that made up the works. The steelmaking complex itself was the be-all and end-all. The area around it, at least initially, was seen simply as a place to warehouse workers. Only when the dimensions of the factory grew to gigantic size did officials put forward the claim that they were creating a "socialist city." But, as Kotkin pointed out, "the two [ideas] were really one and the same."

In fact, the state's concept of the city never changed. In 1929, before Ernst May was hired to design Magnitogorsk, Gipromez (the State Institute for the Design of Metallurgical Factories) had already published an artist's conception of the future city. In the drawing, the city's streets emerge out of the mill, radiating from the factory gate. This graphically represented the Bolsheviks' belief that everything in the city would flow naturally from the steel plant. "Build a steel plant," Kotkin commented, "and civilization would follow." More exactly, he added, "build a steel plant, and that *is* civilization." But given where they started in the process of making history, the Bolsheviks could not see much beyond the factory gates. Magnitka provided the material needed for industrialization. The workers were the means, but the steel plant was the end. For Marx and his followers, however, steel plants were only a means, created by capitalism, for the attainment of a more civilized and humane life beyond the confines of factories.

Not surprisingly, while the Bolsheviks conceived Magnitogorsk and the other new industrial centers as cities of the future, they resembled nothing so much as gigantic copies of that primitive form of capitalist urbanization, the company town. Like the coal-mining settlements of Appalachia, the textile mill towns of the Carolinas, or the larger and more modern Pullman in Illinois, company towns were owned or controlled lock, stock, and barrel by the local employer. Workers lived in company houses, bought their necessities in company stores, and were educated, if at all, in company schools. In Soviet cities, where the state (meaning the party) was the employer, the same system prevailed. The

Bolsheviks called this socialism. But in the United States it was seen, especially by Socialists, as just the opposite. American workers experienced company towns as a semi-feudal form of capitalism, as an archaic throwback to the days when serfs were tied to their domiciles—as well as to their jobs—by the local lord. In company towns, of course, corporate serfs had neither the freedom to form their own unions nor to elect their own government. In other words, as in feudalism, the economic and political relationships were one and the same. Despite these restrictions, American workers were able to fight against, and finally to eliminate, company towns because the surrounding society was more advanced. In the Soviet Union, however, the steel mill was more advanced than anything around it.

III

In the United States the rights and liberties of a civil society were seen as the birthright of all citizens, and the conditions that existed in company towns were seen as un-American. Euro-Americans have always taken the existence of civil society for granted. But neither the Soviet state, nor the tsarist state from which it emerged, allowed independent citizen associations to exist, much less to intervene in matters of social policy. Thus, having no concept of civil society, the Soviets also did not even have a common term for it. Nevertheless, in the 1980s, many democratic reformers in the Soviet Union understood civil society as the heart of democracy. As democratic reformer Oleg Rumyantsev argued in the early days of Perestroika, democratization could only be achieved in the Soviet Union through the development of independent social movements of ordinary citizens; in other words, through the creation of a civil society.

In the West, on the other hand, this process had required no conscious political intervention on the part of reformers. As Marx's analysis implied, civil society arose naturally as part of capitalist development and the operation of a free labor market, while the state, and especially the bureaucratic Soviet state, separated itself from and stifled civil society. "Freedom," Marx wrote, "consists in converting the state from an organ superimposed on society into one completely subordinate to it." That required democracy, which he saw as the highest form of political organization. American Socialists, who grew up in a society without the remnants of feudalism and class-imposed limitations on social mobility and action— which, however, did exist in many of Europe's emerging capitalisms— arrived at this same view without any knowledge of Marx's writings.

Many American Socialists instinctively shared Marx's view of the state as a restraint on freedom. In this view, decentralization was an implicit good. The American Socialist Party organized itself in conformity with this principle. Thus, while the American party had an elected national leadership, each state organization enjoyed a high degree of autonomy. So, too, did each of the party's 5,000 locals. And, exemplifying the party's belief in open discussion and democratic participation in policymaking, the party press was also highly decentralized. Of the 323 daily, weekly, and monthly periodicals that constituted the Socialist press in 1916, only one, the *American Socialist,* was an official national party publication, and it did not start publishing until 1914. Many party locals published their own weekly papers, but the majority of Socialist publications, especially the more widely circulated ones with a national audience, were privately owned. These publications ranged in size from the local weeklies published in towns with as few as 200 inhabitants to the privately published weekly *Appeal to Reason,* which in 1913 had 761,747 subscribers throughout the United States.

The party press also reflected a high level of openness to and tolerance of opposing views. Some periodicals—of which the *Appeal* was the prime example—focused on news and socialist education and consciously avoided factional disputes. Others, including many of the most interesting smaller publications, participated heatedly in the constant intra-party debates about tactics and strategy. Yet even the more partisan periodicals opened their pages to contributors of many tendencies. No one considered it strange, for example, that Debs should be an editor of the left-wing, semi-populist *National Rip-Saw* and of the neutral *Appeal,* while he was also a regular contributor to the *Christian Socialist* and to

Victor Berger's "right-wing *"Milwaukee Leader.* Nor did anyone question the *International Socialist Review's* practice of featuring among its contributors such non-socialist reformers as Clarence Darrow and Cleveland's Frederick C. Howe; moderate Socialists like Carl Sandburg, Upton Sinclair, and Gustavus Myers; and left-wingers such as Jack London, Big Bill Haywood, birth control advocate Margaret Sanger, and Christian-Socialist-turned-Bolshevik Sen Katayama.

Socialists also took an active part in the whole range of reform movements of the Progressive Era. A majority of the founders of the NAACP were Socialists, among them the great sociologist and historian, W. E. B. DuBois. Socialist men and women were active suffragists—indeed, the party provided the winning margin for women's suffrage in Nevada in 1914 and in New York in 1917. And, of course, Socialists played a major role in the trade union movement, both inside and outside of the American Federation of Labor.

Russians, on the other hand, had never experienced the freedoms that underlay civil society. Unlike the Western socialist parties, the Bolsheviks had been forced to operate as an illegal, underground organization until the tsar was overthrown in February 1917. Deprived of the context in which Western Socialists developed their principles and characteristics, the Bolsheviks knew only the habits and culture of tsarism. They operated in a quasi-military manner, even in the early days when they enjoyed a high degree of formal democracy within their ranks. And they carried this style and the principles it reflected into the post–civil war years. Furthermore, with no popular base experienced in the habits of civil society, and only a quite small working class (one that had gone through few of the struggles universally associated with capitalist development), there was no force in the larger society to challenge Bolshevik practice. In other words, there was virtually no popular pressure to counter the Bolsheviks' tendency to suppress all aspects of civil society, at least not until the 1980s.

Only after Mikhail Gorbachev came to power in 1985 and initiated the process that led to the Soviet Union's collapse did Soviet citizens enjoy even the most elementary aspects of a civil society. Before that private citizens—or should I say, would-be private citizens—could not possess so much as a typewriter, or more than a few sheets of writing paper, without state sanction. To be caught using a copying machine for private purposes, or owning a computer without official government permission, was to court imprisonment, even as late as 1988, when I visited Moscow to interview the New Democrats. True, samizdat (self-published) newsletters and pamphlets did exist in the decades after Stalin's death, but they had to be reproduced by painfully crude and slow methods. Some were typed with five or six carbon copies at a time. Others were reproduced by photographing a typed copy and then making multiple prints from the negatives. Even in the early years of Mikhail Gorbachev's tenure, if officials discovered a samizdat publisher, the culprit was visited and warned to stop. If he didn't, he was subject to arrest.

Initially, when Stalin was driving everyone to create a basic industrial infrastructure, the absence of civil liberties and rights was not a great hindrance to development. Indeed, the absence of a tradition of organized resistance to authority facilitated Stalin's ruthless efforts. But once the drive for the basic industrialization of the country had been completed, this system militated against the kind of innovation required for continued progress. Even in the post-Stalin years, change could come only on orders from above. And the more Soviet industry developed, the more debilitating the lack of a civil society became. Neither Stalin nor his successors could handle, or even begin to understand, the complexity of modern technology. Nor could the Soviet people, trained as they were in passivity and routine, rise to the occasion. The result, after Stalin died and Khrushchev was deposed, was the stagnation of the Brezhnev years, during which, once again, the Soviet Union's lag behind as the West accelerated.

Nowhere was the absence of a civil society more obviously frustrating than in the field of science. To drive, or inspire, workers during the years of forced industrialization, Soviet leaders required a high level of belief in what was described as "building socialism." This was a matter beyond debate. It required habits of strict conformity to the views and orders of party and state officials, which, within the narrow limits prescribed by Bolshevism's "historic task," worked fairly well. But science requires creative thought and inquiring minds. Scientists do not do well when subjected to the dictates of political leaders, especially leaders like Stalin and his cohort, none of whom had any background in the methods or content of the physical sciences, and most of whom distrusted the scientists' petit-bourgeois provenance and their ideological commitment to Bolshevism.

The havoc that a highly ideologized science can wreak was most striking in the case of Soviet genetics. This was a highly politicized scientific field, but—for Stalin—not a very important one. That situation enabled a scientific fraud, Trofim Lysenko, to attack Mendelian genetics as "bourgeois" science, and to win Stalin's support for his ideas about the ability of plant species to acquire new characteristics based on their immediate environment. Lysenko's theory was rejected and widely ridiculed by Soviet and Western geneticists, but he ignored them and, in the words of Soviet Nobel Laureate Nikolai Semenov, "transferred the struggle against those with different ideas from the level of scientific discussion to the level of demagogy and political accusations." In short, Lysenko appealed to political authority, rather than to the scientific community. Stalin liked his ideas—they paralleled his own. So with Stalin's imprimatur Lysenko became the Soviet Union's chief geneticist and Soviet genetics suffered the consequences.

Soviet physics was lucky to escape the same fate, perhaps because there was no Lysenko in the field, but more likely because the results of false theories in physics were easier to detect and had much more detrimental consequences for Soviet industry. Nevertheless, even physicists were subject to ideological monitoring and to occasional arrest during the late 1930s.

Ironically, it was World War II—and especially the American atom bomb—that granted Soviet scientists the only space of intellectual autonomy won by any significant section of Soviet society before Gorbachev came to power. This was just the opposite of Western experience. In the West, wars have normally brought with them great restrictions on free speech. Certainly that was true in the United States during the two world wars, especially the first. In the Soviet Union, however, where there was virtually no intellectual freedom before the war, the government's dependence on its scientists created what David Holloway called "an embryonic civil society" (though, as he noted in *Stalin and the Bomb*, the physicists did not use the term).

One of the reasons for distrusting Soviet scientists, especially physicists, was their tradition of internationalism. In the mid-1930s, when they were actively pursuing nuclear physics, Soviet scientists were closely attuned to the work of their counterparts in the West. Even then, however, they were relatively isolated—it took months for Western scientific journals to pass through the censors and reach them, and, therefore, they generally lagged behind their foreign colleagues. Nevertheless, Soviet physicists were doing high-quality work. In 1939, for example, Georgii Flerov and Konstantin Petrzhak were the first in the world to verify the existence of spontaneous nuclear fission—fission achieved without bombarding uranium with neutrons. By that time, Igor Kurchatov, the future scientific director of the Soviet nuclear project, his colleague, Iulii Khariton, and others were working on the physics of nuclear chain reactions. They understood this as a potential source of tremendous energy. But while they were aware of the possibility of its being used for a powerful bomb, their main interest was in the use of nuclear power as a source of heat with which to generate electricity.

Like all Soviet intellectuals, physicists were frequently vetted for their ideological reliability. Party "philosophers" attempted to control them by distinguishing between bourgeois and proletarian science. But the better scientists generally did their best not to get entangled in these discussions. One brave exception was Iakov Frenkel, who in 1931 was summoned to explain his views by the party faction at a scientific congress. What he had read in Engels and Lenin did not delight him at all: "Neither Lenin nor Engels is an authority for physicists," he said, adding that Lenin's book [*Materialism and Empirio-Criticism*] amounted to "little more than the assertion of elementary truths that it's not worth breaking a lance over." As Holloway commented, no other physicist was so outspoken or so courageous in criticizing dialectical materialism. Frenkel insisted that "there cannot be proletarian mathematics, proletarian physics, etc." And, he said, as "a Soviet person," he could not sympathize with an opinion that was harmful to science. Not surprisingly, these views won Frenkel the enmity of party ideologues, who made him their chief target among the physicists for the next twenty years. Fortunately for him, as a first-rate physicist—and unlike people in other fields—Frenkel escaped arrest and possible execution.

During World War II, leading Soviet scientists, most notably Peter Kapitsa, called for collaborations with Western scientists. This wish was a reflection of a broad desire among Soviet intellectuals for greater contact with the rest of the world, which the wartime Soviet alliance with Britain and the United States seemed for a time to foreshadow. Indeed, at a 1945 celebration, Molotov promised the "most favorable conditions" for closer ties between Soviet and world science. But in 1946, as the Cold War began, Stalin made it clear that the relative intellectual tolerance allowed during the war would be ended. As Stalin began to tighten party control over the intelligentsia, the less ideological scholars and officials came under renewed criticism for their alleged subservience to Western ideas.

This reversion to the pre-war political climate had a profound effect on Soviet science. Lysenko, whose political position at the end of the war had been weakened—in 1946 one of his main opponents had been elected a corresponding member of the Academy of Agricultural Science—now had the opportunity to revive his fortunes. Charging his opponents with political disloyalty and with being in thrall to foreign ideas, he linked his crusade against genetics to Stalin's campaign for ideological purity and once again won Stalin's support. At a special session of the academy, Lysenko read a report that Stalin himself had not only vetted but edited. The science of genetics, Lysenko claimed, was a bourgeois fabrication and incompatible with Marxism-Leninism. Several scientists argued forcefully against Lysenko, but at the end of the conference he declared that "the Party Central Committee has examined my report and approved it." In other words, challenge me and you challenge Stalin, the final arbiter of all matters cultural and scientific. Of course, no one challenged him, but in the purge that followed, thousands of plant biologists who had argued against him at the conference, or in the past, were removed from their teaching and research positions.

As Holloway noted, Lysenko's victory encouraged others to do for their disciplines what he had done for his. In the next two years conferences were organized on physiology, astronomy, chemistry, and ethnography to root out foreign ideological influences. The bourgeois sin of "cosmopolitanism" was attacked, and ludicrous claims of discovery and invention were made for Russian and Soviet scientists and engineers.

Physics, too, came under attack, and the discipline's ideological police also called a conference at which to promote dialectical materialism and to badmouth the leading figures in the field. One issue was the rivalry between the physicists from Moscow University and those from the Academy of Sciences. The leading physicists, those working on the atom bomb, were almost all from the academy and the university scientists were jealous. Angry that their work had not received the recognition they thought it deserved, they followed Lysenko's lead and prepared to accuse the academicians of spreading cosmopolitanism and idealism, of not citing Russian scientists sufficiently, and even of spying for Germany. Frenkel was a particular target for his 1931 remarks on the irrelevance of dialectical materialism.

These accusations put the president of the academy, S. I. Vavilov, in a difficult position. As a competent physicist he understood the absurdity of the charges made by the university faculty. But as academy president he could not ignore a campaign mandated by the political authorities. Fortunately for the academicians, they were now working on the Soviet bomb, which was Stalin's highest priority. Had the conference been held it would clearly have disrupted that work. So, after the organizing committee had met forty-two times in the two and a half months of early 1949, the conference was suddenly called off only five days before it was scheduled to begin. As Holloway wrote, only Stalin could have made this decision, probably as the result of a request by Lavrenti Beria, the head of the NKVD and the director of the atom bomb project.

Beria was a true believer and one of Stalin's most trusted sycophants. He was in charge of getting the atom bomb made as quickly as possible, and, like Stalin, he didn't trust his scientists. But he needed them. So, according to General Makhnev, head of the secretariat of the Special Committee on the Atomic Bomb, Beria decided to make his own investigation. He asked Kurchatov whether it was true, as Lysenko's allies were charging, that quantum mechanics and relativity theory were idealist (anti-materialist). Kurchatov avoided a direct answer, but replied that if quantum mechanics and relativity theory were rejected, then the bomb would also have to be rejected. Apparently, Beria got the point and asked Stalin to call off the conference.

(Holloway also provided what he said was a more circumstantial account, based on a report of a conversation between Beria and atomic physicist Lev Artsimovich, just after Stalin died. According to Artsimovich, Beria told him that three of the leading physicists had approached him and asked him to call off the conference and that he had told them he could not make that decision but would speak to Stalin. He did, and Stalin agreed to cancel the conference. "Leave them in peace," Stalin told Beria. "We can always shoot them later.")

As nuclear physicist Lev Landau joked, the survival of the Soviet physicists was the first example of a successful nuclear deterrence. Stalin needed the bomb to enhance the power of the state. That was the top priority. But the physicists also used the building of the bomb, and then the creation of a hydrogen bomb of their own design, to build what Holloway called "a small island of intellectual autonomy" in the midst of a society where the state claimed control of all intellectual life.

The bomb also did something else that no one acknowledged publicly: It exploded the myth of scientific socialism. Stalin had used Lysenko to impose his idea that socialist science was distinct from and superior to capitalist science. This served his nationalist aims and his propaganda needs. But his actions in regard to the physicists belied his words. As Kapitsa, who at the time was under virtual house arrest, wrote in a letter to Stalin, the Soviet Union had fallen behind the West in science because its leaders did not trust its scientists. Soviet scientists, Kapitsa wrote, had developed many of the basic ideas for technologies also developed in the West during the war, but the government deprived them of the support needed to carry their ideas to fruition. Only after the Western scientists had achieved success in these fields did Stalin allocate resources to the Soviet scientists. Stalin claimed that socialist science was superior, but he routinely undermined it and instead copied Western technology. Then he trumpeted the copies as original Soviet achievements. Given this mode of operation, however, the Soviet Union was always catching up, but could never "catch up with," let alone "surpass" the West.

This was the case with the atom bomb. Not only did Stalin ignore pre-war suggestions from some Soviet physicist that nuclear energy be developed—a good case could be made that it made more sense to pursue other things, given the country's limited resources. But even when he and Beria were told about the American atom bomb project, they did nothing because they didn't trust their own spies. In early 1945, Klaus Fuchs, one of the Los Alamos nuclear scientists, told the Soviets about the plutonium bomb. Six months later he gave a full description of the bomb, and of the process by which it was put together. In May 1945, Kurchatov, who had only been allowed to see some of Fuchs's material, but who knew that a bomb was feasible, wrote to Stalin proposing that extraordinary measures be taken to develop a bomb. The nuclear project, he wrote, should be given "the most favorable and advantageous conditions." But Beria, and apparently Stalin, suspected that Fuchs's report was disinformation, designed to induce the Soviets to squander precious resources on a wild goose chase. Stalin did not even reply to Kurchatov's letter. It took the explosion of the American bomb over Hiroshima to convince Stalin that the bomb was real—and that it posed a political threat to the Soviet Union. Then he mobilized a full-court press, in an effort, once again, to "catch up."

To make the bomb, Stalin gave Kurchatov and his colleagues massive resources and privileged living conditions. Yet, even with the project under Beria's highly competent direction, party leaders continued to distrust the scientists. One incident in 1949, only weeks away from the explosion of the Soviet's first bomb, was particularly revealing. A delegation that included Mikhail Peruvkin, People's Commissar of the Chemical Industry, came to the chemical separation plant at Cheliabinsk–40, where Anatoli Aleksandrov, the director of the plant, was nickel-coating the plutonium hemispheres for the first bomb. They asked him what he was doing. Aleksandrov told them. Then they asked why he thought it was plutonium. Aleksandrov explained that he had been involved in the process of producing it and that it could not be anything else. "But why are you sure that some piece of iron hasn't been substituted for it?" they asked. Aleksandrov held a geiger-counter to the plutonium and it crackled. "Look," he said, "it's alpha-active." But, said one of them, "perhaps it has just been rubbed with plutonium on the outside." Aleksandrov got angry. He took the piece and held it out to them, saying "Feel it, it's hot." One of them replied: It doesn't take long to heat a piece of iron. Finally, the fuming Aleksandrov said that if they wished they could sit there until morning and wait for it to cool, but he was going home. This apparently convinced them and they went away.

These visitors to Aleksandrov's chemical plant were among the country's top technological people. What, then, must the level of familiarity with the workings of a modern industrial science have been among the political leaders?

IV

The disconnect between the culture of Soviet scientists and their political leaders is striking, but it is only one example of the extreme disparities that ran through the core of Soviet society. To start with, the revolution was made by socialists rooted in the Marxist, or materialist, side of socialist tradition. Yet the very idea that a socialist revolution could be made in a country lacking the social, political, and economical prerequisites was glaringly utopian. True, Marx had speculated that perhaps Russian socialists could act as a catalyst for a revolution in Western Europe, but neither he nor any other socialist ever entertained the idea that the Russians alone could achieve a socialist society.

Furthermore, Marx's idea of socialism and that of the Soviet leaders were fundamentally incompatible. Soviet socialism was both nationalist and statist. Marx, as he wrote in the *Communist Manifesto*, envisioned socialism as "an association in which the free development of each is the condition for the free development of all." This idea, of course, was a transcendence of capitalist individualism, which had earlier cracked open the social and political rigidity of feudalism, and a return to community, this time in a society of social equals. The Soviets also sought to eradicate bourgeois individualism, but they did so by returning to a pre-capitalist tradition in which the private sphere was indistinguishable from the public. That was the essence of feudalism, which, as Marx pointed out, had no private sphere because everyone existed in an essentially inflexible social grid. In feudalism, as in the Soviet Union, commerce, social relations, stratification, and even the private individual related in a fixed political hierarchy. The owners (the party-state bureaucrats, and, ultimately, Stalin) were lords of various stations; the propertyless were serfs, existing in an increasingly immutable political hierarchy.

This arrangement was characteristic of ancient Russia, and, in regard to matters of state, of Bolshevism. As Victor Doroshenko, a Soviet historian, explained in an interview with Adam Hochschild, who wrote *The Unquiet Ghost,* Stalinism had made great changes in Russian life, but it was firmly within the old Russian tradition in terms of property relations and political hierarchy.

In Russia, "Relations between people were *never* dependent on the market," Doroshenko explained, They were based instead "on one person obeying the other. This pyramid existed in the fifteenth century and it exists in the twentieth. Peter the Great would gather people from different walks of life—the boyar, the merchants, the free peasants—and say to them, 'I need ships, so you chip in. One ship from five boyars, one ship from fifteen merchants, one ship from one hundred peasants.' So who's property did he commandeer? No one's property! All property belonged to the czar." This was Russia's olden way. And what triumphed because of the revolution, Doroshenko asked rhetorically: The idea that "always existed in Russia over the centuries," that everything was "the property of the czar." Or, as Lewin observed, the so-called socialist method of "direct" appropriation and distribution of products "that was supposed to be superior was actually a principle that operated on any manor of the Middle Ages."

Stalin's reign of terror also followed Russia's czarist tradition. When Stalin's favorite czar, Ivan the Terrible, executed his enemies, real or imagined, he also killed their wives and children. Stalin not only did the same, but went a bit further. He had the NKVD kill all the relatives they could find. When, in 1936, after the first of Stalin's public show trials, Lev Kamenev was executed, every member of his family, save one, was hunted down and killed. Four years old at the time, his son, Vladimir Glebov, escaped execution only because a kindly person at the orphanage to which he was sent gave him his mother's last name—and then lost him in the bureaucratic maze.

By 1936 Stalin had eliminated the last of his real rivals, yet in 1937 the terror, which had started several years earlier, became wider and more intense. The earlier terror had been devised to cover the disastrous mistakes of the leaders. As Lewin wrote of the late 1920s and early 1930s, the huge country had been transformed quite suddenly into an impressive building site. That presented a picture "extolled by many," but it also created "a national catastrophe of major proportions." Agriculture was utterly disorganized and huge rural areas were plunged into severe famine. Inflation, black markets, and a drop in the nation's standard of living "unheard of in conditions of peace" shattered the whole social fabric. To "keep the kettle from blowing up," Lewin wrote, drastic measures had to be taken. To prevent a popular opposition from developing, the powers of the dictatorship were vastly enhanced. "Mass coercion, a set of terroristic laws, persecutions of whole categories of the populations" became necessary to keep the lid on, while fake trials, mass shootings, and a witch hunt that swept the country diverted attention from those responsible. For the first time—still several years before the great purge of 1937–1938—dozens of top government officials, themselves party members, were shot for alleged sabotage.

This was more than a diversion. It was also Stalin's attempt to control, if not eliminate, the pervasive corruption and inefficiency of the whole new social layer of managers and bureaucrats created overnight by the mad rush to industrialize. But the terror only made matters worse. It petrified bureaucrats and made them even more careful and cautious in the often-vain hope of remaining invisible.

In 1937, a new campaign of terror—known as the blood purge— began after NKVD chief Nikolai Ezhov assumed complete control over the process of political vetting within the party. Previously, the party had brought charges against inefficient or corrupt officials and the NKVD had conducted the prosecutions. But local party bodies were often reluctant to single out victims. They dragged their feet and pursued the search for internal enemies only with considerable prodding from above. The NKVD, on the other hand, needed no prodding. It strived to find as many enemies as possible. NKVD leaders in Magnitogorsk, for example, were under direct pressure from Moscow to maximize the number of arrests. To fulfill their quotas in 1938, they even "arrested" (and presumably executed) large numbers of convicts already in the city's criminal labor colony.

Magnitogorsk was different from the rest of the country only in details. Anatoly Spragovsky, a retired KGB agent (the KGB was the NKVD's successor), who in the late 1950s was a rehabilitations investigator, told Hochschild how the NKVD operated in Siberia. "Everything was planned in Moscow," he recalled. "On the walls of [local NKVD offices] there were charts of counterrevolutionary organizations." These organizations were, of course, imaginary. But people who were arrested had to be charged with being agents of something. In Moscow or Leningrad, the victims were often accused of being spies for some foreign power; engineers were charged with sabotaging the factories where they worked; and so on.

But for rural, western Siberia, with few factories or nearby foreign powers, this wouldn't do. Instead, the major enemy was a group called the Counterrevolutionary Cadet Monarchist Organization. According to Spragovsky, the local NKVD decided to declare that all prisoners who had been arrested were members of this organization. Hochschild commented that Spragovsky's description was consistent with what he had been told by an artist in the region whose executed father had indeed been falsely charged with being a monarchist.

This new purge was very efficient at killing people, but its purpose remains obscure. Just like everything else in the Soviet economy, the purge was conducted with quotas. In the documents Spragovsky examined in the course of his work, were orders with exact numbers given. "You

would be ordered to arrest and shoot, say, ten thousand people,"
Spragovsky said. "But you could arrest twenty, thirty, forty [thousand].
The more 'enemies of the people' you arrested, the higher your score."
As a result of such orders, Spragovsky recalled, the Tomsk NKVD challenged Novokuznetsk to a socialist competition to see who could arrest
more people. "It turned out that Tomsk arrested and executed more people than Novokuznetsk." And the NKVD leaders in Tomsk won a medal.

This purge was directed primarily at party members, many of whom
were hated for their petty tyrannies, and so, while terrifying for millions
of people, the arrests were not entirely unwelcome by millions more. Indeed, the purge had an element of macabre populist justice. Kotkin described this well. As he wrote, the terror came to resemble "a kind of
'socialist' class war," although "such a direct formulation was precluded
by the official ideology." Initially this war was inspired by the new layer
of corrupt or inefficient managers, technicians, and other white-collar
employees who made up what Milovan Djilas, the Yugoslav theoretician,
called the "new class." These "new men," as Soviet leaders called them,
were mostly young, inexperienced, and saddled with colossal responsibil-
ities for getting things done under almost impossible conditions. By observing their own superiors, they learned to boss by making arrogant
demands and threats. The workers, in turn, saw them as "exploiters" and
"blood-suckers."

For example, one early victim of the new purge in Magnitogorsk was
KBU chief Lukashevich. (KBU was the Everyday-Life Administration, responsible for living conditions.) Lukashevich was expelled from the party
and arrested in April 1937. This event was accompanied by a torrent of
attacks on him in the local newspaper, which, somewhat tardily, wrote
that it was "impossible to describe all the outrages [he] committed in one
article." The newspaper charged that Lukashevich and other members of
the "KBU gang" had not only been inefficient, but had "awarded themselves and their friends choice apartments, received special food supplies
at state prices or gratis, rode around in chauffeur-driven cars on personal
business, built personal cottages at state expense, took frequent "business
trips" to Moscow, and helped themselves to petty cash for pocket money.

By directly encouraging workers to speak out against bosses like this, Stalin unleashed a massive wave of accusations and arrests. Many of these were against real petty tyrants; many others, however, were acts of personal revenge, jealousy, or simply self-protection—better to accuse someone else than wait to be accused yourself. In short, the whole process became wildly out of hand. Finally, in late 1938, Stalin removed Ezhov and appointed Lavrenti Beria as the new NKVD chief. Beria abruptly stopped the purge, which had clearly become counter-productive.

When encouraging workers to express themselves, Stalin had, of course, repeated the official myths that there were now but two classes in the Soviet Union, workers and peasants, and that the state was run for the benefit of the workers, who, he said, owned everything. In fact, as Lewin observed, Stalin and his colleagues treated most workers simply as *rabsila*—a formless mass of labor power, to be used as the leaders willed—while they treated a smaller, even more oppressed mass as forced, unpaid labor. The idea for this latter group first surfaced in 1925, when the first Bolshevik chief of police, Feliks Dzerzinsky, considered the question of using prisoners to exploit Siberia's mineral-rich far North. It wasn't until the end of the 1920s—after Stalin put the GPU (the NKVD's predecessor) in charge of forced labor—that prisoners became a significant part of the economy. After that the NKVD used them to save money on projects to which a normal labor force could be attracted only with very high wages, if at all.

The first official regulation on forced labor camps was issued in 1930, and the first group of deportees were not political prisoners but dekulakized peasants exiled to camps in Eastern Siberia. From these humble beginnings grew a vast network of prison camps, or gulags. Researchers in the Soviet archives have identified some 476 such camps, though the total number is still unknown. Some camps were very small, but some were made up of hundreds, even thousands, of units, spread over endless miles of otherwise empty tundra.

The importance of the gulag can hardly be exaggerated. Consider, for example, that in 1937, unpaid and barely fed prisoners produced 37 percent of the country's gold, and in 1940, prisoners cut 40 percent of the country's timber. Or, that by 1942, there were some 4.34 million prisoners laboring on projects all over the Soviet Union. Like other aspects of Soviet reality, this labor system was part of the Soviet process of primitive capital accumulation. In that regard, it is reminiscent of slavery in the British colonies in America and in ante-bellum America—though, of course, there were substantial differences. American slavery was limited to people kidnapped in Africa and shipped to the New World, where they became the personal property of plantation owners. They were valuable property—strong young males were sold for several thousand dollars— and unless a slave fought against his fate, as many did, the investment was protected. Along the Mississippi River levees, for example, where giant bales of cotton were pushed down slides to the river barges below, a bale would occasionally careen off a slide and crush a worker on the receiving end. So slaves worked the top and free Irish workers, replaceable at no cost, worked the bottom.

The NKVD, on the other hand, did not have to buy its prisoners, it just arrested them as needed. And it was an equal-opportunity slaveowner. It kidnapped Russians, Armenians, Ukrainians, Azers, Georgians—indeed the whole range of nationalities that made up the nation—indiscriminately. The victims were then sentenced to periods of three to ten years, during which they were fed as little as possible, and many of them, if not most, were worked to death. Michael Solomon, a former prisoner in Kolyma, the Siberian gulag the size of France, described the treatment of those newly arrived at the transit camp: The prisoners were paraded naked in front of the mine managers who "pinched our muscles, opened our jaws, and felt our teeth." If satisfied, they told the board, "I'll take him." An NKVD doctor told Solomon: "Your lives are reckoned to last ten years. If you live longer, it means that you are guilty of one of two things: Either you worked less than was assigned to you, or you ate more than your proper share."

As documented in a spate of recent works on the gulag by Russian historians, prisoners were treated worse than slaves. Like slaves, they ceased to be regarded as human beings; unlike them they were calculated as units of expendable labor, to be fed as little as possible and worked as hard as possible. Their use was promoted by NKVD officials as a way of making investments affordable. The only concern for their well-being that appears in the surviving records was whether the high percentage of ill and dying lowered the efficiency of the work. This was Beria's concern when he took over the NKVD and ordered food rations to be raised. According to Galina Ivanova, however, he did so only to increase productivity, and, thereby, to prove that his NKVD could be an important and stable part of the overall economy.

In fact, the feasibility of many projects depended on prison labor, as Stalin's letters to Molotov reveal. For example, in 1930, at Stalin's urging, the Politburo approved the construction of a major canal between the Baltic and the White seas. Molotov had privately suggested to Stalin that the project might cost more than they could afford. Stalin shared this concern. He wrote to Molotov acknowledging that "the financial plan has to be cut as much as possible." But, he added, "it's still a crime to squelch the matter." His solution was to build the canal "relying mainly on GPU [prisoners]." Similarly, in 1935, OGPU chief Genrikh Yagoda assured Stalin that a road then being built by prisoners would cut 50,000 rubles per kilometer from its cost. Stalin found these savings irresistible, so the practice continued to expand until he died, reaching its high point only in the early 1950s, when the gulag became a full-fledged "camp-industrial complex."

This was the Soviet Union's "real existing socialism." The official language still had echoes of Marx's dream of an egalitarian revolution—a dream shared by many Communists in Europe and the United States. But it had become nothing more than rhetoric designed to mask Soviet reality and to pacify the remaining true believers.

Tragically, Soviet reality not only turned the meaning of socialism on its head, but also totally distorted the intellectual and political development of socialists in the West. As we've seen, under the Communists, socialism came to mean the push for industrial development under a hierarchical, dictatorial regime. The best that can be said of Bolshevism is that it greatly reduced illiteracy and provided a level of popular education unmatched except in the most developed capitalist countries of the West and Japan. True, the Soviet Union was the first country to introduce universal health care. It made great advances in the quality of public health, although, as with forced industrialization, the initial gains were not sustained. The political structure of this regime was unique in world history. It was an amalgam of the worst aspects of feudalism, the harshest practices of capitalism, and social protections associated with socialism—a curious mixture of progressive ideas and social policies and brutally retrograde political culture. The Soviet experience is thus a true tragedy, in fact a double tragedy, the first of which facilitated the second. First, the founders embarked on the path of revolution under conditions that made its success impossible despite the best intentions of many of its leaders. Second, the man who led and epitomized Soviet society for most of its existence, while probably the only one who could have done so, was himself fatally flawed.

The Soviet experience—and especially the political intrigues of the late 1920s—put the finishing touches on the American left. On the one hand, like millions of people in Western Communist parties and on their peripheries, most pro-Soviet Americans sincerely believed what Soviet officials told them about their efforts to build a new society. On the other hand, the increasing numbers of anti-Communists spent their energies exposing the horrors of Soviet reality and attacking American communism's domestic followers. Worse, as socialism came to be equated with Soviet "real existing socialism," socialists of all stripes in the United States gave less and less thought to the transcendence of the world's most developed capitalism, or to socialism as the means of fulfilling the democratic promise inherent in American life. Then, in 1929, just as socialists—particularly the self-styled "Marxists" among them—had predicted throughout the 1920s, American capitalism collapsed and the Great Depression began. This crisis of the system, the deepest and most profound of American capitalism's cyclical depressions, was the socialist left's big opportunity, or so one might have thought.

6

CAPITALISM COLLAPSES: WHATEVER HAPPENED TO SOCIALISM?

I

ONLY A DOZEN YEARS AFTER THE RUSSIAN REVOLUTION, the American stock market crash triggered the Great Depression. Many on the left saw this collapse as opportunity. In fact, after an initial period of shock and paralysis, Americans spawned an unprecedented array of radical activity, much of which drew on the residue of principles and programs espoused earlier by the Socialist Party. The party itself, however, could do little more than stand on the sidelines and watch as these new movements created the pressure that spurred Franklin D. Roosevelt to adopt his New Deal measures.

Roosevelt, his allies, and even the Louisiana radical Huey Long argued that they were proposing their reforms in order to save capitalism from itself. Indeed, that is what they did. But to do so it was necessary to infuse the old system with principles that brought social need to the fore. That drew the ire of free-market conservatives whose first principle was today's bottom line. As Milton Friedman, the dean of free-market economists, complained decades later, New Deal reforms created a government that is now responsible for 45 percent of national spending. And, he added, that "doesn't [even] allow for the effect, not of spending, but of regulations—the Clean Air Act, the Aid to Disabilities Act and so on—so that, in fact, we are more than half socialist today." As a result, Friedman argued, "more than half of the total output of the country is being distributed in a way that is determined by the government."

This, of course, is not socialism, though Friedman was not entirely mistaken. Many of the reforms that humanized capitalism during the Depression were, indeed, based on principles that were first proposed by Socialists. While the changes were enacted to secure the people's loyalty to the existing system, we are all better off for them. True, also, as Friedman's complaint suggested, these principles have become widely accepted as a necessary means of humanizing the "free market" capitalism that created the Great Depression and that champions of parasitic enrichment continue to practice today.

II

In any case, the severity of the Great Depression revealed unrestrained capitalism's weakness. In the first year following the crash, 26,355 businesses failed. This was just the beginning. By 1933, as David Kennedy reminded us in *Freedom from Fear*, industrial production had plummeted. Gross national product fell to half of its 1929 level, and spending for new plants and equipment ground to a virtual standstill. Steel production had dropped 60 percent from pre-crash levels, machine-tool makers had reduced their output by two-thirds, and residential and industrial construction had shriveled to one-fifth its pre-Depression level. Overall, businesses invested only $3 billion in new plants and equipment in 1933—a mere 12.5 percent of the capital invested in 1929. Things did not get much better for a full decade, and then only because of government military spending for World War II.

When Franklin Roosevelt took office in 1933, one out of every four workers was on the street. As industry collapsed, poverty and destitution also swept the American countryside. Already depressed throughout the 1920s, agriculture now experienced disaster. Millions of farmers and tenant farmers, especially in the South and Southwest, starved and were driven off their land. In Oklahoma, the wheat harvest that had brought in $1.2 million in one county in 1931 brought in only $7,000 in 1933. In Mississippi, income per capita dropped from a pathetic $239 in 1929 to $117 in 1933. Millions of families were disrupted as millions of men left home hoping to find a job somewhere else. Many of the unemployed, young boys and girls as well as their brothers and fathers, rode the rails from town to town looking for work of any kind.

Sociologist Thomas Minehan had a special interest in the children. He spent three years hopping on and off freight cars in the guise of a fellow tramp studying how they were faring during this economic downturn. Living with these children, hearing their stories and sharing their experiences, disturbed him deeply. In *Boy and Girl Tramps in America* he wrote about the "flesh and blood youngsters who should be in high schools and homes [but] were in boxcars and [hobo] jungles." As a sociologist, Minehan drew graphs and provided the tables required by his discipline, but he found it "totally inadequate" simply to report that 324 youths [from his sample of 509] had left home because the father was unable to support his family, or that fourteen shoeless boys he met had no recourse but to steal shoes from others, or that nine of the sixteen girls in his sample sold their bodies to get bread. He had "seen pictures of the Wild Children in Revolution-wracked Russia," and he had read of the "free youth" in the post-war chaos of Germany. But he had always believed that "in America we managed things better." The sheer number of children he had seen on the road, and the way they had been forced to live, convinced him otherwise.

Yet the hundreds of thousands of men, women, and children riding the rails and living in hobo jungles were only a small part of the dispossessed. Many families who had lost their homes lived in corrugated packing crates, and other slapped-together shacks in the Hoovervilles (named after President Herbert Hoover) that sprung up in every city. Most of these were at the edges of towns, but sometimes they were right under the noses of the wealthy. In New York, for example, a packing crate village in Central Park lay directly under the eyes of apartment dwellers high above Fifth Avenue and Central Park West. That one, however, was soon torn down and its residents transferred out of sight.

The depth and suddenness of the Depression shocked everyone. Throughout the 1920s, Communists had predicted that a financial and business crisis was just around the corner, but they, too, were caught by surprise. Even so, many Socialists may have found some satisfaction that the natural workings of modern capitalism had finally offered them this opportunity. If so, they were deluded, for while many people saw these events as an omen of the system's imminent demise, neither the Socialists nor the Communists enjoyed more than a short bounce in popularity from the disaster. True, in 1932 Socialist Norman Thomas received 884,000 votes for president, a big increase over his vote in 1928, but still fewer than Debs had received in 1912 (when the electorate was half as large). More importantly, a vote for Thomas was seen as little more than a way to protest the conservatism of both major parties, while in 1912 Debs was competing against Theodore Roosevelt and Woodrow Wilson, both running as Progressives.

In 1932, William Z. Foster, the Communists' candidate for president, did much worse than Thomas; he garnered only some 102,000 votes (his party's all-time high). Still, later in the depression decade and helped by their identification with the Soviet Union, which alone among nations in this time of international crisis was busily engaged in a building boom of new industry and infrastructure, the Communists fared somewhat better than the Socialists.

III

When the Depression began, however, the American Communist Party was in bad shape. The 1929 stock market crash had by chance coincided with the most traumatic and defining internal crisis in the party's early history. Split by what they thought were doctrinal disputes about the nature of the world capitalist economy, the rival factions were only unwitting pawns in Stalin's machinations aimed at consolidating his absolute power. In the American party, each of the two factions tried frantically to divine Stalin's position. But when Stalin took the sharp turn toward the ultra-sectarianism that came to be known as the Third Period, the leaders of the American majority faction found themselves out on a limb. Bravely, they held their ground and argued against Stalin. This was a fatal mistake. He easily humbled them and went on to nullify a recent leadership election in which Jay Lovestone, Benjamin Gitlow, and their closest allies had received a 90 percent majority.

The denouement of this affair came when Stalin challenged the Americans at a meeting of the executive committee of the Comintern in Moscow on May 14, 1929. The 90 percent majority, he told Lovestone and Gitlow, was not really theirs. They had been elected not for their intrinsic virtues, but simply because their members had seen them as the most loyal supporters of the Communist International. What will happen, he asked, when "the American workers learn that [by thinking for yourselves and fighting against its executive bodies] you intend to break the unity of the ranks of the Comintern?" Do you think your members "will prefer the interests of your factional group to the interests of the Comintern?" At present, he taunted them, "you still have a formal majority," but if you attempt to challenge us, "tomorrow you will have no majority and you will find yourselves completely isolated. You may be certain of that, dear comrades."

True to his warning, Stalin saw to it that Lovestone's and Gitlow's support at home evaporated. Abandoned by their previous followers, they were expelled and vilified. And then, to leave no room for doubt about who called the shots, Stalin ignored not only Lovestone and Gitlow, but also their factional rivals and coronated Earl Browder—a still relatively unknown outsider—as the new party leader.

These events affected the future and grabbed the attention of every American party official. When the struggle was over, as Theodore Draper accurately concluded in his *American Communism and Soviet Russia*, the lesson of Lovestone's defeat was "burned into the consciousness of the founding generation of American Communist leaders." It taught them, Draper wrote, "that resistance against the Russian leadership of the world Communist movement was futile and barren." Ten years after its founding, "nothing and no one could alter the fact that the American Communist party had become the hapless instrument of the Russian Communist party."

And yet, despite the party leadership's subservience to Moscow and the paucity of its popular presence, the Communists far outdid the Socialists in their level of activity throughout the Depression. During these years— and, indeed, until well after World War II—young people disenchanted with the iniquity of corporate capitalism and imbued with the egalitarian spirit of socialism flocked to the party associated with the world's first— and only—successful "socialist" revolution. The vast majority of these new members knew nothing of events within the Soviet party or the Comintern. In the late 1920s, during the height of the leadership conflicts in Moscow, negative reports in the American press about the Soviet Union seemed simply to be a continuation of the anti-socialist slanders that had dominated the media at least since 1917, and especially during the 1919 Palmer Raids and the deportation of socialists and anarchists. After the 1929 crash many on the left saw Communist policies simply as a rational reaction to growing signs of capitalism's final crisis.

For American Communists the practical issue that Stalin chose—and that divided the factional fighters in the late 1920s—was how to form a popular front. In party jargon, a popular front from below meant working with the rank-and-file of other left or liberal organizations in order to recruit their members and undermine their "corrupt" leaders, while a popular front from above simply meant cooperating with other organizations to achieve a particular goal. From the beginning, especially in regard to the Socialists, the party's instinct had been to attack the group's leaders while trying to lure away its members. The one exception was in trade union work. Most Communist leaders in the early 1920s opposed dual unionism, at least in principle. William Z. Foster, the party's expert on trade unionism, had long opposed the IWW as a dual union and had worked with some success in the AFL. In 1919, he had been appointed by Gompers to lead the AFL attempt to organize American steel workers, and he joined the Communist Party only after the Second Comintern Congress in 1920 repudiated dual unionism. In 1927, just before Stalin changed the rules, Foster reiterated that it would be a "basic error to

reject existing trade unions." There is, he insisted, "no room for a genuine dual union movement in the United States."

But, as Irving Howe and Lewis Coser explained in *The American Communist Party,* because the federation refused to organize the vast bulk of
unskilled workers, cooperation with AFL affiliates was not always possible. "Unskilled labor must become skilled before it can gain its rights,"
wrote AFL executive committee member John P. Frey in one expression
of federation policy. So, like it or not, organizing the unskilled tended
naturally toward dual unionism. Indeed, when United Mine Workers
president John L. Lewis created the Congress of Industrial Organizations
(CIO) in 1936 it was in large part a dual union. But in the '20s the time
was not yet ripe for any such effort—and in any case the Communists'
vehicle for union organizing, a thinly disguised labor front group called
the Trade Union Educational League, was too marginal to do the job.

Nevertheless, the party thrust the job on the TUEL when delegates at
its 1925 convention adopted an ambiguous resolution instructing its leaders to organize textile workers both by "strengthening the existing organization" (the AFL Textile Workers Union) and by creating new unions
where none existed. This led the next year to a party-led strike that began
at the unorganized Botany Mills in Passaic, New Jersey.

Conditions in these mills had deteriorated ever since textile mills started
moving South, where wages were lower. When the company made things
worse by announcing a 10 percent wage cut, the party took the initiative
and called a strike. Foster and others opposed the move. An openly Communist campaign had little or no chance of success, Foster argued, but the
party leadership overruled him. They ordered the TUEL to take the lead
and they appointed Albert Weisbord, a recent convert from the Young Socialists and a Harvard law student, to assume command. Weisbord was an
articulate, energetic, and charismatic youth who knew little about unions
and less about textile workers. No matter, the party's needle trades group
told him what to do. Following instructions he set up a United Front Textile Committee, made up mostly of Communists and their sympathizers,
which, in turn, sent a committee of forty-five workers to Botany management with a demand for the restoration of company wage cuts.

The company refused the demand and fired the entire committee. That provoked 5,000 workers at the Botany Mills to walk out, and they were followed by thousands of other workers from other mills in the Passaic area. Howe and Coser related what followed: "Police and deputy sheriffs attacked strikers with clubs, fire hoses, tear gas, guns. Injunctions were issued, picket lines broken, union halls closed." Nearly a thousand strikers were arrested. Mayors, magistrates, U.S. senators, a local "citizens committee," the U.S. secretary of labor—"the whole apparatus of 'public opinion'"—joined against the strikers. But the thing that hurt the most was an AFL denunciation of the strike and its leaders.

Aware that party leadership of the strike furnished the employers with their major ammunition, the Communists still refused to relinquish control. Instead the party set in motion an impressive machine for popularizing the strike and raising relief funds. Passaic was swamped with left-wing and liberal journalists who wrote passionate reports in support of the strikers. A barrage of stories and pictures in the press documented strikers being clubbed, prominent liberals being arrested for talking to pickets, and many TUEL-organized veterans and young girls from the mills parading Passaic's streets in support of the strikers.

The strike dragged on indecisively for almost a year, closely managed by party leaders in New York. "The most intimate questions of strike policy were settled," Gitlow admitted, "without even consulting the general strike committee, let alone the strikers." Finally, however, it became inescapably clear that the strike could not be won and that the Communists had to hand the workers over to the AFL Textile Workers Union. In the end, even after the AFL took over, many strikers lost their jobs. Within two years the Communists were gone and the AFL local had only 100 members.

The Passaic strike set a pattern for other textile strikes in New Bedford, Massachusetts, and Gastonia, North Carolina. The main difference was that by the time of the later strikes, the organizers had been put in an even more untenable position by the Comintern's decision openly to promote dual unionism. Against overwhelming odds, Communists fearlessly led workers into hopeless battle—all the time denouncing the AFL as enemies of the workers and even as fascist agents. In the end no gains were made in textile, but the party did enjoy a substantial measure of success in the New York garment industry. There they established control over the International Ladies Garment Workers Union local and almost won control of the ILGWU international. And they gained permanent control of the furriers' union New York local, led by the openly Communist Ben Gold.

During these years, too, the Communists organized unemployment councils in many cities, led rent strikes, fought evictions of unemployed workers from their homes, and led demonstrations and hunger marches calling for more government aid to the dispossessed. Despite heavy recruiting in the course of such activity, however, party membership never reached as high as 80,000 at any one time—though some have estimated that as many as a million people passed through the party's ranks in the twenty years after 1929. Relatively large numbers of industrial workers and African-Americans joined and left the party in a steady stream throughout the '30s and early '40s. Young radicals, some of them high school dropouts, also joined, and many of them were educated in party schools and remained loyal to the party until Nikita Khrushchev condemned Stalin's crimes at the Soviet party's twentieth congress in 1956.

IV

A word here needs to be said about the Communist Party's relationship to blacks, because the party was the first white political group to champion their cause and to create a largely interracial organization. The early years of the century, as Southern historian C. Vann Woodward wrote, was "Progressivism for whites only." This caught the dominant spirit of the era in the North as well as the South. Almost without exception, progressive and trade union movements of the era were impregnated with racist ideology and shot through with hostility toward African-Americans, Asians, and Mexicans. A steady succession of racist acts permeated

American society in the decades preceding World War I. In the South, the Jim Crow system as it existed until the mid-1960s was constructed in the late nineteenth and early twentieth centuries. With the inauguration of Democrat Woodrow Wilson in 1913, the Southern caste system came to Washington, and segregation became the official policy in most government agencies. In part, as a concomitant to America's entrance onto the stage of world power, racist theories were used to justify not only the seizing of Spain's colonies, but also domestic reform. Progressive Republicans as well as Democrats, men such as Theodore Roosevelt, Albert J. Beveridge, Hiram Johnson, and the Kansas journalist William Allen White, explained America's greatness in terms of the nation's "race life" and racial institutions. Extolling the American's "instinctive race revulsion to cross breeding" with "inferior races," White wrote that reform upheld the purity of America's "clean Aryan blood."

Organized labor was also far from immune to racism, although its leaders tended to be pragmatic. Seeing the low standard of living of Oriental immigrants as a threat to the gains made by unions, AFL President Samuel Gompers wrote anti-Chinese and anti-Japanese pamphlets and proposed resolutions promoting Oriental exclusion. He supported actions like the segregation of Japanese children in San Francisco's public schools in 1907 by Mayor E. Z. Schmitz of the Union Labor Party. And despite the AFL's constitutionally stated principle of racial equality, African-Americans felt the sting of Gompers's tongue and the discrimination of organized labor. Rather than criticizing unions that excluded blacks from membership, or employers who hired them to break strikes, he attacked the blacks. With typical bombast, Gompers "served notice" that he would not let "Caucasian civilization"—and the "uplifting process" of labor—be interfered with in this way.

Not surprisingly, in this pervasive atmosphere, tension existed in the Socialist Party over the question of race. As a loosely organized popular movement, its members reflected a wide range of contemporary attitudes, especially in the party's early years. Not until the early teens, despite the party's official principle of racial equality, did more than a few party leaders challenge labor's dominant views on race. Indeed, not until

1913 did the national party office develop enough interest in its African-American membership to query the state party secretaries about the status of blacks in their domains.

The results were mixed. Northern state secretaries all said that they had some integrated locals, but none provided details because their membership records did not specify race. Secretaries of nine Southern states and the District of Columbia reported a range of relationships with blacks. South Carolina had no black members, while Florida, Georgia, and Mississippi had black members in segregated locals or as members at large. Arkansas, Kentucky, Louisiana, Maryland, and Tennessee all allowed mixed locals, though only Kentucky had more than a handful of active blacks—mostly in the state's mining camps and in the Louisville local, where members of the geographically based black and white branches attended joint local meetings. Only in Oklahoma—the Socialists' strongest state—did the party put up a real fight for black enfranchisement. In 1910, the state party tried valiantly to defeat a referendum that placed a "grandfather clause" in the state constitution disenfranchising former slaves and their descendants.

Occasionally, before the world war, Southern party officials decried racism. The Tennessee platform of 1912, for example, stated that "the question of race superiority" had been "injected into the mind of the white wage-worker" only as a weapon of the capitalist class to keep "workers divided on the economic field." As we have noted, in 1914 individual Socialists played a leading role in the formation of the NAACP. As editor of its journal *Crisis,* W. E. B. DuBois wrote that "slowly but surely colored folk [were] beginning to realize the possible meaning of socialism for them," and in 1916, he commented that the Socialist candidates were "excellent leaders of an excellent party," although, he thought, a vote for them would be "thrown away."

In their early years, Communists—most of whom were Eastern European immigrants—showed even less awareness of blacks than did the Socialists. Despite prodding by Lenin and the Comintern, the American party had only two dozen black members as late as 1927. Starting in 1920, there had been a running debate among Communists on the

"Negro question," but it had taken place at meetings in Moscow. Finally, in late 1928, the Russians concluded that Negroes in the Southern black belt of the United States constituted a nation. As the *Daily Worker* then dutifully explained, this meant that "while continuing and intensifying the struggle under the slogan of full social and political equality for Negroes," the party "must come out openly and unreservedly for the right of Negroes for self-determination in the Southern states where Negroes form a majority of the population."

This decision, part of the International's one-size-fits-all program for building revolutionary movements in the "colonies and semi-colonies," profoundly changed the attitude of the American party toward African-Americans. During previous years Communists had made sporadic attempts to attract blacks, most notably when Cyril Briggs and other members of the predominantly West Indian African Blood Brotherhood had joined in 1921, and again in 1924, when the party tried to establish fraternal relations with Marcus Garvey's Universal Negro Improvement Association. But Briggs and other black nationalists in the party found that they could get a serious hearing only in Moscow.

Pushed by the Comintern, and even though the party's call for an independent black nation in the South attracted little support, the party's new concentration on the "Negro Question" quickly gained it a following among blacks. The party provided legal defense, agitated for aid to the unemployed, and fought discrimination in hiring and in the AFL unions. The *Scottsboro* case, a frame-up on rape charges of nine teenage blacks in Alabama in 1931, was the most publicized of Communist defense activities during the Third Period. The party's sectarian control of the case won them the distrust of all the liberals also working on it, but its dedication to the "boys" won them a measure of respect among African-Americans and brought in many new black members. In the Midwest, party membership grew from 50 in 1930 to 700 by 1932. By the late 1930s blacks composed more than 10 percent of national party membership. Although most of these new members were in Harlem and Chicago, the party did succeed—for the first time in the nation's history—in building a largely interracial social movement.

V

Despite all this activity, the Third Period was filled with contradictory results. Until the import of Hitler's rise to power in Germany sank in, the Comintern insisted that worldwide depression had made capitalism ripe for revolution and that fascism was a transitory threat. "After Hitler us" was the German party's slogan, and in the United States Communists also saw the depression as opportunity. But shock and fear, not revolutionary zeal, initially gripped the American nation and traumatized its people. Indeed, their profound passivity confounded observers. Many top American officials marveled at the way their fellow countrymen simply accepted the desperate situation caused by industry's collapse. In 1932, Franklin D. Roosevelt—still governor of New York—found it "enormously puzzling" that Americans had endured the three-year ordeal that followed the '29 crash "so peaceably." Searching for an answer, David Kennedy suggested that American society's "vaunted celebration of individualism" was one reason for this. In a culture that attributed all success to "individual striving," he wrote, it should be no surprise that personal failure was understood as the result of individual inadequacy.

Kennedy added that this phenomenon was most pronounced among newly poor white-collar workers who only a few short years before had been the "chief acolytes and beneficiaries of the individualistic creed." Their sudden descent from security, self-sufficiency, and pride to uncertainty, dependency, and shame did not anger or radicalize them, as many observers expected. It simply left them "dumb with misery." Blaming themselves, many of them could barely manage to ask for help. As the mayor of Toledo, Ohio, testified in 1932, he had seen thousands of such "defeated, discouraged, hopeless men and women, cringing as they come to ask for public aid." It was, he said, "a spectacle of national degeneration."

Such scenes were replicated everywhere. Lorena Hickok, relief administrator Harry Hopkins's personal investigator, told him that an insurance man she had interviewed "lived on bread and water for three weeks" before he could bring himself to seek aid; that an Alabama lumberman she met had walked down to the local relief office many times but had gone past the place again and again without going in. In Texas, she reported, a twenty-eight-year-old college-educated woman, unemployed after eight years as a teacher, could only blame herself: "If I can't make a living, I'm just no good, I guess."

After a few years of continuing misery and the rise of left-wing agitation, however, anger replaced passivity. By the middle of Roosevelt's first term as president, millions of Americans were supporting radical social movements. Workers were eagerly joining unions. Others were flocking to Huey Long's "Share the Wealth" campaign or Francis Townsend's old age clubs. Still others were working and voting for Upton Sinclair and his "End Poverty in California" crusade or for Minnesota Governor Floyd Olson's Farmer-Labor Party.

By 1935, public sentiment had turned sharply to the left. Ironically, however, while new movements were proliferating and socialism's earlier programs were being assimilated into the left-liberal political agenda, the Socialist and Communist parties remained on the outer margins of popular discourse. Both parties, identified as they were with debates over the nature of the Soviet Union, had little relevance to Americans obsessed with reviving and humanizing their own economy. In any case, though Socialists and Communists played important roles as experienced, dedicated, and knowledgeable organizers in the new industrial unions, neither party played a significant role in the new popular movements.

VI

In the mid-1920s, John L. Lewis, the longtime president of the United Mine Workers, had contributed to the marginalization of socialism by identifying and denouncing his left-wing rivals as un-Americans who regularly received their orders from Moscow. That was in the years of Republican ascendancy, when Lewis was considered labor's leading Republican and when he faced strong left opposition within the UMW. When Section 7(a) of the National Industrial Recovery Act of 1933 was adopted all that changed. Section 7(a) gave workers the right to organize and bargain collectively through representatives of their own choosing, and it created a new Lewis. Overnight, he became an ardent supporter of Franklin Roosevelt—and a hero of the left.

Lewis hailed 7(a) as the greatest single advance for human rights in the United States since Abraham Lincoln's Emancipation Proclamation. He had worked hard for its inclusion in the act. And he seized on the opportunity it provided to rebuild his nearly moribund union by boldly throwing his slender resources into a massive drive to unionize the coal fields. Lewis's organizers swept through Appalachia proclaiming: "The president wants you to join the union." Join they did. As Melvin Dubofsky and Warren Van Tine have written, the organizers "did not have to plead with miners to join the union; all they had to do was sign up recruits as fast as they appeared."

Nor did Lewis have to rouse the miners to action once they had joined the UMW. Throughout the summer of 1933, militant miners led spontaneous "wildcat" strikes for union recognition throughout the coal fields. Lewis shrewdly used the threat of uncontrollable chaos to win concessions from Roosevelt and the coal companies. Wittingly or unwittingly, Dubofsky and Van Tine asserted, *New York Times* reporter Louis Stark played Lewis's game. He told Roosevelt that "seething discontent in the [coal] fields may break out worse than ever" and that "From coal it will spread to steel and autos." But Stark reassuringly told the president that Lewis was aware that conflagration "may be disastrous for everybody" and that he was "holding tight." In this situation, Stark advised, the key to peace was "an agreement between the union and the southern operators."

Amazingly, that, and more than that, is what Lewis got. Using rank-and-file rebelliousness to pressure both the operators and Roosevelt, he won the first code written under the NIRA that gave the union substantial concessions, as well as a role in their implementation. The bituminous coal code, approved by the president, granted the UMW what it had fruitlessly struggled for since its founding in 1890: a contract that covered all the major soft-coal producing districts. That was not all. As a result of the code other benefits also flowed to the miners. Statutory law now instituted the eight-hour, five-day week and the right of miners to choose their own checkweighmen, (men who checked the weight of each miner's coal) and it banned wage payment in scrip and the requirement to trade at company stores and to live in company houses. The code also outlawed child labor (defined as under age seventeen) in the mines and granted a grievance and arbitration procedure to settle disputes.

The miners' eagerness to join the union and to fight for a contract had its parallels in San Francisco and Minneapolis, and this, too, must have encouraged Lewis in his desire to organize other unions along industrial lines. In San Francisco, in 1934, 130,000 workers defied their conservative leaders and endorsed Harry Bridges's call for a general strike. Bridges, the Australian-born local president of the city's International Longshoremen's Association (ILA), then led a four-day uprising that paralyzed all nonessential commercial activity in the city. In the end, as a result of overwhelming support from rank-and-file workers, the employers were forced to abandon their discriminatory "shape-up" hiring system and to turn hiring over to a union-run hiring hall, where hiring was based on strict rotation rather than favoritism.

A month later, Minneapolis also erupted, when a Trotskyist-led Teamsters local fought the savagely anti-union employers association for thirty-six days. In the end the Teamsters also won an unprecedented victory for the industrial labor movement—but only after a series of gun battles, in one of which dozens of strikers were shot in the back while fleeing company thugs. As in San Francisco, a union-led funeral march for a slain worker foretold victory. Still, despite the outpouring of 100,000 mourners, the strike boiled on and the city's central market remained closed.

It took federal mediators, Minnesota Governor Floyd Olson, and then President Roosevelt himself to get the employers association to accept the end of its unchallenged rule. Roosevelt proved decisive. After meeting with Olson, he ordered the Reconstruction Finance Corporation to withdraw its loans to the St. Paul banks that were financing employer resistance to the union. Having lost on all fronts, the employers had no alternative but to surrender. The union had broken "the historic dictatorship over Minneapolis and the lives of its workers by the tightly organized" employers association. The settlement, Irving Bernstein wrote in *Turbulent Years*, was not only a great victory for Teamster Local 574, but also for trade unionism throughout the Northwest.

The San Francisco and Minneapolis workers had three things in common with Lewis's miners that spurred him to break with AFL craft unionism and to organize a new federation along industry-wide lines. First, young radicals had led both strikes. Bridges, though not himself a party member, worked closely with Communists, while in Minneapolis, Local 574's strike was led by Trotskyists. Second, in both strikes, workers had defied their old craft-union leaders and had established industrial unions. In San Francisco, AFL officials opposed Bridges's call for a general strike and Joseph Ryan, international president of the ILA, fired Bridges as an organizer—using his association with Communists as an excuse. Similarly, in Minneapolis, the AFL refused to support Local 574's leader when he appointed the radical Dunne brothers to lead the drive to create an industrial union. Like Ryan, the conservative international Teamster president, Dan Tobin, attempted to expel the local from his union.

Third, and most important, rank-and-file members had fought tenaciously against the concerted efforts of militantly anti-union employers. Tens of thousands had poured out onto the streets behind new leaders committed to industry-wide organization. Together they had defeated the best efforts of employers associations to squash both strikes.

VII

In 1935, Lewis made his move for a new federation of industrial unions. As Len De Caux, an Oxford-educated Communist and the long-time editor of the *CIO News*, told it, everyone had been guessing about Lewis's intentions when he arrived in Atlantic City for the 1935 AFL convention. Some of the young industrial unionists, present as delegates of federated labor unions, didn't expect much of Lewis. "They knew his Old Guard record—a Coolidge-Hoover Republican, a redbaiting reactionary, in fact one of the flashiest of red scare showmen." Despite the talk in Washington of a "new Lewis," De Caux also had doubts about Lewis's conversion. But when the young rebels "came away glowing" after visiting Lewis's headquarters, De Caux began to sense a real change in the man. These "youngsters," he wrote, were used to being "shut out, pushed in the face by those in power," but Lewis welcomed them, "asked their problems, offered his help."

The old guard craft unionists had also heard the rumors of a new Lewis. "Disturbed but not upset," they expected Lewis to put on a show and play to the new militants, but they did not expect him to bolt. After all Lewis "was one of them." He had always "stood against the 'reds,' even led the fight." He might "shoot off," but since he didn't have the votes, they believed that he'd have to compromise. And, as they had done so often, they expected to "bury the rebellion in a whoop-dadoop of anticommunism."

But Lewis had out-thought the old guard. He pushed hard for a resolution calling for the organization of unions that ignored craft lines and included all the workers in an industry. As expected, he lost. As expected, he didn't bolt. Instead, he provoked a symbolic fight with "Big Bill" Hutcheson—the powerful head of the carpenters' union and a hard-line defender of craft jurisdiction. The fight ended when Lewis shot a right jab to Hutcheson's face and knocked him off his feet. Lewis then calmly lit a cigar, sauntered out of the hall, and waited for the old liners to expel him—and to assume the onus of splitting the movement.

Meanwhile, immediately after the convention, he called together seven unions beside the UMW and set up a Committee for Industrial Organization within the federation. This led to the unions' expulsion from the AFL—and to organizing drives that created the United Automobile Workers, the United Steel Workers of America, the United Electrical Workers, United Rubber Workers, and several other unions. Together these unions then changed their name from the Committee for Industrial Organization to the Congress of Industrial Organizations, and went on to organize millions more industrial workers.

After being hired by Lewis as editor of the CIO's newspaper, De Caux came to realize that all of Lewis's actions before and after the convention had been calculated. "[E]very move, word, and gesture," De Caux wrote, had been carefully—and often secretively—thought out, and then worked out as part of his strategy for launching the big CIO drive. Part of that calculation, as the hiring of De Caux made clear, included the wooing and use of Socialists and Communists as organizers in the drives to unionize America's major industrial giants. Criticized even by some of his allies for doing this, Lewis responded that he wasn't worried. "Who gets the bird," he asked, "the hunter or the dog?"

In the CIO, as Lewis's story suggested, ideology played only a small role. The shared goal was industry-wide organization, regardless of skill, and the organizers' desired attributes were commitment, zeal, and ability. Thus, it should be no surprise that despite his past militant anticommunism, Lewis hired Communists, Socialists, and a smattering of other radicals to work for him. In the process, several Communists became leaders of such CIO affiliates as the United Electrical Workers, the National Maritime Union, and the Transport Workers Union. But in their roles as presidents of their unions most of these Communists played down their political beliefs, and—when push came to shove during the early Cold War years—disavowed them entirely.

VIII

Unlike the new unions, the other popular movements of the 1930s were both ideological and transitory. But neither the Socialist nor Communist parties played direct roles in any of these movements, despite the fact that each proudly and vociferously embraced social principles clearly rooted in the old socialist movement. Indeed, some of the new leaders had been members or followers of the old party, or of successors such as the Nonpartisan League and the Farmer-Labor parties.

Upton Sinclair, for example, had been a lifelong Socialist, as well as the author of dozens of educational novels, of which *The Jungle*, written in 1905, had been most influential. A story about life and work in Chicago's meat-packing industry, Sinclair's book vividly described the grisly conditions in the city's slaughterhouses. He had written it, he said, to convert people to socialism, but while he aimed at his readers' heads, he had hit them in the stomach. Despite its popularity, *The Jungle* produced few converts to the party, but it was credited with playing a major role in developing popular support for the 1906 Pure Food and Drug Act.

In 1934, still going strong, Sinclair quit the moribund Socialist Party to run for governor of California as a Democrat. Reacting to the way in which the Soviet experience had changed socialist discourse, he suggested that American workers didn't understand words like "proletariat," and that only "a movement based upon American conditions, and speaking the American language" could succeed. American workers, he explained, "act and speak and dress middle-class." Still, in the face of the Depression, he argued, Americans were "looking for help and ready to join anybody who shows them the way."

And, of course, Sinclair knew the way. He knew, he wrote, "exactly" how to end poverty. If elected governor, he promised, he would "put the job through"—and not take more than one or two years of his four-year term to do so. As Arthur Schlesinger related, Sinclair's brief and direct slogan "End Poverty in California" represented an equally brief and direct plan, all laid out in a book, *I, Governor of California*. "Taking a leaf from Edward Bellamy's *Looking Backward*, Sinclair wrote in classic utopian style, and concocted a program that was a mix of Henry George, Robert Owen, and the 1897 Western state colonizers," Schlesinger wrote. The problem, according to Sinclair, was idle land, idle factories, and idle people, and the solution was for the state to take over unoccupied land, much of it already in tax delinquency, and to rent or purchase unused factories. The unemployed could then grow their own food and make their own clothes and shelter, all in a closed system of exchange. "Let the people go to work again, and take themselves off the backs of the taxpayers," he wrote.

Sinclair looked to the ultimate establishment of a network of land colonies, model factories, and workers' villages that in time would become "self-governing communities, production units managed by the workers under charter from the state." This production-for-use system would then compete with the production-for-profit system of capitalism. Public industry, he was certain, would put private industry out of business everywhere it was given a fair chance. By 1938, Sinclair believed, the old order would have "crumbled like a dry-rotted log," first in California and then in the rest of the nation. And the political situation would be "changed forever."

By 1938 the old system had changed a bit, and, by giving the political establishment a run for its money, Sinclair had contributed some impetus to the changes. But the changes that occurred were not at all what he had hoped for. However, in July of 1934, for a brief time, Sinclair appeared to have a good chance of being elected. More than two hundred thousand copies of *I, Governor of California* were circulating in the state. The End Poverty League, Inc., was publishing a weekly paper. Hundreds of EPIC clubs had been set up by a corps of organizers who were busily launching barbecues, picnics, and sewing circles.

Sinclair's opponent in the Democratic primary was George Creel, a protege of Woodrow Wilson's son-in-law, William Gibbs MacAdoo. Creel was no pushover. An anti-socialist liberal who had run Wilson's Committee on Public Education—the agency charged with whipping up popular support for World War I—he had powerful backing. Yet to just about everyone's surprise Sinclair not only beat Creel but won more votes than all eight of his primary opponents put together. At the subsequent party convention, with Creel's uneasy support, Sinclair was chosen as the Democratic candidate for governor.

At first, the campaign went well. Sinclair went to Hyde Park for a chat with President Roosevelt, who, according to Schlesinger, charmed him by telling the story (which, however unlikely, was endorsed by Eleanor Roosevelt) that his mother used to spoil young Franklin's breakfast by reading to him from *The Jungle*. Roosevelt also showed interest in Sinclair's idea of production-for-use, which he compared to an Ohio program, allegedly along this line, that was receiving federal support. Like so many others who visited with Roosevelt, Sinclair was convinced by his cordiality and enthusiasm that the president shared his views.

The rest of his trip was also encouraging. From Hyde Park, Sinclair traveled down to New York City, and was pleasantly surprised when Postmaster General James Farley—the Democratic Party's chief patronage dispenser—held out his hand and said, "Call me Jim." Then he went to Washington, where he met with Harry Hopkins and other administration leaders. On his way back to California he stopped in Michigan and picked up an endorsement of EPIC from the radio priest, Father Charles Coughlin, then still in the New Deal camp.

All of this put Sinclair in an optimistic mood. But he had not reckoned with his opposition in California. There, Schlesinger wrote, the "propertied classes saw in EPIC the threat of social revolution by a rabble of crazed bankrupts and paupers—a horrid upheaval from below" that "could only end up in driving all wealth and respectability from the state." They were not about to let this happen. In a public relations campaign led by the Republican state chairman, Louis B. Mayer, of Metro-Goldwyn-Mayer, the state's smartest advertising people were mobilized to discredit and destroy Sinclair. And in a portent of Richard Nixon's dirty tricks campaigns against Rep. Jerry Voorhis for the House in 1946 and then against Rep. Helen Gahagan Douglas for the Senate in 1950, the Republicans smeared Sinclair "as an atheist, a Communist, an anarchist, a vegetarian, a believer in telepathy and free love, and an enemy of Catholics, Christian Scientists, Mormons, Seventh Day Adventists and Boy Scouts." Fliers endorsing Sinclair by a nonexistent "Young Peoples Communist League" and signed by a fictitious Vladimir Kosloff were widely distributed. False affidavits asserted that Sinclair had trampled the American flag, cursed the Constitution, and, when forty-eight sailors had been killed in an explosion on the battleship Mississippi, said he wished it had been forty-eight hundred.

Many years later advertising man Leone Baxter lamented that "because he was a good man, we were sorry we had to do it that way." It was all justified, however, by the need to keep Sinclair from becoming governor. In the face of all this, Democratic officials, glad to see Sinclair go down to defeat, beat a hasty retreat. First, California party leaders abandoned Sinclair. Then Farley repudiated his endorsement. And finally Roosevelt quietly let it be known that Sinclair could be sacrificed.

IX

Floyd Olson of Minnesota was everything that Sinclair was not. Where Sinclair was a lifelong visionary, a man of many enthusiasms, Olson was a consummate politician, a man who expressed his beliefs within the framework of carefully calculated possibilities. He knew not to get caught far enough out on a limb to be cut down, but when it served his cause to express his principles, he did so boldly.

By the time Olson was forty-five he had spent ten years as the Hennepin County (Minneapolis) attorney and had been elected to three two-year terms as Minnesota governor on the Farmer-Labor Party ticket. In 1936, he was preparing to run for the U.S. Senate, an election he would certainly have won, had he not died suddenly of pancreatic cancer.

Olson was the only child of Scandinavian immigrants—a Norwegian father and a Swedish mother. His father, an easygoing man, worked as a checker for the Northern Pacific Railroad. His mother, who was better educated, was determined that Floyd would go further in life than her husband. Floyd absorbed both his father's taste for what his biographer calls "the more conventional vices," and his mother's ambition. From high school he went to the University of Minnesota, but after a year of quarrels with the authorities over his refusal to participate in compulsory military training, he quit school and spent the next year on the road. Ending up in Seattle, he briefly joined the IWW and is said to have absorbed the Wobblies' "smoldering indignation against capitalistic exploitation of the workers."

In 1913, Olson returned to Minneapolis, where he worked as a law clerk and attended Northwestern Law College at night. After being admitted to the bar and working for a brief time as a lawyer in private practice, he sought public office. Years later he told friends that this decision had been prompted by a desire to protest the conviction and sentencing of a colleague for having written a book critical of American participation in World War I. But while he shared the Farmer-Labor Party's views, Olson first tried unsuccessfully for the Democratic nomination for Congress, and then switched parties and won the Republican nomination for county attorney. His biographer, George H. Mayer, suggested that he took this leaf from the Nonpartisan League book because in 1919 the Farmer-Labor Party was still suffering from its wartime pummeling at the hands of the state's super-patriots.

After five years, however, smoke from the war had cleared, the antiwar forces had been vindicated in the realm of public opinion, and Olson turned to the party nearest his heart and secured the Farmer-Labor nomination for governor. He lost that year in a close race, but two years later he was elected, and was then twice reelected.

In his first term, Olson proceeded cautiously. The legislature was still under Republican control, and farmers and workers were on the opposite side of several issues. Farmers, already hard-pressed, were opposed to new or increased taxes. Labor, suffering from high unemployment, wanted higher wages on state contract work and more state jobs. This created a treacherous political terrain for a Farmer-Laborite.

In his second and third terms, however, with the Depression in full swing and popular radicalism on the rise, Olson was able to lead a parade for reform. Seeing capitalism as a system "steeped in the most dismal stupidity," he looked to government as the solution to the problems of working people. His legislative proposals were aimed at keeping farmers from losing their farms, at helping workers find jobs or get unemployment insurance if they were laid off, and at aiding consumers by keeping prices low. To stem the tide of farm evictions, Olson pushed legislation for mortgage adjustments and a two-year grace period between delinquency and foreclosure. And for those who had lost their farms, he proposed legislation to mandate low rental rates on foreclosed farms. To raise money for relief of the unemployed, Olson called for a state income tax on high-income brackets. And he advocated an anti-injunction bill to protect workers on strike. To help small businesses being squeezed by competition from out-of-state corporations, Olson sought a graduated tax on chain stores. And to aid consumers he proposed a constitutional amendment to allow state ownership of power-generating facilities.

Asserting, in a speech at Red Wing, that the "old pioneer idea of government as confined to police power has passed off the stage," Olson argued, "We have now reached the socialized state." The only issue was how far it would extend. For him, this was not "a matter of theory, but a problem of practice and expediency." The present economic system, having "shown its inability to provide employment and even food and shelter for millions of Americans," has clearly demonstrated that "only government can cope with this situation." Still, Olson rejected socialism except as a last resort. Instead, he called for heavy taxation to redistribute wealth and to provide funds for social investment, which he saw as the only alternative to the complete socialization of wealth.

In national politics, Olson was a strong supporter of the New Deal, but also a constant critic. In Minnesota, he embraced the Farmer-Labor Party as a third party, but he opposed any attempt to form a national third party, because Minnesota was alone in having a third party capable to winning state-wide elections. Had he lived in North Dakota he would have followed the Nonpartisan League's strategy, but his state's election laws made that impossible. Instead, in 1932, Olson reached an understanding with the Democrats whereby Farmer-Laborites would tacitly support Roosevelt, and the Democrats would not seriously challenge Olson. Eventually, such cooperation led to the present Democratic-Farmer-Labor Party of Minnesota.

X

Of all the 1930s radical politicians, Louisiana Governor Huey Pierce Long Jr. was by far the most successful. A charismatic figure, he is often mistakenly remembered as the first American dictator or the first great native fascist. As his biographer T. Harry Williams wrote, Long was in fact a uniquely democratic politician who had nothing in common with the dictators except their popularity. As a consistent champion of working people and an implacable enemy of the corporate monopolies and Eastern banks, he commanded one of the largest mass followings in the country.

A consummate, and sometimes ruthless, politician, Long was elected to the U.S. Senate in 1930 at the midpoint of his term as governor. But he did not go to Washington to be sworn in until 1932, when he secured the election of a satisfactorily compliant successor in Louisiana and a full slate of other loyal state officeholders. That same year he helped Roosevelt win the Democratic presidential nomination by holding critical Southern delegates in line at the Democratic convention. He did so in part because of Roosevelt's progressive record as New York governor, but also because, like many others, he initially believed that Roosevelt was just a genial dilettante who could be used to further Long's own presidential ambitions. Like many others, however, Long quickly found out that Roosevelt had an iron will of his own and was an equally great politician. From then on, Long considered Roosevelt his mortal enemy.

Part of Long's hostility to FDR, Williams wrote, also came from his belief that "the President was moving far too slowly toward the goal of economic democracy." Like Sinclair in California and Olson in Minnesota, Long had put forward programs far to the left of the New Deal, and he had demonstrated their great public appeal. After 1932, he was a presence on the national scene, and especially in the solidly Democratic South. Roosevelt feared him as a conventional political operator, a direct rival, "who might unseat him from the presidency" fair and square, and who was thus much more dangerous than a second Mussolini would have been. If the New Deal "failed to solve the problems of capitalism," Roosevelt feared, "the restless factions of the American left might erupt into some kind of revolution under Long's leadership." Indeed, Long was popular enough to seem invincible, or at least capable of winning control of the Democratic Party's Southern bastion.

Then, on a warm September night in 1935, in the Louisiana capital of Baton Rouge, Huey Long was shot down by an assassin and Roosevelt was secure in his office.

Huey Pierce Long Jr. started life in a real log cabin, the son of a relatively successful dirt farmer in Winn parish, Louisiana. Even by the standards of hardscrabble northern Louisiana, Winn was poverty stricken—"pathetically, almost sensationally poor," Williams wrote, so much so that its impoverished condition became "almost a byword in the state." People in the parish even joked about their poverty, saying that they made a living by taking in each other's washing. But Huey's father was a good farmer and shrewd businessman. He managed to scratch out enough to move to Winnfield, the metropolis of Winn parish, and to build one of the town's biggest houses. That, of course, was not much in a place that in 1910, with a population of 2,900, had a large lumber mill but only seven brick buildings, dirt streets and no sidewalks, and in which cows, hogs, and goats roamed freely in the business district. Winnfield had no municipal electric, water, or sewer system. Still, it was a cut more cosmopolitan than most northern Louisiana towns. Half a dozen Italian families operated fruit stands, 200 Mexicans worked on the railroad or in the mills, and there were one or two Jewish store owners and two clans of Syrian foot peddlers, in addition to some French Cajuns from southern Louisiana and several Chinese laundrymen.

Huey's father had acquired hundreds of acres of land and enough wealth to furnish his many children with something more than a high school education. He was an avid reader with an unusually large library for his time and place, and Huey, a child of insatiable curiosity, read everything he could get his hands on. With a photographic memory he did well in school almost despite himself. In an early example of his brash self-confidence, Huey did the unthinkable by skipping a grade on his own initiative. When the Winnfield school was upgraded to include a high school, he had just finished the sixth grade. After studying the curriculum for the seventh grade, he decided it offered him nothing. So when school opened he simply presented himself to the eighth-grade teacher. This created an uproar from fellow students, but the teacher took it in stride, quizzed him in history, civics, and English, concluded that he could do the work, and enrolled him.

While still in school, Huey had already decided on a political career. He wrote his name as "Hon. Huey P. Long" in his textbooks and boasted to the principal's wife that he would go on to be governor, United States senator, and president. But from the beginning he was determined to be a special kind of politician, one who would fight for working people— with whom he always identified—and use the power of democratic politics—of numbers—to oppose the corrupting power of big money. This idea was not his alone, it had permeated northern Louisiana in the late nineteenth century, when the Populist party was at its height and Winn parish was its stronghold. In 1892, for example, the Populist candidate for governor, who came from Winnfield, swept the parish by almost five to one. And the Populists carried every subsequent election in Winn until the party collapsed in 1900. Huey's father shared most of the Populists' ideas and he instilled them in Huey, though he also believed that third parties were ephemeral and that it was best to make a fight from a vantage where he could win. In Louisiana, that meant the Democratic Party. And that was the ground on which father and son fought their battles.

After the turn of the century, the Socialist Party replaced the Populists in many parts of the South, including northern Louisiana. "In these parishes," Williams wrote, "a swelling sentiment of farmer resentment threatened to elevate Socialism to the status of a major party." As Huey was growing up, Winnfield was at the center of Louisiana Socialists' strength. In 1908, the Socialists elected half of Winn parish's officers and several ward posts in the town. Yet, despite his agreement with the Socialists' values, and with much of their program, Huey was not attracted to the party. Still in high school, he had already fixed his eye on the main chance.

His first chance to make a public splash came when a touring Socialist lecturer challenged the local state senator and state representative to debate the merits of his cause. These worthies both declined, and in their place local Democratic leaders asked Huey and his best friend, Harley Bozeman, both still in high school, to take on the task. Huey jumped at the opportunity, and he apparently won the debate. Rejecting socialism, he nevertheless attacked big corporations and monopolies while espousing the small-capitalist philosophy that Southern Populists carried into the Socialist Party with them—and in which his audience of farmers believed.

Too restless to finish high school, Huey quit before graduating, and, after a stint as a door-to-door salesman, went to Tulane Law School. After only nine months of intense study there he took his bar exam, became a lawyer, and returned to Winnfield, where his practice at first consisted mostly of workmen's compensation cases for poor white and black clients. His first big break as a lawyer came when a widow, having been turned down by all the town's other lawyers, asked Huey to sue his uncle George's Winnfield bank. The suit was for insurance money that had been deposited years before in another bank, since absorbed by his uncle's institution. Winnfield's other lawyers had refused the widow partly because her case was shaky, at best, but also because they feared to offend the town's most powerful institution—or to go up against the high-powered attorneys who represented it.

But this was grist for Huey's mill. Revealing a technique that he would use time and again in his meteoric rise to political power, he jumped at the chance, took the case, and won. Overnight, from being "the littlest and the least" in Winnfield, he had become known as the smartest lawyer in town. Soon, he had all the law business he could handle, and before long he had gained a reputation throughout northern Louisiana as a sharp, idealistic young lawyer who defended wronged humble clients against big evil corporations.

In 1918, at the age of twenty-five, Long rode this reputation to election as the northern Louisiana member of the state Railroad Commission (later changed to the Public Service Commission). For decades the commission had been an almost moribund repository of prominent political has-beens. Constitutionally empowered to regulate the practices and rates of railroads, steamboats, sleeping cars, telephone and telegraph companies, and pipelines, it had traditionally given industry free reign. But Huey, who was building a career as a tenacious champion of workers' rights and a fearless opponent of corporate greed, changed all that.

On the commission, Huey, as he was universally known, fought to reduce utility rates for telephones, gas, and electricity and to increase the severance tax (a tax on extracted natural resources), especially that paid by Standard Oil. And he used his position to attack conservative politicians and officeholders, from the governor on down, as tools of major corporations. He also paid meticulous attention to the mass of cases brought by municipalities and to requests filed by individuals. Huey's activities in small cases won him favorable attention around the state. Newspapers regularly chronicled victories for the people won by the energetic young commissioner. Typical headlines, Williams reported, proclaimed "Long to Fine Rails That Don't Give Service," "Long Wins Rate Fight for Sugar," "Long Answers Farmers' Plea." But Huey's major efforts went into attempts to regulate Standard Oil's pipelines, through which the state's many independent producers had to send their oil. This was a fight that dragged on for many years—and one that merged principle and benefit to Huey's advantage.

In 1924, Long ran for governor for the first time. He lost, but not by much, and in 1928, after improving his electoral machine, he was elected. The next year, when he presented his first legislative program as governor, it included a proposed five-cent-a-barrel manufacturers' tax on refined oil. This infuriated Standard Oil, whose gigantic Louisiana refinery was Huey's main target. The giant company pulled out all the stops in an effort not only to defeat the tax, but also to get rid of this young irritant. To facilitate its campaign, the company hired an agent who went to Baton Rouge, rented a floor in the city's biggest hotel, and ran an open house at which legislators received instructions and bribes. As one legislator later told Williams, "The money spent was terrific. You could pick up $15,000 or $20,000 any evening." Estimates of the amount of direct bribes ran into the hundreds of thousands, and that was only one of several means that Standard Oil had of pressuring legislators. The company's campaign did the trick. The oil tax was easily defeated. Then Huey's enemies decided to seize the time and rid themselves of this low-life outsider. In a raucous procedure, the assembly voted to impeach Long, but against seemingly heavy odds he rallied his forces and narrowly blocked a conviction in the senate.

It was a close call for Long, who had deeply offended most of the state's traditional elite. Appalled by him, they had tolerated his rhetoric, but not his refusal once in office to play the game and allow the state government to continue being used to promote their interests. Long knew all too well the power that his enemies' resources gave them. But he was determined to beat them and proceeded to build a political machine powerful enough to immunize himself against their attacks. Nothing in his methods was original. He simply pushed the traditional Louisiana practice of building patronage-based machines to its limits. He ruthlessly removed enemies and unreliable supporters from their jobs in state agencies and replaced them with loyal followers. He increased the number of patronage jobs to a new level.

Huey's machine enabled him to push through his program, which was prodigious. At the top of his list was education. He had always seen Louisiana's poverty-stricken school system and high level of illiteracy as a severe restriction on popular democracy and had consistently stressed educational reform. In his first run for governor he promised to increase state support for public schools and to provide all school children with free books. When elected four years later, he did both. Nor did he stop at improving grade schools. He established night schools to teach adult literacy. And he realized his long-time goal to make Louisiana State University into a first-rate school—and to make its facilities available to every poor boy and girl in the state who wanted a college education.

Rebuilding LSU became one of his favorite projects. Before he began, LSU was getting a "C" rating from the Intercollegiate Association of State Universities. With only 168 not-very-distinguished faculty members, an enrollment of 1,800 students, and, in 1928, a skimpy operating budget of $800,000, LSU ranked eighty-eighth in size among American universities. Long changed all that when he began rebuilding in 1930. First, he created a medical school as part of the university. Then, through creative financing (of sometimes questionable legality), he found the funds for further expansion and improvements. As a result of Long's constant efforts, the university's budget jumped to $2,870,000 and its faculty grew to 394, many of whom were established scholars from Northern schools. By 1935, LSU had raised its rating from "C" to "A," had grown to 5,200 students, and had risen to twentieth in size (and among state universities, to eleventh). Best of all, LSU charged practically no tuition and provided a generous number of scholarships. Huey had come close to his goal of making a college education accessible to all.

To fight the Depression and to bring Louisiana into the modern era, Huey also constructed 2,300 miles of paved roads and 2,816 miles of gravel roads, as well as 111 bridges throughout the state. This project took up two-thirds of the state budget and employed some 22,200 men, more than in any other state in the early years of the Depression. Next in importance, according to Huey, were his efforts to improve the quality and increase the capacity of the state's hospitals. The Charity Hospital in New Orleans, for example, had the number of patients it could handle daily raised from 1,600 to 3,800. He also constructed a state-of-the-art airport in New Orleans and made natural gas available to the city's residents.

After January 1932, when he was sworn in as a senator, Long made his presence felt in Washington. In his first few months he called for redistribution of wealth through higher income and inheritance taxes. And he attacked President Hoover's effort to cut the cost of government in order to balance the budget. In an impassioned speech entitled "The Doom of America's Dream," he warned that the great dream of America—that all men are created free and equal—had almost gone out of sight. Everyone in Congress knew this, he said, but few were willing to do anything about it. The situation called for Congress to enact legislation to redistribute wealth. If it didn't, Huey warned, the country would face a revolution. And when that happened there would be no need to worry about budget deficits.

Huey's speech, as one journalist wrote, was "strong, bitter, merciless, and inflaming." It was, another wrote, a stirring "plea for the impoverished masses." Unlike anything heard in the Senate for many years, the speech alarmed conservatives, who had hoped to dismiss Long as just another demagogue. But it established him as a leading member of the Senate's progressive bloc, made up mostly of older Republicans, one of whom, George W. Norris of Iowa, became his closest colleague (and soon switched to the Democrats). Others included Robert M. LaFollette Jr. of Wisconsin, William Borah of Idaho, and Democrat Burton K. Wheeler of Montana.

Seeing his tenure in the Senate as a stepping stone to the presidency, Huey had no need to curry favor with the conservative leadership. On the contrary, he went out of his way to twit his Democratic opponents for being tools of the same big banking interests that ruled the Republicans. Majority Leader Joe Robinson, Arkansas' senior senator, was

Long's favorite target. Huey easily provoked Robinson into passionate outbursts against him. But when Robinson challenged him, Huey avoided engaging the majority leader on his Senate turf. He would make that test on more congenial ground.

The opportunity was not long in coming. Arkansas's junior senator, Thaddeus Carraway, had died shortly before Long took his seat. In Arkansas the governor could appoint a replacement for a senatorial incumbent if he died within a year of his term's expiration. Carraway had died three days too soon, so an election was mandated. However, the time was too short for anyone to establish himself as a front-runner. Instead, the Democrats anointed Carraway's widow, Hattie (who thus became the first woman senator) to serve out the term.

She was in office when Huey arrived. And as the next junior member, she was seated next to him. On his arrival, she greeted him cordially, but Huey paid her little attention until he noticed that not only did she vote with the progressive bloc most of the time, but that she also dared to stand with the small group of senators who voted for his bill to limit incomes to $1 million a year. Still, though he liked Hattie, he assumed that she did not intend to run for reelection. A few months later, however, when Arkansas politicians started competing for the nomination to fill her seat, Hattie surprised everybody by announcing her intention to run. This raised eyebrows in Arkansas but not much anxiety. Unlike her six opponents, she had no money, no organization, no prominent supporters, and no experience in the electoral arena. She was, in other words, very much an underdog, which, of course, was what Huey liked. While others might have shied away from this situation, to Huey it was a delectable opportunity. Hattie was his friend. He wanted to help her. And if he could get her elected he would also help himself to become a much bigger force in the Democratic South, and thus in national politics.

In July, Huey mobilized his forces for an invasion of Arkansas. He was going to help Hattie and help himself, and he pulled out all the stops. On August 1, his caravan, led by a big black car (in which he rode with a bodyguard from the state police) and followed by seven trucks, left Louisiana and headed for Arkansas. Five trucks carried hundreds of thousands of leaflets, and the other two were sound trucks that leapfrogged towns as the caravan crisscrossed the state. Huey held several meetings a day. As he spoke in a town from one of the trucks, the other was setting up in his next meeting place, and his advance men were already covering the town's walls with posters and passing out leaflets. When Huey arrived huge crowds had already gathered to see and hear him—and to cheer Hattie, who spoke only a few words after Huey finished

With only minor variations, Long gave the same speech over and over again. Holding up a bible, he would begin by saying "We're all here to pull a lot of pot-bellied politicians off a little woman's neck." Then he would recite the theme that struck a new note in Southern politics:

We have more food in this country . . . than we could eat up in two years . . . and yet people are starving. We have more cotton, and wool and leather than we could wear out in two years . . . and yet people are ragged and naked. We have more houses than ever before in this country's history and more of them are unoccupied than ever before—and yet people are homeless.

Why was this? Because "540 men on Wall street" made a million dollars a year, more than all the nation's farmers combined. Furthermore, these men on Wall Street controlled Congress, told it what laws to pass and not to pass.

And what was the solution? To limit income and redistribute wealth. The crowds ate it up. And, of course, Hattie Carraway was reelected, and with more votes than her six opponents combined. In the process she became the first woman elected to the Senate in her own right. And Huey Long became a man to be feared by those in the White House and in control of Congress.

Two years later, Long unveiled his Share the Wealth/Every Man a King society in a thirty-minute national radio broadcast. He talked about his new organization as if it had been founded by people he identified only as "we," and he urged people to get together and form local chapters. But there was as yet no organization. The "we" consisted of Huey alone. Within a month, however, the society had enrolled more than 200,000 members, and by 1935, with Share the Wealth clubs in every state, it had a membership of 4,684,000, with 3 million more contacts on its files. Not surprisingly, membership was greatest in Louisiana, Arkansas, Mississippi, and the other Southern states. Outside the South the greatest concentration of clubs—also not surprisingly—was in Floyd Olson's Minnesota and its surrounding Nonpartisan League and Republican Progressive states.

In this process, Huey avoided race-baiting, and even made efforts to recruit blacks. Even though only some 2,000 blacks were allowed to vote in Louisiana, Huey wanted them in his clubs. He did, T. Harry Williams wrote, because Share Our Wealth "was for poor people and the Negroes were poor, poorer even than the poorest whites." In the North, where it was a bit easier for blacks to vote, Negro clubs were organized by black leaders who heard Huey on the radio or read one of his speeches. One of New York's fifteen Share Our Wealth clubs was organized by a black minister, who was asked by a reporter if Huey knew that he was a Negro. He replied: "The color question never came up. I address him as a man, and he addresses me as a man."

That had long been Huey's practice. His call for the organization of African-American clubs was consistent with his usual avoidance of racism and his lifelong disdain for the Ku Klux Klan. Still, his attitude was met with hostility from some of his Southern supporters, and, of course, from his enemies. Among the latter, the Ku Klux Klan denounced him at its 1934 "imperial klonvocation" in Atlanta as having an "un-American attitude" toward authority. And the Klan's Imperial Wizard, Dr. Hiram W. Evans, pledged to come to Louisiana to campaign against Huey. This was an empty threat by a Klan that had seen better days. Nevertheless, in the press gallery of the Louisiana state senate, Huey ostentatiously denounced Evans. "Quote me as saying," Long challenged, "that Imperial bastard will never set foot in Louisiana, and that when I call him a sonofabitch I am not using profanity, but am referring to the circumstances of his birth."

The program of Share Our Wealth was also consistent with Long's views and policies as governor. First, Huey proposed a federal capital-levy that would prevent a family from owning a fortune of more than $5 million and an income tax to limit family income to $1 million a year. The government would then provide every family with a "homestead" of $5,000 a year, or enough to buy "a home, an automobile, a radio, and the ordinary conveniences." The government would also guarantee every family an annual income of $2,000 to $3,000, or one-third of the average family income in 1934. Other benefits furnished by the government would include pensions of $30 per month to the aged, college tuition for all qualified students, and generous veteran bonuses. The work week was to be limited to thirty hours, and the working year to eleven months, thus providing more jobs. And the government would buy and store surplus crops in order to aid farmers by balancing supply with demand.

Some critics denounced the plan as a form of socialism that would reduce everyone to the same income level, but Huey indignantly denied the charge. Using Soviet practice as his idea of socialism, he claimed that the socialists advocated government ownership of all wealth. That, he said, was equivalent to the destruction of individual wealth. In contrast, he would retain the profit motive and by limiting its concentration in the hands of few, would create more individual wealth, more evenly distributed. Furthermore, by removing the worst abuses of the system, his plan would not destroy capitalism but save it. This, of course, is what the New Deal also sought to do, though with much milder reforms.

Huey was much closer to traditional populism—to a radical defense of small, largely agrarian, capitalists—than to socialism. And he had good political reasons to differentiate himself from the Socialists now that the movement's principles had been transformed in the popular mind by the Soviet experience. Still, like Sinclair, Townsend, and Floyd, he had absorbed much from the Socialist movement. That showed in his differences from the Populists: his refusal to retreat into virulent racism; his emphasis on propertyless workers' rights and needs; and his emphasis on universal access to higher education and health care as basic rights. Nevertheless, even while Huey and his fellow radicals in other states drew on the ideas and principles of the earlier socialists, they all disclaimed any purpose other than to save capitalism.

7

FRONTS, DECAY, AMNESIA, AND A NEW LEFT

I

BY 1936 THE PARTIES WERE OVER. American Socialists and Communists in the United States had each failed to develop a substantial popular following, and neither had any prospect of doing so. Both parties played some role in the social and political developments of the recent and coming decades—Communists more so than Socialists—but neither party had any significant ideas about transcending corporate capitalism or any strategies that might alter the system's underlying priorities. Many of the old Socialist Party's proposals had been internalized by corporate liberal reformers, which contributed to the amelioration of corporate capitalism's harshness and the development of the New Deal. The eight-hour workday, women's suffrage, unemployment insurance, workmen's compensation, Social Security, legal protection of unions' right to organize, a progressive income tax, prohibition of child labor, the legal right to advocate birth control were all being partially adopted by Congress or granted by the courts. The same was true on a state and city scale. Regulation or municipal ownership of electric power and public transit had become widespread, but, as Walter Lippmann had predicted, that too stole the Socialists' thunder.

Of course, a few of the old demands, such as public health and safety, environmental protection, and universal health care remained to be won, but such reforms had also become the stock in trade of many progressive reformers and would even be addressed after World War II by Richard M. Nixon.

That left the Socialists with an intractable problem. Their pre-war ideas and proposals had become the coin of liberal politics, but their understanding of American society had not gone beyond that of the years when large-scale corporate leaders had just begun to reshape the nation. In part this analytical failure was endemic. The party's great strength had lain in electoral activity solidly grounded on principles derived from nineteenth-century Christian idealism and in loyalty to working people. In that situation, the old party seemed to have no immediate need for intellectual work. Few party leaders had anything but the most superficial understanding of the transformation that capitalism had been undergoing in the early 1900s—when the party was enjoying its greatest success—nor did they see a need to think deeply about such matters. Indeed, like the vast majority of Americans, most Socialists leaned heavily toward a popular (and Populist) anti-intellectualism.

Furthermore, the Soviets had redefined socialism as a highly centralized, undemocratic forced period of industrialization and embroiled the Socialists in nearly constant conflicts with the American branch of the Communist Party. On the defensive as radicals and liberals euphorically rushed toward the idea of Bolshevism, and then victimized by the Communists' virulent hostility to those who rejected the strictures of the new International, the Socialist Party was unable to revive itself. Caught up, willy-nilly, in debates with Communists about the nature of Soviet society, socialists were unprepared to articulate the underlying difference between the Bolsheviks' imperative to industrialize—to catch up with the West at all costs—and American socialists' need to adjust their policies to the changing social reality of the world's most advanced industrialized nation.

If Socialists had difficulty seeing the need to understand the changes in American society brought about before and during the First and Second World Wars, Communists were totally clueless. It was not only that the Communist parties (three of them emerged from the split with the Socialists in 1919) were initially comprised almost entirely of first-generation radical immigrants from Russia and the rest of Eastern Europe—many of whom followed events in their former homelands more closely than those in the United States. More importantly, party members were forbidden by the new International to think seriously on their own. After all, as Zinoviev had told them in 1919, the new International was not a hotel where everyone could bring his own baggage.

While the new Communist parties had no independent thinkers, they did have a plethora of young "theoreticians." Their job, however, was not to think about American conditions and their implications for strategy. They had tried a bit of that before 1924, with disastrous results. After that, "theory" was used only to rationalize the frequent changes in the party's tactics. What was called theory was, in fact, a process of providing "theoretical" (or scriptural) justification for the changes in political line thrust upon them from abroad.

In the 1920s these changes of political line frequently created tragicomic errors that left the Communists isolated and, with a few exceptions, generally ineffectual. Finally, in the mid-1930s, after the threat of German and Italian fascism became clear to the Soviets, the Communists abandoned their "Third Period" ultra-sectarianism (during which they had seen all socialists and liberals as "social fascists"). Their new policy, known in the jargon of the day as the "Popular Front," was (in the same jargon) a "United Front from Above." This was mandated by Moscow (although the American party, to its credit, had begun to realize the untenable nature of Third-Period tactics on its own and was pleased with the new line). As a result of the change, Communists now ceased to criticize its hoped-for tactical allies, at least in public.

But when the party slogan of the Third Period—"Toward a Soviet America"—was abandoned, or, rather went underground, so, too, did discussion of socialism (except for the occasional mandatory mention of the word at party rallies or in publications aimed at party members). Unable to talk about their own vision of the future, Communists could not tolerate anyone talking about non-Soviet visions of socialism. Those who did so were attacked or belittled. After all, even though it was not a subject for polite discourse, there was only one true socialism, and it had only one true apostle. Anyone advocating an alternative version was sharply reminded of that.

Yet, despite the Popular Front's effective ban on discussion of the true faith, or, more accurately, because it refrained from such propaganda, the Popular Front was the best thing that ever happened to the party. Public activity consisted of good works, which ranged over a wide range of democratic reform movements. And, to the extent that the party behaved well (its ingrained habits militated against such behavior), it gained respect and influence, at least for the moment.

Of course, where it could, the party assumed sub-rosa organizational control of the groups in which its members operated, and in that sense Communists remained sectarian. This became a source of distrust among those who knew how the party operated. Still, in the CIO unions, especially before World War II, when John L. Lewis was firmly in control, the Communists worked as his loyal lieutenants. And in the several international unions where the Communists gained control, they consistently downplayed or denied their affiliation with the party—and their radicalism. Beyond the unions, which were the party's main area of concentration, Communists also actively opposed racial segregation in employment and housing and generally participated in other issue-oriented groups. Within these democratic movements, they often worked diligently and effectively. Yet, while the party grew and prospered in these years, its members rarely acknowledged their affiliation. As Daniel Bell has observed, the party was unique in this respect. It was (and, except for its sectarian progeny, is) the only political party in history whose members have consistently been embarrassed to admit their membership. (This, of course, contrasted starkly with the old Socialist Party, whose members participated proudly and openly in all their activities.)

To broaden their influence, even in their most sectarian days, Communists had set up tightly controlled front groups that were only thinly disguised as independent organizations. The most important of these were the International Workers Order (IWO), a mostly immigrant fraternal group that supplied its members with low-cost insurance; the International Labor Defense (ILD), the party's legal arm; and the Trade Union Unity League, the party's dual union. These consisted of party members and close followers who accepted party leadership. But the groups remained narrow and isolated. The one major exception before the Popular Front days was the American League against War and Fascism, which the party created in 1933 and which carried over into the new period and developed into the party's most successful and influential "mass organization." Initially, the league's base was mostly other party fronts, but despite that and the open role played by party leader Earl Browder, the league became a visible presence even before the Popular Front period began in 1935. After that, as it broadened its base and leadership, it became a force to be reckoned with, even in Washington.

In its initial stage, the league was openly anti-capitalist. At its third congress in 1935, the league's chairman, Harry F. Ward, a Methodist minister and professor of Christian ethics at Union Theological Seminary, said that new members frequently asked if the American League opposed capitalism. Of course it did, Ward replied. "How else could it stop war? How could we be against fascism without being against capitalism, since fascism is an organized expression of capitalism in its declining period?"

Only a few months later, however, in a League Program Against War and Fascism, the answer to Ward's question had been officially changed to: "An anti-capitalist attitude is not a requirement for membership. Our only concern with capitalism is at the points where it breeds war and fascism. We are obliged to expose these points." Two years later, in 1937, as the league continued to grow, anti-capitalist words were stricken from its program, the Communist Party formally withdrew as a participating organization (though it retained control), and the league changed its name to the American League for Peace and Democracy.

By 1939, organizations with a combined membership of seven million were affiliated with the league, which also had 20,000 individual members. Its fifth congress that year marked the peak of its influence. Held in Washington, D.C., the congress received greetings from Secretary of the Interior Harold Ickes, Judith Epstein, national president of Hadassah, and J. Finley Wilson, Grand Exalted Ruler of the Elks. A league labor committee included not only leaders of numerous Communist and fellow-traveling CIO affiliates, but also A. F. Whitney of the Trainmen's Brotherhood, Jack Berry of the AFL painters union, and A. Philip Randolph of the AFL Sleeping Car Porters. Two congressmen, Montana Democratic Rep. Jerry O'Connell and Minnesota Farmer-Laborite Rep. John T. Bernard, served on the league's national committee. (O'Connell was a party fellow traveler who had written for the *New Masses*, and Bernard, a native of Corsica and a former fireman in Eveleth, Minnesota, may or may not have been a party member. In any case he openly announced his membership forty years later—in 1977—when he was eighty-five.)

But the party's great success in organizing this anti-fascist front group was short-lived. Just after the fifth congress, on August 23, 1939, Berlin and Moscow announced the signing of a nonaggression pact that included secret protocols agreeing to the partition of Poland and to Soviet absorption of the Baltic states and parts of Finland and Bessarabia (most of which Russia had lost as a result of World War I). Nine days later, Hitler invaded Poland and two days after that Britain and France declared war on Germany. World War II had begin.

Now Stalin was Hitler's ally—for the moment—and whatever Stalin may have thought of Hitler, antagonizing him was not on his agenda. So the Comintern made its most famous about-face, and overnight Communist parties throughout the world loyally reversed directions. Suddenly, anti-fascism had become a bad idea, the Nazis had become benign, and the American Communists had joined the ranks of the nation's isolationists. Those formerly anathema to the Communists became their temporary allies. Those formerly their allies became anathema. And the American League for Peace and Democracy became an embarrassment. The Communists no longer had absolute control, however, so the league's facade lingered for a while. But, with its major supports removed, its infrastructure crumbled and the league collapsed.

The Communists had made an about face like this before—in 1924—when after many months of supporting the Farmer-Laborites and urging Sen. Robert M. LaFollette to run for president, they had unexpectedly been ordered by Moscow to reverse field and oppose him. At that time, as party theoretician Alexander Bittleman boasted, his party had "changed within one day, almost, fundamentally, our main political line." Bittleman saw this feat as "proof not only of the political flexibility of the Central Executive Committee, but also of the discipline and Communist quality of the party as a whole."

The 1924 maneuver created many anti-Communists on the left. But the party was still small in 1924 (it had been operating in the open for only two years), so few people beyond Progressive circles in Minnesota and Wisconsin noticed. In 1939, however, the stakes were much higher. The Nazi-Soviet pact and the party's sudden change from interventionism to mindless isolationism initiated a tailspin to disaster. After Germany invaded the Soviet Union in June 1941 and the Japanese bombed Pearl Harbor on December 7, the Soviet-American wartime alliance provided a brief respite of relatively good feelings. Even so, the Communists never recovered the trust of most people outside their depleted ranks.

II

In the late '30s, as the Communists gained fleeting prestige and influence, the Socialist Party all but disappeared. As James Thurber's laconic character asked, in a 1937 *New Yorker* cartoon, "Whatever Happened to the Socialist Party?" And in the 1960s, when a new left emerged around the civil rights and anti–Vietnam War movements, New Leftists tended to see the Socialists—whose intense anti-communism initially led them to support the war against Vietnam—as political dinosaurs. Obsession with the evils of the Soviet experience impressed most student radicals as a relic of bygone infighting, a habit of times past. Similarly, Communists—except for the Viet Cong, who were widely admired for heroically resisting American imperial aggression—had no appeal to New Leftists. American Communists were viewed with bemused indifference (at a campus meeting of the Berkeley Vietnam Day Committee that I attended in 1965, an older man from across the bay got up to dispute a point. When he proclaimed his CP membership as bona fides of his radicalism, the audience just laughed.)

Nor did New Leftists admire or respect the Soviet Union. On the contrary, they generally regarded it with indifferent repugnance. Indeed, New Left activity clearly suggested a plague-on-both-your-houses that reflected an inherent understanding of the Soviet system's weakness and the emptiness of its ostensible threat to the West. In that regard, the New Left was a quarter of a century in advance both of the traditional left and of mainstream American ideologues. This attitude was a sign of the New

Left's political strength, at least until it self-destructed in the atavistic emergence of the Weathermen and other radical "crazies" in 1969 and the early 1970s.

Still, despite the New Left's disdain for the Soviet Union, the American Communists had a perversely debilitating influence on the movement and on the identity politics that is its legacy. The New Left's fundamental weakness—which it bequeathed to radical feminism, gay and lesbian liberation, and the separatist wing of the black power movement—flowed from its unwitting replication of popular frontism and the aversion to universal principles at its heart. For the Communists this approach to politics was necessary. The party operated through single-issue movements because it could not proclaim its underlying loyalties or principles. While the party had come out from underground in the early '20s (actually, it was pushed into the open by orders from the International), it never tested its principles by exposing them to public scrutiny, by running in elections and thereby providing the public with the means of choosing or rejecting them.

But the party developed a theory that made a virtue of this necessity. It deluded itself and its fellow-travelers into believing that a pre-ordained historical trajectory made popular exposure to its principles unnecessary. A "strong and consistent fight for democratic rights under conditions of decaying capitalism must ultimately lead the American people to the choice of a socialist path," the party proclaimed at its ninth convention in 1936. Or, as party leader Earl Browder said more mechanistically, "History marches toward socialism." Thus Communists believed that even in an open democratic society such as the United States, a tiny political party could gain power in a time of crisis simply by being strategically placed in popular social movements. The memory that the Russian party, with only 17,000 members at the beginning of 1917, could pull off a revolution comforted them. If the Russians took power by seizing the moment when the tsarist regime collapsed, why couldn't they?

Because Communist leaders could neither be open nor honest about Soviet reality, they also could not explore corporate capitalism's path of development and the ways in which it provided possibilities of a more humane and socially responsible future. Indeed, to have the true religion required a private rejection of the more humane aspects of capitalist development—open, multiparty elections, politically independent trade unions, free speech and all the other civil rights and liberties that had been won in the United States by working people over a century and a half of struggles, and even the virtues of market economics. Most of these things were nonexistent in the Soviet Union, and, therefore, absent from the true believer's concept of socialism. Indeed, insofar as the Communists had a vision of socialism it was closer to corporate capitalism's most undemocratic features: massive corporate and state bureaucracies, a militarized state apparatus controlled by economic giants and run in their interest, a one-party state (though in American capitalism's case this is only a tendency in a legally structured two-party system).

This way of thinking was never subjected to serious examination, either in or out of party ranks. In any case, over time, the Popular Front became a custom that those immersed in communism's faux theorizing rationalized as principle. Old-timers, as well as members who had joined largely because they saw the party as a sincere and effective fighter for its various popular causes, internalized this view. Younger members knew little or nothing about the Soviet Union's true nature, nor did they believe the lies (or what they saw as lies) in the "bourgeois press" about the Soviet Union. Even a leader as high up in party ranks as John Gates, the post–World War II editor of the *Daily Worker*, reported in his autobiography that he joined because of the party's defense of labor, civil rights, and civil liberties and that he never knew the true dimensions of Stalinism.

Yet even party members such as these also thought of themselves as revolutionaries. During the Popular Front days, they, too, accepted the party's theory that militant activity—whether unionism, fighting for racial equality, or for various social benefits—would eventually lead the masses to revolutionary consciousness, thereby obviating the need to explore the ideas and principles that sustain large-scale corporate capitalism. Thus, in the late '30s and '40s, style, rhetoric, and the degree of political commitment and self-sacrifice became the only public distinction between Communists and other organizers or activists in the trade unions and other social movements.

Something similar happened in the New Left. Few New Leftists thought much about a different form of society. Many may have had vague ideas about being revolutionaries, but they operated simply as militant interest groups. In the New Left, as in the old, style, rhetoric, and the degree of commitment and self-sacrifice also became the badges of radicalism. Few New Leftists were concerned about the class nature of American society, fewer still about the need to gain political power. This produced a kind of negative politics. The New Left was against the Vietnam War, against racial discrimination, and later, as the feminist and gay and lesbian movements developed, against sexism, heterosexism, even agism. But if asked what they were for, what positive changes they would make in society, members of the Students for a Democratic Society tended to answer that was the job of political officeholders. Having no interest in contesting for public office or in taking responsibility for the nation's welfare, their job was to create pressure on the president and Congress to implement their demands. In other words, like the Popular Frontists, they operated as traditional, if militant, interest groups. In effect they simply lobbied those in power to make changes for them. That, of course, was something that public officials liked to do. It left them in place. It did not threaten their power, and it allowed them to make adjustments in social policy without altering the underlying principles on which their policies were made.

III

Still, many leaders of the New Left thought of themselves as revolutionaries and saw their various issue movements as surrogates for a revolutionary party. Jerry Rubin, then a leader of Berkeley's Vietnam Day Committee, clearly expressed this view at a planning meeting of the antiwar movement, held in the Eucalyptus Grove on the university campus in 1965. The meeting had been called to discuss demonstrations designed to stop the troop trains on their way to the debarcation point in nearby Oakland. As the discussion progressed, a liberal professor of American history excitedly expressed the hope that by stopping the trains the VDC might end the war. This suggestion startled Rubin. Unable to contain himself, he blurted out: "We can't do that! If the war ended, what would happen to our movement?"

But what was their movement? What were its aims? How had it begun?

The 1950s began as the Cold War decade of conformity. Marked by witch-hunting, blacklisting, and fear, it was a time of congressional inquisitions, epitomized by Wisconsin's infamous Senator Joe McCarthy. Anyone who lacked impeccable credentials as a militant Cold Warrior was meat for the anti-Communist grinder. As David Caute notes in *The Great Fear*, few were exempt from accusations of disloyalty. Like the Cold War itself, the Red Scare was a device to quash the left. McCarthy, for example, accused the Democratic Party of "twenty years of treason" because it had presided over the wartime alliance with the Soviet Union. To save their skins, Democratic politicians strived to outdo McCarthy in ferreting out "un-American" liberals and leftists in all walks of life. But in 1954, with Dwight D. Eisenhower in the White House, McCarthy went too far. He attacked the army as soft on communism.

That led to his downfall. After a series of hearings, the Senate censured him and he faded away, along with the fear that had gripped much of the nation. Two years later, in 1956, Soviet Premier Nikita Khrushchev accomplished what McCarthy could not. By telling, at the Soviet party's twentieth congress, some of the truth about Stalin's crimes, he delivered the final blow to the American Communist Party. Within a year, it and its front groups had all but disappeared. These events cleared the way for something new, and almost immediately, from Harvard to Berkeley, militant student groups popped up on the campuses of elite universities. In 1959 the first independent socialist journal, *Studies on the Left*, appeared at the University of Wisconsin.

These developments seemed unrelated and were in fact largely unconnected. But a new left was in the making, though it remained unrecognized—even by its organizers—until the Student Nonviolent Coordinating Committee (SNCC) emerged from the sit-ins of 1960–1961, and the Students for a Democratic Society (SDS) issued its founding manifesto at Port Huron, Michigan, in 1961. These events provided a basis for popular awareness that a new generation of leftists had come into being and that it was fundamentally different from the old, both in its politics and its social composition. The Communist and Socialist parties had concentrated on trade unions, immigrant national groups, and, to a lesser extent, on African-Americans in Harlem and on Chicago's South Side. The New Left grew up among white college campuses in the North and black and white college students who worked for civil rights, mostly in the rural South.

New Left organizations were also starkly different from the old in their structure. Where the Communist Party and its several offshoots were centralized and disciplined with clear lines of decisionmaking and little or no initiative from the members, the New Left was decentralized and espoused a grassroots participatory democracy, at least in the early years. Taken in its best light, the New Left aversion to structure and lines of organizational responsibility flowed from its founders' belief that diversity and equal participation were necessary to arrive at a new and potentially popular "radicalism." Of course this formal anti-elitism did not usually prevent de facto elites from developing. And since the process of decisionmaking in SDS and other groups was often mysterious, it certainly did not eliminate manipulation by the elites.

Nor could the New Left entirely escape the mistakes of the old, especially as few New Leftists displayed an interest in understanding the experience of their predecessors. Having set about to reinvent the wheel, the New Left fell, willy-nilly, into some of the habits of the old. The worst of these was the Popular Front idea that single-issue movements were inherently revolutionary. That internalized old-left belief led Rubin to fear that if the anti-war movement actually succeeded in ending the war, *his* movement (which he privately believed was revolutionary) would collapse. James Forman, a leader of SNCC, expressed a similar understanding in his 1972 book, *The Making of Black Revolutionaries*. Forman wrote that SNCC workers who worked in Mississippi in the early 1960s "were interested in trying to register voters so as to expose the dirt of the United States and thus alienate black people from the whole system."

The idea that demands for full civil rights inherently threatened the fabric of capitalism had come from straight from the Communists. It was an argument that Communist historian Herbert Aptheker (in good Popular-Front-think) had made many times.

From the vantage point of the new century, of course, this belief was an illusion that served to obviate the need for honest thought about the kind of change that leftists wanted to make in our society—or even if they wanted to make changes beyond the very important issues of racial equality and ending the Vietnam War. In fact, most African-Americans were simply fighting for human rights so long denied them—rights that characterize liberal capitalist society—the right to equal public education, full access to all public facilities, and the right to vote and run for office.

These demands were opposed by the traditional racists in the old economies of the South and in its remnants in the North, but far from being threatened by the demand for civil rights, liberal capitalists saw them as part of the logical development of our society. Civil rights were a necessary part of integrating a mostly rural, semi-feudal workforce into the highly industrialized, consumer-oriented marketplace. After all, 15 million blacks represented a large potential market for the new consumer-based economy, and unlike the other U.S. colonial markets, these potential consumers had little choice but to buy American.

Then, too, from the point of view of American foreign policy makers, overt racial oppression was a liability. In the Cold War contest with the Soviet Union, the semi-colonial treatment of American blacks was more than an embarrassment. It threatened to throw the emerging nations in Africa and Asia into the Soviet camp. The granting of civil rights, therefore, offered something to everyone but the racists rooted in the arcane social order of a rapidly changing world.

IV

There are many ways of understanding when the civil rights movement began. From the liberal corporate establishment's vantage point, the

1954 decision of the Earl Warren Supreme Court (*Brown v. Board of Education*) was the beginning of a new era in race relations, led by themselves. From the blacks' point of view, North as well as South, the movement has been a continuous struggle for equality, with many ups and downs, ever since slavery was abolished and the slaves were granted the formal status of free laborers. Some New Leftists liked to think that the turning point was the series of student sit-ins throughout the South that started at a lunch counter in Greensboro, North Carolina, on February 1, 1960. But the lunch counter sit-ins followed the Montgomery bus boycott by five years and the Little Rock school struggle—during which President Eisenhower called in federal troops to protect black students—by three. Still, the 1960 activity set the stage for a distinct New Left. As student leader James Forman wrote, it laid the groundwork for organizations that students "could control and direct and which would not be subject to the authority of anyone but themselves."

That need, which students white and black, North and South, clearly expressed in the '60s, led student leaders at a South-wide Student Leadership Conference in Raleigh, North Carolina, during Easter week of 1960, to reject Martin Luther King Jr.'s request that they join him as a student branch of the Southern Christian Leadership Conference (SCLC). This, however, was not a decision motivated by a different set of immediate goals. At the time of SNCC's formation, Ella Baker, an early leader, made that clear. She wrote that whatever their differences, "Negro and white students, North and South [were] seeking to rid America of the scourge of racial segregation and discrimination—not only at lunch counters but in every aspect of life"—a goal entirely consistent with King's.

Still, in their hearts, and in their private conversations, there was a difference. Many of the new activists questioned whether integration into the existing society was a sufficient goal—whether their purpose should not be larger. The problem was that the people they were trying to organize and serve clearly had no larger social goal than equality within existing society. And the organization they had just created had emerged simply from that immediate need. So, even though the contradiction between the immediate purpose of their activity and their own underlying desires for a new society often intruded itself into their thoughts, they never had the time to sit back and discuss the relevance of these desires to their work.

SNCC's voter registration work, its major area of activity, illustrates this point. For Southern blacks the drive to register and vote during the early 1960s was analogous to mass production workers' drive to organize industrial unions thirty years earlier. Both efforts sought to reduce the powerlessness of the actors and to achieve a modicum of respect and influence over their own lives. For the blacks, registering to vote and voting was a way of gaining a measure of power—just as organizing unions had been for auto, steel, and rubber workers. In some ways the role of SNCC in this process was similar to that of the Communist Party in the '30s. Like the Communists, SNCC organizers worked selflessly in conditions of poverty and constant danger. Often their lives were threatened. Always they were vulnerable to arbitrary and wanton violence. And while their underlying ideology was much less coherent than the Communists', many SNCC workers also had to suppress their underlying revolutionary desires.

Even so, despite the problem of a dual purpose, half of which remained unspoken, the New Left's true independence and its commitment to a public radicalism provided the possibility of a genuinely new left politics. And the experience of the civil rights movement, and, especially after 1965, that of the anti-war movement, greatly strengthened the tendency of New Leftists to see their activity as directed against the ruling principles of corporate capitalism.

V

The quintessential hero of this strain of the New Left was Mario Savio, a former altar boy from New York and the leader of Berkeley's Free Speech Movement. He started at Manhattan College, in New York, where he had not been happy. His roommate was a Goldwater conservative, and there was nobody on campus that he could communicate with about anything he considered important. The kind of people he wanted to know were involved in SNCC. They were, he wrote, people like himself who seemed to have "a well-developed sense of justice and injustice." In the summer of 1963, he worked for a Catholic relief orga-nization in rural Mexico. The next summer he taught at a SNCC freedom school in McComb, Mississippi. It was easy to see, he later wrote, how white, middle-class youths could identify with the civil rights movement. To him, as to people who shared his passions but were passive, it was a way to be an actor in his own life. Such activity was a "real wedding of thought and action," he said, "very different from watching television or being a spectator at sports." And Berkeley, to which he transferred in his junior year—when his machinist father got a job in Los Angeles and his parents moved there—came "close to being [his] idea of what college should be like."

But it wasn't long after Savio got to Berkeley that something happened that infuriated him and hundreds of fellow students. While Savio was still in Mississippi, other students had been involved in civil rights demonstrations and sit-ins against the *Oakland Tribune* and against San Francisco's Sheraton Palace hotel. To support these activities, they had passed out leaflets and set up tables in Sproul Plaza (located inside the Sather gate on the south side of the Berkeley campus). Disturbed by this activity, university President Clark Kerr issued a fiat designed to stop the distribution of literature and the solicitation of money on campus. Initially the ban was justified by the claim that tables interfered with the flow of pedestrian traffic onto and off the campus. This claim created a minor uproar and was challenged by the students, who were then allowed to have tables.

But then the ruling was qualified. Students could now set up tables, but they were forbidden "to aid projects not directly connected with some authorized activity of the university." It was not permissible, the dean of students declared, for leaflets distributed on university property "to urge a specific vote, call for direct social or political action, or to seek to recruit individuals." Such activity, the dean asserted, violated the clause in the state constitution providing that the "University of California shall be kept free of all political and sectarian influence." Once again, however, the university administration had been disingenuous. As Jackie Goldberg, one of the Free Speech leaders, pointed out, the dean had only quoted half of the constitutional sentence. The other half read: "in the selection of its regents and officers." The constitution said nothing about student activity.

As Savio saw it, Berkeley and Mississippi were two fronts in the same war. At stake was "the right to participate as citizens in a democratic society," express individuality, and be actors in the making of history. Savio understood that this was not the university's view of itself. As he said, after World War II, the university had become a gigantic bureaucracy that was "part and parcel of this particular stage in the history of American society." The university, he charged, now simply served "the needs of American industry; it is a factory that turns out a certain product needed by industry and government." As that product, the student was intended to be an unthinking and unquestioning cog in the vast bureaucratic machine. The "'futures' and 'careers' for which American students now prepare," Savio complained, were "for the most part, intellectual and moral wastelands."

Savio's description of the university's role matched the one that Clark Kerr had given in 1962. Since the end of the world war, Kerr wrote, a "previously unimagined numbers of students" were attending college. As a result, the university had "to merge its activities with industry as never before," because it was no longer an elite institution whose main social function was preparing a new cadre of the ruling class, but one that educated workers for a more complex economy. "Characteristic of this transformation," Kerr explained, "is the growth of the knowledge industry, which is coming to permeate government and business, and to draw into it more and more people raised to higher and higher levels of skills." In its new role, he added, "The production, distribution and consumption of knowledge is said to account for 29 percent of gross national product, and knowledge production is growing at twice the rate of the rest of the economy." In short, the knowledge industry was now "to serve as the focal point for national growth."

But the students who founded SDS, like Savio, had a different view of education's role. In their 1962 Port Huron Statement SDS leaders affirmed the "human potential for self-cultivation, self-direction, self-understanding and creativity." And they insisted that "the first task of any social movement is to convince people that the search for orienting theories and the creation of human values is complex but worthwhile." This clearly implied a view of higher education that differed from Kerr's. As Savio said in his first big (and spontaneous) speech at Berkeley, "President Kerr has referred to the University as a factory; a knowledge factory— that's his words—engaged in the knowledge industry. And just like any factory, in any industry—again his words—you have to have a certain product." The products, Savio explained, were intended to be unthinking members of various businesses, and "never, at any point, is provision made" for the expression of individuality. "You just can't [display individuality] unless you have no intention of making it in this society."

Savio and his FSM comrades were part of a general movement among students in response to the changing nature of higher education. In 1940, just before the war, only 12 percent of eighteen-to twenty-year-olds were in college. By 1970 about 50 percent were enrolled. This vast increase in the student population served two purposes: to delay the entry of millions of youth into the workforce for several years (thus protecting against high unemployment rates), and to train millions of new workers, no longer needed for the direct production of goods, for jobs in sales promotion and service, social control, administration, and various kinds of research and development. As Kerr noted—and Savio resisted—the meaning of being a college student and the nature of work that college-trained people did after graduation had changed dramatically with the rapid expansion of higher education. Two decades earlier, most college students were from families of independent professionals, small entrepreneurs, or upper-level managers, and were being trained to take their places as part of a ruling elite. Now, the students were from a much wider spectrum of society and, Savio explained, were being trained to become "cogs" in corporate or government bureaucracies.

One way of seeing the New Left is that it was a protest against impending proletarianization. Just as workers' movements during the Industrial Revolution were a protest against their being forced into factories as wage earners, now students were protesting against their projected role as skilled workers. The clearest expression of this view was articulated by SDS president Greg Calvert in a speech at Princeton University in 1967. Revolutionary consciousness, Calvert argued, "is the perception of oneself as unfree . . . as one of the oppressed," combined with an awareness of the gap between "what one could be" (given the social potential at the historical moment), and "what is" (the ways in which that potential is frustrated by the existing society). "New working-class theory," Calvert said, was a powerful part of this process. It enabled students to understand their special role in relation to the present structure of corporate capitalism. "Students," he said, "are the 'trainees' for the new working class, and the factory-like multiversities are the institutions that prepare them for their slots in the bureaucratic machinery of corporate capitalism."

Within SDS against such leaders as Tom Hayden (who had pushed for students to leave school and organize in poor communities), Calvert argued that SDS "must stop apologizing for being students or for organizing students." Students were a "key group in the creation of the productive forces of the super-technological capitalism," Calvert explained. And the demand for student control, he said, was a demand to end student alienation in the same way that demands for workers' control were a way of reducing alienation in a factory. If this was true, Calvert concluded, it was a mistake to assume that the only radical role that students could play would be "as organizers of other classes." Instead, students should understand themselves as part of a "broad range of social strata" that included members of the old and new working class, as well as the under-class of racial or ethnic minorities—all of whom must move together to transform the United States into a more democratic society.

This insight might have helped New Leftists develop a sense of solidarity with American workers, as well as with blacks and Third World victims of U.S. imperialism. But Savio never went much beyond his FSM speeches, nor did the founders of SDS go much beyond the Port Huron Statement's call to "search for orienting theories." They were too busy with the day-to-day demands of their movements to reflect on the larger questions involved concerning the transformation of American society. Even so, their activity around issues like civil rights and the Vietnam War soon began to reveal the limitations of liberalism and its proposals.

Events in the early 1960s ate away young people's innocence. One early SDS community organizer, for example, observing that blacks were segregated and discriminated against in the North despite their attainment of formal rights, commented that "civil rights gets the Negro in the South no more than a Harlem." And in 1961, when the Kennedy administration denied its responsibility for the CIA-planned and directed invasion of Cuba, people's faith in John F. Kennedy's professions of support for national independence and self-determination was undermined. In the mid-'60s the war against Vietnamese independence swept away their belief in American virtue and brought many in the New Left to imagine themselves as revolutionaries. Facing an array of opponents that included not only the corporate media and the Republican and Democratic parties, but even the leaders of the trade union movement, students fighting against the war came face-to-face with the entire American establishment. This created a unique consciousness, for not only did this make the New Left the first "revolutionary" movement in modern times to exclude the working class—and even to be hostile to "hard hats"—but it also made it appear (to the few that thought about such things) that their only allies were in the ghettos of the North and in the Third World. Fundamental social change, many began to think, would come about only as a result of action outside the United States, and in urban ghettoes.

Of course, having no theory of class (and being mostly middle class) they could think of themselves as revolutionaries only so long as they faced the entire establishment. So, in 1968, when popular pressure against the war grew strong enough to allow some Democrats openly to oppose the war, it created a crisis for the New Left. Jerry Rubin's nightmare now became real. Even if the war would not end, liberals would now become the popular leaders of the anti-war movement. Democratic Senator Eugene McCarthy was the first to challenge President Lyndon Johnson. He almost won the New Hampshire primary, which led Senator Robert F. Kennedy to enter the anti-war ranks. These events resulted in a rush of anti-war forces back into the Democratic Party and foretold the end of New Left illusions of popular revolution.

It also led to chaos in the remnants. Since 1966, the Progressive Labor Party—a Maoist offshoot of the American Communist Party—had been trying to gain a foothold in SDS. In 1966 and 1967, when the new working-class theorists were in the leadership of SDS, PL had tried to gain recruits based on its theory that the "old" working class (industrial workers) was the "key" revolutionary agent. That had little appeal. Indeed, it simply led to a debate with the new working-class theorists about which working class was the key to left success—as if there were two working classes. In any case, neither working-class theory had much of a following among the more active students. But when McCarthy and Kennedy entered the anti-war fray, they undermined SDS's revolutionary bona fides. PL and its Maoism (and identification with China and the Third World) suddenly posed a real threat to the leadership in the SDS national office. Now PLers' open espousal of communism and its waving of Chairman Mao's Little Red Book suddenly began to attract radical students who sought more than an end to the war. This, in turn, led the remaining SDS leaders to revolutionary one-up-manship in the hope of heading off PL.

One attempt to outmaneuver PL was put forward by Mike Klonsky, SDS national secretary in 1968–1969. Klonsky merged PL's working-class theory and an identification with "revolutionary youth." This had the virtue of moving to coopt Progressive Labor while retaining youth as a key revolutionary force. It meant, Klonsky argued, that SDS's "struggles must be integrated into the struggles of working people." This formulation was similar enough to PL's own Worker-Student Alliance to appeal to many of the same students, but different enough to appeal also to many youth-culture adherents. In itself, Klonsky's approach probably would not have sufficed to head off PL. But just in time PL lent a helping hand in its own demise by condemning black nationalism as reactionary and by specifically condemning black student groups and the Black Panther Party.

Meanwhile, the National Office Collective was developing an alternative proposal that stressed anti-imperialism and identification with the

Black Panthers. This group, which came to be known as the Weather-men, was led by the SDS interorganization secretary, Bernardine Dohrn. She had developed close relations with the Black Panthers in Chicago, where Panther leader Fred Hampton (later murdered in cold blood by the Chicago police) worked closely with SDS. In March 1969, at the SDS national council meeting, the Black Panthers were officially recognized as "the vanguard force" in the black liberation movement. The identifica-tion of revolutionary white youth—seen as the key force among white Americans—with the Panthers and revolutionary nationalists in Cuba, Vietnam, and other Third World countries temporarily sufficed to distin-guish the national office collective from PL. It gained membership sup-port as the best means of ridding SDS of the threat of a PL takeover.

Still, at SDS's last convention, in June 1969, PL came with the largest bloc of delegates. As I described the situation in *Ambiguous Legacy, the Left in American Politics,* the national office collective delegation, desperate at the prospect of losing control, called on the Panthers for help and they responded by appearing at the convention to denounce PL. For a few moments, it appeared that PL was finished. But then the Panther spokesman started talking about "pussy power." He explained that women's role was to deny sex to men who were not sufficiently revolu-tionary and then defended the notion in the face of an overwhelmingly shocked response—and PL-led cheers to "fight male chauvinism." In the face of this uproar, the Panthers found it necessary to retreat, but they soon returned with a pronouncement from Bobby Seale stating baldly that any movement that included the Panthers had no room for PL. This gave Klonsky and the Weathermen a pretext for walking out of the con-vention and reassembling in an adjoining hall. There they proceeded as if they had expelled PL from SDS.

All of this tactical maneuvering was justified by "theoretical" argu-ments, though the last thing that any of the factions wanted was a seri-ous open discussion of any question. Mystification and ritual language were the order of the day, as the split between Weatherman "theory" and its actions soon demonstrated. Bernardine Dohrn and Mark Rudd, a Columbia University student militant, proclaimed that the blacks were the vanguard of the revolution, as they allegedly had been of radical social forces throughout American history, and that white workers and the white middle class were racist and corrupted by "white skin privilege." This excused the Weathermen from organizing among whites, not only because it was a waste of time (which it certainly would have been), but also because doing so would have been "objectively" racist. In the light of this contempt for the great mass of working Americans, the order of the day, Rudd concluded in a pathetically revealing slogan, was the martyrdom of "two, three, many John Browns."

(I attended this convention, as I had a few others, as a friend of SDS and a partisan of the anti-PL groups. As I sat at the Weathermen meeting a story about Louis Boudin—exactly fifty years earlier—kept going through my mind. As David Shannon recounted it in *The Socialist Party of America*, Boudin, a left-winger and an eminent legal scholar, had attended the Socialist Party's 1919 emergency convention at the Machinists' Hall in Chicago. When the majority refused to seat the left-wing delegates, Boudin walked out with them and reassembled downstairs to form the Communist Labor Party. A few hours later, after an argument with John Reed, he walked out again, explaining, when asked by reporters why he had done so, that he had "not quit a band of crooks to join a band of lunatics." That was irony enough, but more came later. Boudin was the great-uncle of Kathy Boudin, one of the two women who ran naked from the Greenwich Village townhouse bombing, and who later was a member of an underground revolutionary group that robbed a Brinks truck in Nanuet, New York, and murdered three guards. As of this writing, she is still serving a twenty-year sentence for participating in that action.)

Only four weeks after the June convention, the Weathermen's theory was tested in action when the Black Panther Party held a meeting of its own in Oakland, California, and called for a "United Front Against Fascism." Reminiscent of the Communists' shift to the politics of the Popular Front against fascism in 1935, the Panthers' effort was called to mobilize support for the party in the face of FBI and local police efforts to disrupt and destroy it. The Panthers called for a traditional civil libertarian effort. They asked for legal aid and financial support and for community control of the police. And they suggested other measures designed to stop or slow down the lethally illegal attacks coming from the FBI and other government agencies.

Not surprisingly—given the help that the Panthers had given SDS in ridding it of PL, and in light of statements by Weathermen leaders that the Panthers were the revolutionary vanguard—the Panthers expected SDS to support their initiative. But since the Panthers had failed to live up to the revolutionary image assigned them by Dohrn, the Weathermen refused to support their erstwhile partners in such a liberal endeavor. It was not the first time in relation to the left that blacks had been put forward as the leading force until they took some initiative of their own (something like this had also happened in 1942, when A. Philip Randolph led a march on Washington for civil rights that was attacked by the Communists as weakening the war effort). In any case, the Weathermen were now on their own and they proceeded to act out Mark Rudd's cry for martyrdom.

The failure of the New Left to study history, or reflect on the failures of its predecessors, doomed the student radicals to a farcical recapitulation of earlier tragedies. Less than a year later, a bomb factory in the basement of a townhouse on fashionable West Eleventh Street in Manhattan blew up and the building collapsed. At least three Weathermen were killed, and, as noted above, two women escaped and ran naked into a nearby building, from which they then disappeared. The Weathermen then continued in their adolescent fantasy for a few more years. As former Weatherleader Bill Ayers boasted in his recent memoir, *Fugitive Days,* they even exploded a pipe bomb in the Pentagon. But the only thing they succeeded in destroying was the hope of a democratic left in the United States. In its place, in the absence of a left based on universal principles, many little lefts for which the New Left had acted as a catalyst survived and went their own ways. Of these, the women's movement and the gay and lesbian movements were the most significant. Many of these single-issue groups won important victories in the following years. Still, the hope of a left based on universal principles that had raised its head in the early sixties was dead and buried.

8

THIGH BONE CONNECTED
TO THE HIP BONE:
THE WOMEN'S MOVEMENT,
CIVIL RIGHTS, AND THE
WAR MACHINE

I

THE RESURGENT RIGHT OF THE 1980S and 1990s was founded largely on nostalgic appeals to the traditions of a bygone age, aided by the entrepreneurial euphoria that accompanied the explosive growth of electronic technology and Internet startups. But the right also benefited from the collapse of the left, which, by failing to adjust to the changing social realities of the post-industrial age, or to press for demilitarization and the social possibilities opened up by the end of the Cold War, gave right-wingers clear sailing.

As we've seen, such a disconnect with the developmental needs of society had not always characterized the left. In the first half of the twentieth century, socialist ideas had served both the left and the nation well. When Milton Friedman, the prime tribune of laissez-faire, complained that the United States was more than half socialist, he was unwittingly paying tribute to the left's role in those years. That, of course, was not Friedman's intent. On the contrary, like Ronald Reagan, he located the deep insecurities generated by the new consumer-oriented economy at the left's doorstep. "Today," Friedman said, "we're much less safe than we were when I graduated high school. We have much less feeling of security, much less optimism about what the future's going to be like." And this, he suggested, was the left's fault: "All of the problems have been produced by government," he argued. "Consider the schools. The quality of schooling I got in a public high school in 1928 was almost surely a great deal higher than you can get now."

The insecurities that Friedman alluded to—and many more—are real enough. Their underlying cause, however, is not "government" (a euphemism for "the left"), but the steady transition of the economy from a focus on industrialization to one on "value-free" consumerism, military Keynesianism, and empire. The process began decades ago, in the 1920s, but it accelerated greatly during the great leap forward of industrial productivity during and especially after World War II. As production increased steadily in those years, jobs in manufacturing did not keep pace. On the contrary, they relentlessly disappeared. That presented a dilemma to those in the upper reaches of American society. If a return of the Great Depression was to be avoided—and policymakers were seriously concerned with this question after the war—jobs outside of civilian manufacturing had to be found. The deluge of new consumer goods needed to be absorbed. This called for a new ethic of popular conspicuous consumption.

This was something fundamentally new in capitalism. Only a few decades earlier, scarcity—self-restraint in the interest of capital accumulation—had dominated social life. Now, that ethic, and the social habits associated with it, had to be retired and a new social goal—value-free self-fulfillment through consumption—had to be promoted.

In the pre-war years the order of the day had been squeezing capital out of workers. This had been done by keeping wages low and maintaining traditional, one-wage-earner families at subsistence level. Before the war, happiness, or at least satisfaction, lay in having a steady job. But the hallmark of recent decades—the expansion and servicing of compulsive consumption—requires different habits, different family structures, and different attitudes toward work.

These changes made many things possible. One possibility was articulated by Mario Savio and the SDS's Port Huron Statement. Happiness, they said, now required a self-fulfilling job or a meaningful career. But the vast expansion of advertising and consumer credit also promoted the idea that happiness was having a new car, the latest shoes, or the newest electronic gadget. That is what prevailed in most of society. In less developed industries, both at home and abroad, capital is still squeezed out of workers in the old manner. But profits are also sucked out of consumers imbued with new needs created by ubiquitous advertising, media promotion, and the new norm of two-wage-earner households. This fundamental shift in the way people measure their worth and in the nature of the workforce opened up new living choices that wreaked havoc on traditional social relations. This, in turn, created fear and insecurity in large sections of society. For this neoconservatives, unable—or unwilling—to locate the source of these changes, placed the blame on the left.

II

The social changes of the last half of the twentieth century have had their greatest positive impact on women, who as workers and citizens, and in their familial relations, have gained a measure of autonomy and power. World War II provided a prelude of things to come. When men went to war a massive government campaign brought housewives out of their homes and into aircraft factories, auto plants, shipyards, and many other traditionally male workplaces. Hundreds of thousands, perhaps millions, of these "Rosie the Riveters" (as women in industry were popularly called) had new vistas opened before them. They learned that they could do "men's work" as well as men. They met and mingled with people of different ethnicities and cultures. They participated in union affairs. And they became their families' breadwinners.

After the war, however, as men left the armed services and reclaimed their old jobs, government and industry did their best to squeeze women back into their traditional roles. That effort was aided by massive postwar federal subsidies designed to create a new suburban way of life for millions of Americans. The federal government encouraged this process by building new highways and creating mortgage policies that favored easy access to suburbs and the financing of single-family suburban homes—programs that in addition to reinforcing traditional family living were designed to help stimulate the post-war economy by creating huge new markets for automobiles and durable household goods. Two-car families (now three-or-four-car) were a post-war phenomenon, as were dishwashers, in-house clothes washers and dryers, and air conditioners. These developments made housework less demanding, but they also created a way of life that increased women's isolation and reinforced their traditional role as stay-at-home moms.

Not surprisingly, these developments, aided by government and corporate propaganda campaigns, pushed feminist consciousness to an all-time low in the 1950s. However, a reaction to the '50s, one that spurred a new women's movement, was not long in coming. In the '60s this movement would develop into an enduring social achievement.

Changes in higher education also spurred the new women's movement. College students of both sexes who became the New Left in the 1960s had been inculcated in the 1950s with the view of women as mothers and housewives—or as secretaries and servants. But as young women entered colleges and universities alongside men in the post-war boom of college education, they began to chafe at the idea that their education was simply preparing them to become socially trained housewives and mothers. Women went through the same formal process of education as men, but both formally and informally they were instructed that their futures lay in finding a man to whom they were expected to subordinate themselves. Their education prepared them to lead creative and self-determined lives, but their desires for careers and meaningful work were not taken seriously.

Similarly, in New Left groups like SDS, despite the rhetoric of participatory democracy, women were often treated no better than in society at large. In some ways it was worse, because movement women were stripped of traditional protections against sexual exploitation in the New Left's atmosphere of sexual freedom. At movement meetings, women made the sandwiches, cleaned the tables, and provided sex for the men. Not surprisingly, then, the first groups of the new women's movement emerged from an SDS convention at Kewadin, Michigan, in 1965. Also not surprisingly, this was initially a movement concerned with the problems of an educated, middle-class elite.

Still, the situation facing university women had universal roots. The women's ideas struck a chord that resonated among women of different ages and social situations. The speed with which this early phase of the feminist movement spread attests to its perceived relevance to the great majority of women both in the United States and abroad. Although many people saw the new movement as the special province of privileged university students, these new feminists revitalized and transformed a women's movement that had lain largely dormant since the fight for suffrage was won in 1920.

By the early 1970s, as feminism grew into a major new movement in American society, it was the left's one remaining bright spot. Inevitably, however, feminism's new strength caused a backlash among millions of Americans made insecure by the rapidly changing technology and investment patterns that were disrupting their lives and threatening their families' stability. Many working-class and minority families saw feminism, and especially radical feminists, as the cause of the dislocations they experienced. The right seized on this situation to pose as the defenders of stable, traditional family relationships—and to villainize feminists who paraded their hostility to the traditional family structure.

The anti-family attitudes of radical feminists thus became a bedrock issue for the emerging New Right. The right's issue was not women working. After all, women had always worked outside the home. In the early nineteenth century, for example, single farm girls were the main employees of textile factories. Later, many young working-class women worked at routine, brain-numbing jobs as salesclerks, file clerks, or telephone operators. But few of these women saw these jobs as careers. They worked to help support their families in the years before being rescued by marriage. Most hoped that they then would stay home, do the housework, and raise their children. Such traditional women's jobs, however, were not suitable for college graduates, or so many of them felt, nor did many want to play the traditional role of housewife.

III

Under any circumstances, a movement with the goal of changing the way women were seen and treated by society would have met with stiff resistance and open hostility—not only from men, but also from the institutions, religious and secular, that had a vested interest in defending traditional gender-based social relations. The surprise was not this resistance, but the popularity of the idea of gender equality, which rested on the movement's espousal of two universal democratic principles: equality under the law, and the right of personal autonomy. Initially this meant equal rights in employment and in relations within the family, as well as equal access to positions of private and public authority. In the realm of personal autonomy, it meant, among other things, the right of women to control their own persons and bodies, most obviously the right to contraception and to terminate unwanted pregnancies.

The public overwhelmingly embraced these ideas, at least as abstract principles. But the anti-family attitude of the more radical feminists and their insensitivity to the many traumas of abortion, especially in the early phase of the movement, exacerbated hostility to the new movement. This hostility was greatest among traditional Christian families, and Ronald Reagan, a man who barely knew his own children and rarely spoke to them, built his base in the New Right on the defense of the family. He did so by attributing the steady erosion of traditional working-class families and communities to the social policies of the left. And the left fell—or dived—headlong into the trap.

This was, of course, not easy terrain on which to maneuver. Agitation for equal rights by college-educated women was made possible by changes in the economy that tended to push them out of their traditional roles. And basic feminist demands were entirely within the classical framework of American democracy as it has evolved since the adoption of the Constitution in 1786. But, as everything solid was melting into air in the last decades of the twentieth century, millions of Americans were already disoriented and beset with anxiety. Those who had grown up in the homogenous ethnic communities or parishes of the industrializing years were most unsettled. And feminist calls to "smash monogamy," or to destroy the nuclear family, played into existing fears and obscured their universal principles. In short, the left's attacks on traditional institutions and habits—grossly exaggerated by right-wing media—helped create a large working-class constituency of "Reagan Democrats."

The civil rights movement of the 1960s, the left's other enduring democratic achievement, suffered from analogous problems. Many Americans felt threatened by the great gains of the civil rights movement. Legal segregation in education and places of public accommodation finally came to an end in the 1960s—a hundred years after the Civil War. Discrimination in employment was finally declared illegal. The right to vote was officially protected for the first time since Reconstruction ended in 1876—and many African-American and Hispanic candidates were elected to local and national office. Appointments of racial and ethnic minorities at the national and local levels also increased dramatically, especially during the Clinton years, and—at least at the Cabinet level—survived even into the second Bush administration.

Despite a widespread residue of racism in the general population, a huge majority of Americans have favored granting full democratic rights to blacks and Latinos in education, voting, and employment, at least in principle. But conservatives, mostly in the Republican Party, have opposed the full realization of equal rights, especially for poor and working-class blacks and Latinos who tend to support Democrats. And they have relied on a substantial undercurrent of popular racism to help them frustrate affirmative action and—most clearly in Florida—even the right to vote.

Unfortunately, in some instances the left has facilitated this process by supporting policies that pit blacks and Latinos against working-class whites, perhaps most clearly in the fight over mandatory busing to achieve school integration. The principle here was to achieve integration of highly segregated schools by busing white children to heavily black schools and black children to heavily white schools. The pro-busing groups believed, or hoped, that this mechanical solution to separation would produce substantive integration of the races and improve the quality of education for minority (and majority) ethnic groups. But forced busing failed to do that. Where there had been segregation between schools, now there was segregation within schools. Minority students in "integrated" schools were generally relegated to lower-track classes and remained separated. Hostility between ethnic groups stayed as great (in some cases was greater) than before. Educational gains were few and many parents, black as well as white, were discomforted and angered that their children, who had been able to walk to schools within their own communities and be among their neighbors and friends, were now subjected to long bus rides into strange and often hostile territory. This was a stereotypically bureaucratic solution. It was expensive. Worse, the money it required did not go toward improving education, but only to pay for the hiring of buses. And, of course, the left got the blame for all this.

A left based on socialist principles would call for something quite different. It would agitate for equal school financing, equal facilities for schools in all communities, equal pay for teachers, equal class size, and most importantly, for the full range of extracurricular activities that make suburban schools more attractive to children, enrich their lives, and strengthen their communities. Those who might still want to send their children to other schools should have that right, but if schools were brought up to par in deprived communities it is unlikely that many would choose the inconvenience of busing children into schools where, at best, they were outsiders.

The question of affirmative action in higher education has also divided blacks and whites competing for a scarce resource. On a short-term basis and in specific situations this is probably unavoidable. But those on the left should push for greater investment in higher education to make it available to all. Or, in the short term, the left should support systems like that in Texas, where the top 10 percent of graduating students from every high school are automatically admitted to a state university, or like Georgia, where all students who have a "B" average in high school are admitted free to the state university.

IV

But wait, you may ask, where would the money to do all this come from? The answer is that within the framework of current politics the money is not available. If everyone accepts the long-established parameters of government budget-making, the best that a single-issue movement or interest group can do is compete for a slightly bigger slice of a rigidly divided pie. That's what pundits call pluralism. It is not a free exchange of ideas or principles—the corporate media do their best to prevent that—but a political competition for traditionally scarce resources. That has been the operating principle for interest groups and social movements in the post–World War II period, and it is one reason why the left needs to address universal principles as a framework for support of popular needs.

The American political economy did not always function this way. In the early years of industrial growth, the federal government generally left economic and social matters to capitalists, large and small. The government's economic role was pretty much restricted to protecting and subsidizing industry, either by imposing tariffs on imported goods or by providing capital for developmental projects that had no immediate prospects of profitability or were beyond the capacity of private capital to accomplish. Thus, in the nineteenth century, government intervention in the economy was limited to subsidizing the building of canals, financing the construction of railroads, and protecting industry by imposing heavy tariffs on an array of imports.

In those years capitalists kept popular consumption at or near a subsistence level. As Stalin would have said, they squeezed capital out of the workers by paying wages that barely sufficed to keep families housed and fed. (Indeed, in Lawrence, Massachusetts, in 1912, the great textile strike came about because the company discovered that most of its immigrant workers had savings accounts. This led the owners to conclude that their workers were overpaid and could afford a wage cut. But the workers were already living in desperate poverty. Their savings accounts were made up of money squeezed out of near-starvation wages—money they intended to use to return to their homelands. The cut in pay threatened that dream and caused a spontaneous strike, fought so militantly that the workers won a rare and historic victory.)

When the Lawrence strike occurred, government had already begun the process of actively intervening in the economy. Under pressure from farmers, workers, small entrepreneurs, and progressive corporate officials, government's role was expanding. Giant corporations already dominated the nation's economy and agrarian reform movements and the Socialists were demanding social and economic government programs. Indeed, even before the turn of the new century, some regulation of industry had been enacted, most notably the Interstate Commerce Commission in 1887 and the Sherman Anti-Trust Act of 1890. In the Progressive Era of the early 1900s, public agitation for government to regulate and stabilize the economy became widespread. But it wasn't until the passage of New Deal social legislation, and the expansion of the consumer society after World War II, that government became a major vehicle of social and economic regulation, as well as a highly developed system of social support and subsidies for big business.

Half a century of public pressure brought many beneficial reforms, but also a federal budget structured to put tight limits on what can be done in the public interest. With the beginning of the official Cold War in 1947 the structure was propelled forward by two concerns. First, American business and government leaders were deeply worried that the nation, which had been saved from the Depression only by the boom in government spending for World War II, might plunge back into the bad old days of the 1930s. Second, Soviet occupation of Eastern Europe, which appeared to many as Stalin's move to expand the reach of international communism, also appeared to many as a period of Communist aggression.

This made some sense. World War I had created the conditions that made the Russian Revolution possible, and World War II allowed the Chinese Communists to take power—and energized anti-colonial struggles throughout the "Third World." (Is there a lesson here for Bush II?) But, of course, Stalin did not create these conditions, nor did he have much interest in exploiting them. Stalin was a paranoid nationalist. He saw enemies everywhere, but at root his policies were always defensive. As the war ended, he once again feared that his country—which had lost 20 million citizens and seen most of its industry reduced to rubble— would fall prey to the hostile Western victors. He especially feared the United States, whose industry had grown greatly during the war, and who had dropped atomic bombs on Hiroshima and Nagasaki as an apparent first step in a new war aimed at him.

To overcome this not-entirely-paranoid fear, Stalin created his massive buffer zone to the west by subjecting the Eastern European nations to strict Soviet control. And the Soviet takeovers of Poland, Czechoslovakia, and the other Eastern European nations after World War II (as well as the Chinese Communists' threat to take over their country) certainly promised to deprive the Western capitalist nations of potential markets. Whether or not Western leaders believed that these moves threatened U.S. national security (which in retrospect they clearly did not), those concerned about the health of the American economy saw Soviet expansion as the perfect excuse to beat the war drums. That served two purposes. It provided a rationale to re-arm, and it undermined the danger of a strengthened domestic left capable of extending the social reforms begun before the war. Indeed, military spending stimulated the economy. And its benefits went to the right corporations, especially, as Frank Kofsky showed in *Harry S. Truman and the War Scare of 1948*, to the aircraft manufacturers who had profited greatly during the war, but found themselves on the verge of collapse when it ended.

The liberal left in these early Cold War years was not only debilitated by fear of being branded a "comsymp." It was also frustrated by the massive arms spending that left relatively little money in the budget for "discretionary spending." By putting the bulk of the federal budget out of bounds, those who supported the Cold War pauperized education, housing, health and human services, transportation, environmental programs, and medical and scientific research and created a situation in which reformers must compete against each other in the zero-sum game of "practical politics."

V

In fact, the Soviets were paper tigers. They had always lagged far behind the United States in the size and quality of their military technology, and even further behind in the ability of their industry to support another war. Still, American administrations consistently exaggerated the Soviet threat to justify their own opposition to anti-colonial movements all over the globe. During the Cold War years this arrangement was sold to the American people in the name of defending democracy against godless communism. Some of the dumber American leaders may even have believed this, but as Tina Turner might ask, What's democracy got to do with it? And the answer is: Not much.

The United States relationship to the Cuban revolution is a case in point. True, Fidel Castro would become a symbolic Cold War problem for the United States. But when John F. Kennedy took office in 1961, Castro had not yet formed an alliance with the Soviets. In fact, Cuba's Communists had opposed Castro and jumped on the bandwagon only when he was about to win the revolution. And Castro initially had no use for the Communists or the Soviets. After taking power, he traveled first to Washington for support, but was rudely rebuffed. Only after Eisenhower imposed an oil embargo on the island, in the final days of his term, did Castro accept the Soviet offer of oil (and the political subservience that it entailed). The Bay of Pigs invasion of Cuba—which became a Kennedy administration disaster—was bequeathed to him by Eisenhower. As Richard Reeves related in *President Kennedy, Profile of Power,* Eisenhower had decided to invade Cuba soon after Castro defeated the dictator Fulgencio Batista. He had made this decision (his treasury secretary, Robert Anderson, explained to JFK the week he took office) because "Large amounts of U.S. capital now planned for investment in Latin America" were "waiting to see whether or not we can cope with the Cuban situation."

After the embarrassment of the failed Bay of Pigs invasion, Kennedy came up with the idea for another effort to keep Latin America safe for investment. Presented to the media as a move to bolster democracy in the region, Kennedy's Alliance for Progress was simply a new way of maintaining a safe climate for American corporate investment in Latin America. The core of the alliance was the creation of "police academies" in which American army officers and FBI agents were to be instructors on fighting subversion. "Teach them how to control mobs and fight guerrillas," Kennedy said. "Increase the intimacy between our armed forces and the military in Latin America." The first of these secret police academies—long known as the School of the Americas—was established in the Panama Canal Zone in 1962. It trained South American and Central American police forces in riot control, intelligence, and interrogation techniques (read torture). Reeves wrote that these schools, along with Alliance for Progress arms sales to Latin American armies, encouraged "generals to dispose of elected leaders, confident that their new friends in North America might look the other way as long as the coups were presented as anti-communist."

Such policies pushed radical anti-colonial movements throughout the Third World into hatred for the United States and dependency on, and, in some cases, ideological support for, the Soviet Union. That these movements were generally opposed to the interests of American corporations is certainly true—any step toward democracy would have been. But neither Guatemala, Guayana, nor Chile—all of whom had left-wing governments overthrown by the CIA—copied Soviet-style communism. Nor were they anti-capitalist in practice. In any case, to a believer in national self-determination, it would have been irrelevant if they were.

For decades, American presidents slandered Nelson Mandela, the African National Congress leader, as a terrorist, using the congress's alliance with the South African Communist Party as an excuse. They supported the South African apartheid regime's military aid to neocolonial groups in the region. Similarly, to defeat popular democratic movements that threatened corporate interests, the United States intervened directly in the Dominican Republic, Haiti, El Salvador, and Nicaragua, as well as Guatamala, Guyana, and Chile. It trained, armed, and directed counter-revolutionary, terrorist armies and assassins in these and several other "emerging" nations. In Guatemala, the United States actively supported an army that killed 200,000 unarmed peasants in twenty years of civil war. In Chile, because Secretary of State Henry Kissinger couldn't "see why we have to let a country go Marxist because its people are irresponsible," the CIA secretly told its agents that it was "firm and continuing policy that [Salvador] Allende [the democratically elected president] be overthrown by a coup." A few years later, President Reagan succeeded in disorienting and overthrowing Nicaragua's popular government by violating a law passed by Congress (and signed by him) that forbad the financing or aiding of counterrevolutionaries in that benighted country. For all of this the Cold War was a godsend.

But it takes two to tango, and Soviet leaders also had a stake in perpetuating the Cold War. In the early 1960s, after Stalin died, Nikita Khrushchev denounced Stalin's crimes and began to make reforms in the Soviet system. He also made overtures to Eisenhower to negotiate an end to their mutual antagonism. As it turned out, Eisenhower spurned him after Khrushchev caught the president in a lie over the U-2 spy plane incident. In any case, the other Soviet leaders would have frustrated Khrushchev because they needed a foreign enemy as much as the Americans did. As historian Moshe Lewin explained, the "bureaucratic power grid" in Moscow blocked Khrushchev's efforts and replaced the cult of Stalin with a "cult of the state." The bureaucracy achieved a "super monopoly"—a unique Soviet-style bureaucratic absolutism—that had no serious leaders and was ideologically vacuous, demoralized, and in large part corrupt. This government was capable of doing little more than protecting its privileges. These were the years of stagnation and of governments that could keep the population quiet only with fear of an external enemy.

VI

Escalation of the Cold War, fed by politicians on both sides who used it for their own purposes, reached a climax in the 1980s with Ronald Reagan and his massive increase in American military muscle. Reagan, who was still in office when Mikhail Gorbachev instituted glasnost and perestroika (the attempt to rebuild Soviet industry along more modern lines), took credit for the collapse of the old Soviet system. But the Soviet system would have collapsed many years earlier had Soviet leaders not been able to use Cold War patriotism to justify their domestic "security" measures. Far from hastening the Soviet Union's demise, Reagan, like his predecessors, helped to keep a moribund Soviet system alive on the life-support threat of another war.

When the Cold War ended and the United States emerged as the world's last superpower, a new excuse for militarization was required.

The Clinton administration came up with the ludicrous idea that we were threatened by rogue states, epitomized by North Korea and its one or two long-range missiles, or by an essentially demilitarized Iraq. Like Iraq's missiles, that rationale would not fly. Now, shorn of the idea that our nation faces major military threats from abroad, and in the face of unprecedented terrorist attacks on the American people, a bit of reality may begin to creep into public debate about our relationship to the rest of the world.

So far, however, that has not happened. Instead, we are witnessing a debate about whether or not we should openly embrace our role as the last great empire. Some leftover Reaganites actually argue that the United States should openly embrace its role as an imperialist state. Thomas Donnelly of the Washington–based militaristic think tank, the Project for the New American Century, and a spokesman for this notion, pointed out that with 20,000 semi-permanent troops stationed in the Mideast, the United States is a major military power in almost every region of the world. He advocated a "Pax Americana," similar to the ancient Roman and British empires.

Unlike its imperial predecessors, the new American empire does not conquer land or administer colonies, Donnelly assured us. But the United States has a worldwide dominating presence, militarily, economically, and culturally. Therefore, he said in the *New York Times*, American leaders should admit that they are managing an empire, and Americans should think more clearly and openly about the necessity of their imperial mission. If they did, he argued, "We'd better understand the full range of tasks we want our military to do, from the Balkans-like constabulary missions to the no-fly zones over Iraq, to maintaining enough big-war capacity" as a hedge against the emergence of a rival.

Others argue that it's a bad idea for us to blow our own horn. "Realists" such as Nixon's Secretary of State Henry Kissinger, George Bush I's National Security Adviser Brent Scowcroft, and Bill Clinton's National Security Adviser Sandy Berger say that the United States is a new kind of benign colossus. We are, Berger said in a speech to the Council on Foreign Relations, "the first global power in history that is not an imperial power." This is called "realism" in high government circles because it shows some awareness that openly embracing an imperial stance would provoke a backfire of negative foreign and domestic reaction.

But others who acknowledge the downside of openly embracing imperialism see doing so as unavoidable. Andrew Bacevich, a retired army colonel and a professor at Boston University, for example, argued that we must stand up and face reality. Though he said he didn't like the idea of an imperial America, let's face it, like it or not, that is what we are. "I would prefer a non-imperial America," Bacevich told the *New York Times,* one "shorn of global responsibility, a global military and our preposterous expectations of remaking the world in our image." If we could move in this direction, he said we would "have a much better chance of keeping faith with intentions and hopes of the Founders [who, after all, fought a revolution against imperial Britain]." But Bacevich realized that "in all of American public life there is hardly a single prominent figure who finds fault with the notion of the United States remaining the world's sole military superpower to the end of time."

American leaders consistently find it necessary to muddy the situation in their public pronouncements. No wonder then that the American people are hesitant to provide the resources needed to carry out the "constabulary" role of suppressing minor attacks similar to those that British imperial forces encountered so frequently in the nineteenth century. And no wonder that Americans are surprised by the hostility of foreigners to our presence in their lives. Donnelly also doesn't argue that an imperial role is good, just that it's "unavoidable." In fact, no public figures, with the exception of Pat Buchanan, had the courage to speak against this role. Buchanan worried, however, that if we continue on this path "we'll end up paying a higher cost, morally and materially, than we can currently imagine."

Ironically, this exchange of views was published in the *New York Times* less than a month before the catastrophic bombing of the New York World Trade Center on September 11, 2001. In that one horrible moment, it became clear that all the atom bombs, missiles, warships, and even armies of our empire are all but useless when the enemy is not another nation but informal groups of angry fanatics determined to wreak vengeance on what they see as an arrogant, oppressive presence in their lives. If anything provides an argument against our military policies these past fifty years, this should be it. Neither the realists nor the imperialists, however, have a clue about the true cost that our policies have imposed on the American people, much less on other people around the globe. That should now be all too clear, yet, as I write this, the reaction of our elected officials and the media continues to be one of avoidance, if not true blindness.

VII

Perhaps the one good thing that came out of the slaughter at the World Trade Center and the Pentagon was a public inkling that the world is not what our leaders have told us it is—that perhaps, as a nation, we need a new way of relating to the rest of humanity. This was something that couldn't have been done effectively during the Cold War. To have done so would have brought down the power of the corporate media and the political establishment on such "un-Americans." But now there is no reason why leftists cannot challenge the military–oriented foreign and domestic policies of the administration and Congress. Indeed, there is every reason why they should.

Our government's policies have already caused damage here at home and sparked protests, riots, violence, and terrorism in many nations. The Cubans trained by the CIA to overthrow Fidel Castro at the failed Bay of Pigs invasion, for example, later became the burglars at Watergate. And the 35,000 militants from forty Islamic countries that three American administrations bankrolled and trained to fight against the Soviet Union in the Afghan jihad of the 1980s grew into the Taliban who sheltered Osama bin Laden and aided his bombing of the World Trade Center. Nothing could have more forcefully made the point that militarization of the world not only can't stop terrorism, but that it leads to terrorism by those who lack the military resources to oppose dominating nations openly. And, because such terrorism leads to a diminution of democracy in the nations terrorists target, in the end militarism makes losers of us all.

The left's failure to challenge the policy of military overkill militated against anything more than superficial thinking about the larger questions of our domestic priorities and our role in relation to the rest of the world. But lack of imagination on the left is hardly the sole obstacle to moving toward a higher form of society. The primary cause lies in the minds of capitalists who are still preparing for previous wars (hot and cold) and rushing blindly into imperialism's past. American corporations and financial institutions, of course, have been the core beneficiaries of globalization and of the military machine that protects their incursions into underdeveloped nations. But in the long run even they will suffer from the effects of an economy heavily dependent on arms spending, the accumulation of heavy armaments parked around the globe, and the compulsive sales of arms to transitory "friends" everywhere on earth.

VIII

At the turn of the twenty-first century, a stirring of opposition to the World Trade Organization and globalization raised the possibility of a left revival in the United States. The focus was largely on the damage done to targeted nations by "free trade" policies. Many of those participating in the demonstrations understand, however, that free trade (or globalization), per se, is not the issue. Capitalism has always been dependent on trade, and since the end of the nineteenth century, when American industry became highly competitive, the United States has generally opposed protectionism. European nations and England, on the other hand, relied on protected trade with their own colonies to create the markets required for their industrial development. (The Spanish empire was the exception that proves this rule. Spain had no need to develop trade with its colonies because its wealth was not based on industrialization, but on pure plunder: It simply stole the New World's gold and silver. This gave Spain an initial advantage over other European nations, but left it with insufficient incentive to industrialize. And, of course, its plunder was finite and steadily drained away, while growing industries steadily increased Britain's wealth. As Spain's wealth diminished, it lagged further and further behind the rest of Europe.)

The United States alone of major capitalist nations remained anti-colonial in its industrializing phase. In part, this was ideological—the nation was born by freeing itself from the British Empire. But, more to the point, Americans didn't need overseas colonies to have expanding markets. For more than a century, during the nation's period of basic industrialization, American capitalists enjoyed a vast and constantly expanding internal market, one created by the settlement of what they chose to believe was vacant land, inhabited only by savages. It wasn't until the end of the nineteenth century that the frontier was considered to be officially closed. But conveniently, in 1898, the United States went to war and took over the main remnants of Spain's empire. Puerto Rico, Cuba, the Philippines, and Guam then became American colonies in fact, if not name. Hawaii was also annexed.

After the victory over Spain and the annexations that followed, many Americans continued to reject the idea of European-style colonialism. In 1900, William Jennings Bryan fought his presidential campaign largely on this issue. As historian Fred Harvey Harrington has written, the anti-imperialists believed that the taking of colonies violated the principles of the Declaration of Independence, Washington's Farewell Address, and Lincoln's Gettysburg Address—which asserted that government should not rule people without their consent, and that the United States, having been conceived as an instrument of and for its own people, should not imitate the ways of the Old World. As Bryan asked an Omaha audience rhetorically in June of 1900, "Our guns destroyed the Spanish fleet, but can they destroy the self-evident truth that governments derive their just powers from the consent of the governed?" Once again, however, Bryan went down to defeat and, after several years of bitter fighting, the United States had extended its frontiers far out into the Pacific—and had established Manila as a great entrepot for Far Eastern trade. (The Philippines were granted independence in 1946.)

Neither government officials nor the American media are inclined to educate the public about their country's foreign depredations. In 1962, however, Secretary of State Dean Rusk, seeking congressional approval of Kennedy administration plans to overthrow the Castro government in Cuba, argued that such action was nothing unusual. To make his point, Rusk submitted to Congress a list of 168 "instances of the use of United States Armed Forces abroad, 1798–1945." Congress then quickly passed a resolution in support of Kennedy's policy. Here, verbatim, are a few representative samples from this list:

> 1852–3—*Argentina*—*February 3 to 12 1852*—Marines were landed and maintained in Buenos Aires to protect American interests during a revolution.
>
> 1853—*Nicaragua*—*March 11 to 13*—To protect American lives and interests during a revolution.
>
> 1854—*China*—*May 19 to 21 (?)*—To protect American interests in Shanghai.
>
> 1857—*Nicaragua*—*April to May, November to December*—To oppose William Walker's attempt to get control of the country
> . . . .
>
> 1858–59—*Turkey*—Display of naval force along the Levant . . . to remind the authorities (of Turkey) . . . of the power of the United States.
>
> 1867—*Island of Formosa*—*June 13*—To punish a horde of savages who were supposed to have murdered the crew of a wrecked American vessel.
>
> 1876—*Mexico*—*May 18*—To police the town of Matamoros temporarily while it was without other government.
>
> 1888—*Korea*—*June*—To protect American residents in Seoul during unsettled political conditions, when an outbreak of the populace was expected.
>
> 1899–1901—*Philippine Islands*—To protect American interests following the war with Spain, and to conquer the island by defeating the Filippinos in their war for independence.

When these incursions occurred, the United States was still a minor player on the world scene. Now it is not only the most powerful military power on earth, but also has the greatest military presence wherever American capital has interests to protect or new fields to capture. By using military force as a major instrument of policy, successive administrations have set examples and encouraged others to follow suit. It does this both directly and indirectly, openly and surreptitiously. Not surprisingly, this angers many people in many places all around the globe.

Then, too, as the world's leading purveyor of armaments of all kinds, the United States has facilitated armed conflicts everywhere. The government subsidizes arms exports and maintains personnel in its embassies whose only assignment is to sell arms. This has led to many "blowbacks," as the CIA calls policies that come back to haunt them. For example, American administrations armed Iraq for several years before we fought a war against Saddam Hussein. And, as noted, the CIA armed and trained those who became the Taliban when it served their purpose. Since the Kennedy years, the United States has armed and controlled the military forces of just about every country in South and Central America, most of whom use their armies to suppress their own people and prevent democracy. By spreading arms and training foreign armies, the United States undermines democracy around the globe and encourages local disputes to develop into larger, more deadly conflicts.

It was policies and actions like these that led Mahatma Ghandi to argue that the United States was no friend of democracy beyond its borders. "Your wars," he said, "will never ensure safety for democracy," because America's "capitalist owners" could not sustain their overseas holdings "except by violence, veiled if not open." Similarly, the Reverend Martin Luther King Jr.—Ghandi's American disciple—called the American government "the greatest purveyor of violence in the world today." These views have been validated by American actions throughout the Cold War and since.

IX

By undermining self-determination and democracy, U.S. "free trade" and "globalization" policy has gone hand-in-hand with militarization in facilitating the growth of international terrorism. Corporate and political leaders, of course, are all but blind to this situation. They promote their policies not only on the ground of national (read corporate) interest, but also assert that they are helping to modernize the nations impacted by free trade agreements and World Bank policies. This is a mistake—if it isn't simply spin. The financial and trade institutions who call themselves "free traders" enjoy the benefits of new deregulated markets in capital, labor, and goods in this arrangement, but Third World working people are victimized by an unsocialized capitalism that leaves them powerless. In a brilliant article in the *Financial Times*, Benjamin A. Barber, a professor of civil society at the University of Maryland, argued that by imposing unregulated global markets the "free traders" are moving the Third World back to a form of "capitalism uprooted from the humanizing restraints of the democratic nation state." As the events of September 11 demonstrate, both sides suffer from this policy because the conditions from which the globalizers imagine they benefit create the very disorder in which terrorists gain popular support.

"McWorld's neo-liberal antagonism to all political regulation in the global sector," Barber wrote, its opposition to "all institutions of legal and political oversight and, to all attempts at democratizing globalization and institutionalizing economic justice" is proof of indifference to democracy and modernization. Instead, "McWorld" celebrates market ideology's commitment to "the privatization of all things public and the commercialization of all things private." Yet total freedom from government interference in the global economy, and insistence on "the rule of private power over public goods" is "another name for anarchy. And terror is merely one of the contagious diseases that anarchy spawns."

In short, today's globalizers are re-creating a form of capitalism shorn of the benefits brought to our modern social system by the struggles of working people and socialists throughout the history of capitalist industrialization. This is unsocialized capitalism, or, if you prefer, capitalism in its pure form—the thing that ideologues such as Milton Friedman promote. This form of capitalism is not only subject to the social disruptions, violence, and anarchy that American capitalism experienced in the late nineteenth century, but also to the deep resentment that its imposition, often by military force, generates among the victimized populations. The chaos and violence of European and American capitalism during its laissez-faire years of industrialization was bad enough, but it was considerably softened by the struggles for political and social rights in a society free of the foreign domination that protects corrupt and oppressive regimes. People in the Third World have no such luck. Held in abject poverty by outsiders, they also suffer from the conspicuous display of a consumer society opulence through the whole range of cultural media that have also invaded their lives.

To be sure, as Barber explained, democracy and the participation in public life that it affords will not appease the terrorists. As "enemies of the modern," they are "scarcely students of globalization's insufficiencies." The terrorists who bombed the World Trade Center demonstrated instead their desire "to recover the dead past by annihilating the living present." Yet while terrorists themselves cannot be the object of democratic struggle, it is important to understand that they succeed only because "they swim in a sea of tacit support and resentful acquiescence," waters that roil with anger and resentment and that are "buoyant to an ideology of violence and mayhem." Without the "environment of despairing rage that exists in too many places in the Third World," and in "too many third world neighborhoods of first world cities," terrorism would present a much more limited and easily handled threat.

X

Conducted on behalf of those who now control our government, military globalization destabilizes the world and incites terrorist acts by groups of aggrieved people deprived of the means to participate in their own governance. But our globalizers depend on popular lack of interest in—and ignorance of—foreign policy or foreign affairs. During the 2000 presidential elections, polls measuring public concern about the issues found that "defense" and foreign affairs were always far down the list. In poll after poll both before and after the 2000 presidential election, Americans listed education, the economy, Social Security, health care, morals, crime, taxes, and prescription drug benefits before "defense." In an

ABC/*Washington Post* poll taken six weeks before the election, defense was listed eleventh in importance. In a CBS News poll after the election (in August 2001) Americans listed eight issues as the single most important problem for the government. Defense fell below 3 percent and didn't make the list. Still, during the 2000 presidential election, George Bush II constantly promoted increased military spending and his new version of Star Wars. Of course, Al Gore remained mute.

Perhaps now, after the attacks of September 11, Americans will be more inclined to face the stark reality that we are part of a complex world and that our government's policies and actions overseas have consequences for all of us here at home. Indeed there are some signs that Americans are now at least willing to listen to the idea that our nation's role in the world somehow encourages terrorism.

In any case, it should now be clear that traditional military strategies, and especially nuclear bombs and missiles, are all but irrelevant in today's new world order. It boggles the mind that President Bush's controllers can think only of military means to stop the threat of terrorism directed against the territory of the United States, but this is what the administration seems to have meant when it said that the use of ordinary commercial planes as bombs at the World Trade Center and the Pentagon have changed the world and the nature of warfare. Something quite different is needed. As long as people in the Third World are motivated highly enough to work together for a couple of years in total secrecy on a plot as complex as the September 11 bombing, terrorism will continue in some form against Americans. Killing bin Laden and breaking up the top levels of his organization may end this round of terror, but even if every terrorist now active were to be eliminated, it wouldn't be long before a new crop grew up. This is true not because people of the Third World reject Western democratic values, but because of the pain that American imperial policies inflict. As historian Tony Judt has observed, "those who hate us for our values (which in any case are Western, not American) are vastly outnumbered by those who resent our foreign policy." He argues explicitly (as I have) that Bush's efforts to eradicate terrorism "will go for nothing" if we continue to keep "uncritical company" with rulers who consistently commit the "very crimes we abhor."

XI

A century and a half ago, Marx wrote that capitalists, "fanatically bent on making value expand itself," were "ruthlessly forc[ing] the human race to produce for production's sake." He saw this "blind process" driving the development of industry to create the material conditions that alone can form the real basis of a higher form of society, one in which "the full and free development of every individual" would form the ruling principle. The good news is that thanks to the genius of capitalist development a society based on that principle is now technically within our grasp. The bad news is that leftists continue to operate within the parameters of the trap set for them by the defenders of contemporary corporate capitalism. The events of September 11 strongly suggest that the time for the left to examine the social possibilities inherent in our material achievements has arrived. But they can do so only by breaking out of the straightjacket imposed by those frozen in the habits of thought and practices that dominate thinking in the world's last remaining empire.

9

THE HARD PART: SOCIALIST PRINCIPLES IN THE POST-INDUSTRIAL ERA

I

THE INTRODUCTION OF INDIVIDUALISM as a social principle was one of capitalism's great virtues. But in the name of community, the utopian socialists opposed the ruthless, competitive individualism of early capitalism. This was not a rejection of individuality, per se, but of the egocentric drive for personal wealth that capitalists substituted for the traditional social responsibility of feudal society. Indeed, the early communitarians were exceptionally strong and independent people. But they expressed their individualism in the context of interdependence and mutual responsibility for each other's well-being.

Marx shared the communitarian ideal, yet he celebrated the dynamism of individual capitalist initiative during the years of competitive industrialization. The utopians simply hated capitalism. Marx shared their hate of its heartlessness, but loved capitalism for its productive creativity. And within the state created by the modern market, he and his followers consistently sought to humanize capitalism by fighting for the individual civil rights and liberties that permitted working people to associate and organize on their own behalf.

True, Marx's legacy is somewhat ambiguous in this regard. In the *Communist Manifesto*, for example, he wrote about individual development and free association, but he also wrote that after the revolution the working class should "use its political supremacy to wrest, by degrees, all capital from the bourgeoisie, [and then] centralize all instruments of production in the hands of the state." This formulation encouraged his more authoritarian followers to override his first principles. And, of course, the Bolsheviks, led by Stalin, seized on this as doctrinal justification for their suppression of the rights and liberties of civil society in what came to be known as "real existing socialism."

Nor were the Soviets the first socialists to champion such ideas. In the years before the Russian Revolution, socialists of various stripes espoused a variety of utopias, from Edward Bellamy's regimented *Looking Backward* to William Morris's artisanal *News from Nowhere*. Indeed, as I have already noted, illiberal views were common enough in the late nineteenth century to compel Oscar Wilde, in *The Soul of Man under Socialism*, to argue against those who would centralize the state. "If Socialism is Authoritarian," he wrote in 1904, "the state of humanity will be worse than it is now."

Wilde shared Marx's more humanitarian vision of a society dedicated to full and free human development. Like Marx, he understood that under the conditions of industrial capitalism that goal was unattainable. True, he wrote, a few men in society—all of them poets or writers with "private means of their own"—had been able "to realize their personality more or less completely." But these men, benefitting as they as did they did from "private, income-producing property," and never having "done a single day's work for hire" were exceptions.

Wilde was not concerned about these lucky few. His concern was with the great majority of working people whose creativity, "latent and potential in mankind generally," was stifled by capitalism. By making financial gain rather than personal growth its aim, he wrote, capitalism had "crushed true individualism." It debarred those in one part of the community from realizing their individuality by starving them; and it confused the other part by measuring them in terms of what they possessed. Capitalism led people to think "that the important thing [was] to have," rather than "to be." Indeed, Wilde pointed out, English law treated offenses against property much more harshly than offenses against persons, and it made property "the test of complete citizenship." In capitalist England, "property confers immense distinction, social position, honour, respect, titles, and other pleasant things," Wilde wrote. And people, being "naturally ambitious," continue "wearily and tediously accumulating long after [they have gotten] far more than [they] have use for, or can enjoy." Like Marx, Wilde believed that with the abolition of capitalism nobody would have to "waste his life in the accumulation of things, and the symbols for things."

Few socialists fully shared Wilde's take on socialism in 1900 because it was difficult then to see a future where such a system would be possible. But here we are, a hundred and fifty years after Marx wrote the *Manifesto* and a hundred years after Wilde wrote *The Soul of Man under Socialism*. And while even now few envision such a future, the most advanced capitalist nations have nevertheless created the productive capacity for a society such as Marx and Wilde had in mind. The technology and productive capacity exist, but the vision is missing. The problem, then, is how to create a political movement with the will and the ability to realize the vision they shared.

Given the degraded state of the American left, that may well seem a problem incapable of solution. Yet moving in that direction is the only hope for the left as well as for all humanity. The alternatives—as the great Socialist leader Rosa Luxumburg said almost a century ago, and as our recent experience with terrorism and counterterrorism now suggest—are socialism or barbarism.

But where to begin? The social basis for a viable left politics exists, but it is diffuse, directionless, and leaderless. Bringing it into focus and translating underlying principles into a coherent political practice will be a long arduous task, and there will be many false starts. But starts must be made. Groups of interested people with some experience in politics and a commitment to the long haul might form a loose organization to engage in electoral initiatives at the national level. Or it might start with the formation of an institute specifically committed to the development of political programs and strategies that embody social utility as their first principle. How such groups or institutions label themselves is of only tactical importance. What matters is an effort to find or develop a movement that articulates programs that clearly embody underlying forward-looking social principles, and to pursue a strategy aimed at electing legislators who will attempt to realize these principles in social legislation.

In short, what's needed is a coherent left presence in American political life. Nor is this pure pie in the sky. There already is a left presence in Congress, in the form of the progressive and black caucuses, that expresses traditional socialist principles. Many of these members might be part of such a process, but the effort can't be effective so long as it continues to rely solely on individual politician's insights, initiatives, or whims—or on the excitement of a moment. To function effectively in national politics, the left will have to develop constituencies around well-defined current national issues, programs, and principles—constituencies in any given district well-enough educated to withstand the media bombardments and other tactics of better-financed establishment groups and their PR men. We will need, in other words, to follow the New Right's example of establishing institutions devoted to winning the battle of ideas by relating to our natural bases among the American people in terms that they understand and around issues that most concern wider constituencies at any given period.

II

Ironically, in light of the suggestion that the left focus on issues now percolating in the public mind, it seems to me that such a project must begin in an area where Americans have traditionally shown little interest—and about which they are most ignorant—namely, foreign and military policy. This suggestion may seem to be yet another example of the left's quixotic nature, but I think not. The recent terrorist attacks on American soil, and George Bush's war against evil (the goal of which—other than to assure his reelection—remains unclear) seems finally to be leading some Americans to think about their country's relationship to the rest of the world.

Then, too, difficult as it may be to gain the public's attention on these issues, there are compelling reasons to address them. First, it's important to undercut popular support for terrorists throughout the Third World, and to do that we need profound changes in U.S. foreign policy. Second, if we are to have any chance of satisfying the ever-increasing social needs at home, the national budget must be fundamentally reordered. Hundreds of billions of dollars are needed to equalize and improve education and health care. Protecting the environment will also entail major expenses, both to clean up polluted areas and to create employment for those displaced in lumbering, fishing, and other industries. This money can only come from major cuts in the unnecessary, anti-democratic, and ultimately counterproductive military spending that now absorbs more than half of our discretionary federal budget.

The relationship of the United States to the Third World needs to be redirected if the popular base of support for terrorism (and not just the group of terrorists currently targeted) is to be substantially reduced. Present trade and investment policies, and the militarization they entail, not only impose pain and suffering on neocolonial peoples around the globe, but these policies also prevent American working people from enjoying the full benefits of our society's great wealth and productive capacity. Indeed, American foreign policy has become dangerous to our well-being. It undermines our security at home and keeps billions of people outside our borders poor and powerless. Indeed, these policies even undermine the security of the ruling class that imposes them on us all. In short, seen from a broad historical perspective, a fundamental change in American foreign policy would be a win-win achievement for just about everyone on earth, while without such a change, we cannot make much progress toward social justice at home or abroad.

The problem, of course, is not free trade—or globalization—as such. Nor is it trade agreements per se. Rather it is the thrust for world domination by a decreasing number of conglomerations of increasingly large amounts of capital, centered primarily in the United States. Some people believe that these multinational corporations and banks have usurped the power of the national state—that globalization has meant a decline in the ability of a democratic nation to control capital flows and the foreign activities of resident corporations. But just the opposite is true. The federal government not only has a constitutional right to regulate the conditions of capital export and import, but more to the point, corporations depend on federal subsidies and American military intervention to protect their domestic and foreign investments, especially in "developing nations." No matter how large corporations are, they need military force to protect themselves against the wrath of those they exploit around the world. And the armies, navies, and air forces that protect them are courtesy of the U.S. taxpayers. These corporate beneficiaries of our military might, in other words, socialize the cost, while American citizens carry the burden for them in the name of protecting national interests abroad.

Furthermore, the conditions incorporated in so-called free trade and World Bank loan agreements are politically determined and require congressional approval. Naturally, because the gigantic corporations and banks control the government, these agreements now favor capital rather than workers or environmentalists. Ideally, these policies could be reversed by replacing those now in office with a party or coalition that represents the interests of working people. Unfortunately, that's a long-range goal, one not yet on anyone's serious agenda. Still, a political movement could develop enough strength to force significant changes in policy. Already some forces in Congress and outside of government favor doing so. A coherent left—assuming an effort is made to create one—could and should demand changes in trade policy consistent with its principles and in tune with those of existing progressive forces at home and abroad. Such demands would include guarantees in all trade agreements of full civil rights, especially the right of workers to organize unions of their own choosing in trading partner countries, and of environmental standards equal to those in contracting nations with the highest levels of protection. In general, the left should demand that WTO leaders end their hostility to all attempts at democratization of political institutions in targeted developing nations and instead encourage a range of democratic rights—cultural as well as political. Furthermore, these new agreements should be overseen, and disputes under them adjudicated, by the United Nations or the World Court (which, so far, the United States has refused to join).

Most important: If such agreements are to succeed in reducing terrorism they must be accompanied by a worldwide program of demilitarization, led by the United States. To be credible, the first step in this process must be the reduction of our own military to the level required to meet any realistic threat to our national security. It is true that several other nations are major arms purveyors—especially Russia, France, China, and Britain. But by taking the lead, the United States could put great pressure on these countries to follow suit. The United States should cease giving and selling weapons to developing nations and it should negotiate with Russia, France, and Britain, as well as China and other less developed nations, to stop promoting arms sales and to stop selling all but small arms to client states. Finally, to eliminate the military-industrial complex as a powerful lobby, we should remove the profit motive in arms production by nationalizing all military production except small arms.

The realistic military threat to the United States from any other nation, of course, is near zero. The worst threat to our nation that a rational mind could envision could easily be handled by a small fraction of our current forces. True, some military reserves might be required to fight terrorism even after the policies suggested above are adopted, and some troops may be needed as part of international forces to oversee local international disputes. But the size and nature of such forces would be insignificant compared to the current number and size of American overseas military bases.

Cuts in direct military spending and in the tens of billions of dollars in government activities that support our military infrastructure would free up at least $200 billion a year, as well as hundreds of thousands of skilled workers. If not put to productive use, the money and people idled would negatively impact our economy and even threaten a return to recession or depression. But there are many other areas in which our resources, financial and human, could be put to good use in moving us toward a society in which every individual is offered the opportunity to develop to the full extent of his or her potential. I will suggest a couple of these areas—which, not coincidentally, are uppermost in the minds of most Americans.

III

The first area is education, which to most people today simply means preparing their children to do what is needed to earn a decent living. But education, broadly understood, is a prerequisite not only for any person's full and free development, but also for the achievement of a truly democratic society, one in which as many people as possible lead creative, secure, and fulfilling lives. Raising our public schools up to the level now enjoyed by the best suburban schools, and lowering the ratio of teachers to students down to that of those same schools, would be important steps toward that goal. Furthermore, doing so would absorb tens of billions of dollars now squandered on superfluous military hardware, and it could provide interesting, socially useful jobs for all those displaced— everything from scientists to maintenance personnel.

Desirable as this is, it would only begin to fulfill the promise of American democracy. To take a major step in that direction, the curricula of all primary and secondary schools should be greatly enhanced. Public schools should not be further converted—as many "educators" and politicians now implicitly ask—into institutions where the "lower classes" remain segregated and young people are prepared to fill minimally skilled jobs in service industries. As John Dewey, America's greatest educational philosopher, argued in the early 1900s, such schools undermine democracy. Instead, Dewey wrote, supporters of democracy "should be united against every proposition, in whatever form advanced, to separate training of employees from training for citizenship, training of intelligence and character from training for narrow industrial efficiency."

Dewey's ideas had a significant influence on American education, especially in the progressive education movement before World War II. But with the Cold War and the turn to ideological conformity and militarization of the economy, his ideas were derogated. Now Dewey is remembered, if at all, mostly for his ideas about early schooling. However, he was equally involved in debates about education's relationship to democracy. Nor was he alone in this. In a parallel debate, W. E. B. DuBois and Booker T. Washington grappled with similar underlying issues. And, as with Dewey, the conflict between these two leaders arose in part from the conflict between the corporation-dominated drive for docile workers to fill the large number of newly created industrial jobs and the progressive movement's commitment to a more substantive democracy. Unlike Dewey's concerns, however, the Washington-DuBois debate took place in the context of the quest for racial equality in the United States. And while Washington and DuBois shared a burning desire to improve the lives of their people, they pursued that goal in ways that reflected their different backgrounds. Unfortunately, it is a debate that has been muted and remains unresolved.

Booker T. Washington

In his "Compromise Address" at the all-black Atlanta University in 1895, Washington advised his people to remove themselves from civil society and to put economic self-advancement before political or social equality. This retreat into "self-improvement" came in response to fierce attacks on civil rights and the political freedoms of African-Americans that followed Reconstruction's end in 1876. In this increasingly desperate situation, Washington argued, education for work was the black man's "only salvation."

Washington came to this conclusion through his own experience. The son of a slave mother and an unknown white father, he was born in 1856 into the degrading poverty of slave life on a small farm in the Virginia hills. After emancipation, he found work as a houseboy for the cultured wife of a West Virginia river town's leading family. There, Washington's biographer, Louis R. Harlan, wrote, young Booker came to believe that "book learning made the difference between the conditions of whites and blacks." This belief was not his alone. Millions of freed men and women demanded the opportunity to read and write after the war. But few matched the intensity of Washington's desire to read and to escape from the poverty and oppression that remained his people's lot for many long decades after emancipation.

Working as a houseboy provided Washington precious opportunity to read widely and to observe and internalize the social graces of the rural South's upper class. And living in the home of a benevolent white family—when gangs of whites were doing their best to deprive blacks of their newly won rights—taught him that cultured white paternalists were the black man's best friends. More importantly, exposure to his employer's way of life fueled in him a burning ambition to achieve more in life than was possible as a domestic servant. So, when news reached him of Hampton Institute's creation as a school for Negroes more substantial than the one-room shacks that had been his lot, he resolved to attend.

Founded by General Samuel Armstrong as "a manual labor school"— with help from the American Missionary Association and private donations from liberal Northerners—Hampton Institute was but four years old when Washington arrived there in 1873. Armstrong, a Civil War hero and the son of a Presbyterian missionary, ran his school along quasimilitary lines. Its strict schedule began with inspection at 5:45 A.M. and ended with the retiring bell at 9:30 P.M. Like the vocational schools that Dewey would later oppose, Hampton depended "very largely on a routine of industrious work habits, which," Armstrong said, was to individual character as "the foundation is to the pyramid."

Not surprisingly, Hampton's program was "humbler and less ambitious" than its white counterparts. The white schools moved students toward engineering and professions. Hampton concentrated on agriculture and the associated trades. Its curriculum stressed "the dignifying of labor through doing the common things of life . . . without a murmur." Especially because Hampton prepared its students to be teachers for rural primary schools, few of which went beyond the fourth grade, "moral training" was much more important than intellectual instruction. He would "not discourage a bright young dark man from higher education and higher aspirations," Armstrong said. But the race as a whole, he believed, "should abstain from politics and civil rights agitation until industrial education had done its work."

Washington, who arrived at Hampton a disheveled country boy, soon became Armstrong's star pupil. After graduation, he modeled his career—and even the cut of his clothes—on the general. And he was well rewarded. When the Alabama state education commissioners solicited Armstrong's suggestion of a suitable principal for a school being planned at Tuskegee, he took the unprecedented step of proposing his black protege for the job. Washington, he explained, was "a very competent mulatto, clear headed, modest, sensible, polite and a thorough teacher and superior man. The best we have ever had here."

Washington happily accepted the challenge. But when he arrived at Tuskegee he discovered that there was no school and that the $2,000 the Alabama legislature had allocated for Tuskegee in 1881 had already been apportioned among the state's existing schools. Undeterred, Washington conducted classes in a local church while he looked for and found a suitable location at an abandoned farm. After borrowing $200 for a down payment he recruited a group of students who—in lieu of paying for their room and board—agreed to help him clear several acres, rebuild out-buildings, and construct the main hall. Working alongside his students, Washington built his world-famous institute from the ground up. Initially modeled on Hampton, Tuskegee was a highly disciplined, coeducational school that concentrated on preparing country boys and girls to be productive workers on the margins of the New South's industrializing economy.

William Edward Burghardt DuBois

As the creation of a system in which house servants survived by submission and emulation of their paternalistic masters, Washington trod a nonconfrontational path and obsequiously accommodated the Northern industrialists who financed his work. William Edward Burghardt DuBois, however, was the scion of a free colored family that had lived in western Massachusetts since the time of the American Revolution. And his model was the great black abolitionist Frederick Douglass, with whom he shared the ideal of "ultimate assimilation *through* self-assertion."

Like Washington, DuBois was a self-made man. His mother—a member of the Burghardt clan that constituted a majority of the thirty-odd black families around Great Barrington in the mid-1880s—was a poor working woman who had been deserted by her husband. Like most of her relatives she saw no need for formal education and had barely learned to read and write. Her family had been artisans and independent property owners before the Civil War, but the rising tide of post-war industrial development saw them sliding into subsistence. Still, David Levering Lewis wrote in *W. E. B. DuBois: Biography of a Race,* while modernization threatened some with drowning, "in the crucial area of public education it promised to lift all those with enough motivation" to seize the opportunities it offered.

Young Willie DuBois and his mother—who poured all her energies into helping him excel in school—were nothing if not motivated. On his father's side, Willie was descended from James DuBois, a wealthy French physician, and his mulatto slave mistress, and the boy was stirred by what he knew of this background. Willie's grandfather, Alexander, had been born on one of his father James's plantations in the Bahamas (the family had property there and in Haiti). He had been brought to Connecticut in 1812, where James enrolled him at the exclusive Cheshire School. After only two years, however, James died and Alexander, disowned by his white relatives, was forced to quit school. After fending for himself for a few years as a small merchant in New Haven, Alexander went to Haiti to salvage what he could from his once-considerable patrimony. While there he fathered Alfred, but abandoned him when he returned to New Haven. Several years later, apparently on his own, Alfred found his way to Great Barrington where he met, married, and then forsook Willie's mother.

Until he was eighty and a retired merchant and ship's steward in New Bedford, Massachusetts, Alexander showed no interest in Willie. But when his third wife suggested that he best inspect his grandson (beside Alfred, his only natural heir) before it was too late, he summoned DuBois, then fifteen and a junior in high school. This encounter, Lewis suggested, "was one of the turning points of Willie's young life." And DuBois himself wrote, in *The Souls of Black Folk,* that an evening with Alexander and a guest who was one of New Bedford's leading colored citizen deeply affected him. "Suddenly," he wrote, he "sensed what manners meant and how people of breeding behaved and were able to express what we in Great Barrington were loath or unable" to articulate.

Inspired by this meeting and supported by his mother, DuBois went on to finish first in his class of sixteen at Great Barrington's new high school. From there he went to Fisk University as an undergraduate, and finally to Harvard, where in 1896 he became the first African-American to win a doctoral degree. Thereafter, as Lewis recounted, DuBois "cut an amazing swath through four continents." He wrote sixteen pioneering books on sociology, history, politics, and race relations. He was a Lenin Peace Prize laureate, and his birthday was once celebrated as a national holiday in China. He was among the first to grasp the international implications of the struggle for racial justice. As a founder of the NAACP and editor of its journal *Crisis,* he was the premier architect of the civil rights movement in the United States.

Clash of the Titans

Not surprisingly, as time went on, DuBois and Washington increasingly butted heads. In 1895, fourteen years after he founded Tuskegee Institute, Washington emerged on the national scene with the speech in Atlanta that asked black people, at least for the present, to give up civil rights, higher education, and the quest for political power. In place of these things Washington reiterated Armstrong's ideas about his people's role in American society. This, he suggested, was a program from which whites as well as blacks would benefit.

Eight years later, DuBois, lamenting that Washington's "gospel of Work and Money" had overshadowed "the higher aims of life," asked what this strategy had accomplished. The answer was not pretty. In the twenty years between 1880 and 1900, he wrote, Negroes in the South had been disfranchised. They had witnessed the "legal creation of a distinct status of civil inferiority." And they had seen their institutions of higher learning suffer from a steady withdrawal of private and public support. These developments, DuBois hastened to add, were, of course, not the "direct results of Mr. Washington's teachings." Still, "without doubt," Washington had helped prevent 9 million people from making effective progress by pursuing policies that deprived them of political rights, made them a servile caste, and discouraged the education of a potential core of race leaders.

DuBois and Dewey

When DuBois criticized Washington it was not because he disdained industrial education. He understood full well that institutions like Tuskegee were needed to teach Negro youth how to work in the new economy of the South. This was so, DuBois wrote, because "they have less knowledge of working [than whites] and [no one else] to teach them." But it was not a question of choosing between trades or liberal arts. Both were needed, DuBois insisted.

"Teach the workers to work and the thinkers to teach; make carpenters of carpenters, philosophers of philosophers, and fops of fools," he wrote. But, like Dewey, he did not pause there because he was not talking about training isolated individuals but "a living group" of people. The final product of training, he insisted, "must be neither a psychologist or a brick mason, but a man"—or, in Dewey's terms, an active member of democratic society. To make men, DuBois insisted, "we must have ideals, broad, pure, and inspiring ends of living—not sordid money-getting." In a call that resonated with Dewey's philosophy, DuBois wrote that the worker "must work for the glory of his handiwork, not simply for pay; [and] the thinker must think for truth, not for fame."

This required "ceaseless training and education," and the founding of truth on the "unhampered search for Truth." And it required as well, DuBois continued, the founding of the common school on the university, of the industrial school on the common school, and the "weaving thus [of] a system, not a distortion. For this is certain," he explained, "no secure civilization can be built in the South with the Negro as an ignorant, turbulent proletarian." Suppose we teach them to be "laborers and nothing more: they are not fools, they have tasted of the Tree of Life, and they will not cease to think, will not cease attempting to read the riddle of the world. By taking away their best equipped teachers and leaders, by slamming the door of opportunity in the faces of their bolder and brighter minds, will you make them more satisfied with their lot?" Or will you simply lead them "to the hands of untrained demagogues?"

IV

Were Dewey and DuBois speaking into the void when they articulated their democratic ideals and educational principles in 1900? To some it may well have seemed so, for after all, this was a time when their ideals could no more be realized than could Marx's vision of a society of fully and freely developed individuals. But now, a hundred years later, we have reached a level of technological, social, and industrial development that brings these ideals within reach. For those who seek the fulfillment of the promise of American democracy, these ideals are clearly necessary.

This necessity is twofold. First, profound educational reforms are needed to realize the potential implicit in the pronouncement that "all men [meaning people] are created equal." And, second, educational reform offers a partial solution to the problem of how to provide meaningful, creative work for the tens of millions of people being thrown out of work, or into low-paying service jobs, as productivity leaps forward and employment in manufacturing inexorably declines.

There are two potential steps in this process. First, to finance all public schools at the level of those now most well-financed. This would improve the quality of education and provide jobs for thousands of new teachers—and also for architects, artists, musicians, coaches, maintenance workers, counselors, groundkeepers, and many others. Such an upgrade would entail expansion of curricula to a level already existing at many elite private and suburban public schools. The curricula would include the natural sciences from the grades appropriate to the students' developmental level, a range of foreign languages, and a wide spectrum of cultural activities. These should be introduced starting in the early grades and carried through high school. Every school should also be equipped with up-to-date laboratories, computers, and cultural facilities. Intramural athletics should be greatly expanded, while interschool leagues should de-emphasize the increasingly commercialized competitiveness that now focuses on the creation of salable star athletes. Schools should focus instead on sports that are enjoyable for their own sake and teach teamwork and physical skills.

Then, too, the facilities and resources of such schools should cease being isolated reservations for children cut off from their communities. Instead they should become places shared with parents and others as community centers that bring children and adults together in a wide range of daytime and after-school activities. Schools should offer everything from specialized education for adults interested in entering new fields of endeavor to refresher courses for those simply desiring to upgrade their knowledge in any field. And schools should be the locus of free concerts, recitals, plays, art exhibits, antique fairs, and so on.

Such a vast expansion of curricula and the public use of school facilities should be staffed by full-time, paid planners, instructors, coaches, and coordinators. This, too, would provide new employment for hundreds of thousands of people. At first, because inequality is built into systems where public schools are financed by local taxation, all states should be required to provide uniform funding, preferably through a steeply graduated income tax. This is the most equitable means, but since some states are wealthier than others, ability to carry the load would vary and education in the poorer states might suffer. Ultimately, these programs should be paid for with federal funds that are allocated either to the states or directly to local school boards or authorities on a per-capita basis. Local school boards or authorities should have a wide range of discretion on matters based on the specific needs of their communities.

Improving our schools, however, is not simply a matter of infrastructure, faculty ratios, and extracurricula activities. Americans instinctively understand that education for all is a prerequisite for equality and a functioning democracy. Yet, as John Dewey wrote a hundred years ago, our schools, while claiming to prepare future members of an egalitarian social order, are more often institutions in which "the conditions of the social spirit are eminently wanting." He argued then, as he would today, that schools that teach by mind-numbing rote, that simply call upon all students in a classroom to read the same books simultaneously, to recite the same lessons, and pass the same exams, create little opportunity for "each child to work out something specifically his own," something that "may contribute to the common stock." In such conditions, Dewey argued, children's social impulses atrophy, and teachers are denied the ability to take advantage of students' "natural desire" to be creative and to contribute and serve the group.

In today's schools, the stronger children grow "to glory, not in their strength, but [simply] in the fact that they are stronger." And where this is so the natural "social spirit" of humanity is replaced by emotions such as fear, judgments of inferiority, and values of superiority and rivalry. If schools are to foster the "social spirit" in children, if they are to develop democratic character, Dewey insisted, they must be organized as democratic communities. "I believe," he said, "that the best and deepest moral training is precisely that which one gets through having to enter into proper relations with others in the unity of work and thought." Educating for democracy, therefore, means creating schools in which the child is "a member of a community" in which he or she participates and to which all contribute what they can. Such a school "must have a *community* of spirit and purpose realized through a *diversity* of powers and acts." Only in this way, Dewey concluded, "can the cooperative spirit involved in the division of labor be substituted for the competitive spirit [that] inevitably develops when [people] of the same presumed attainments are working to attain the exactly same result."

Not surprisingly, Dewey's ideas, while greatly influential in the first half of the past century, have been out of favor among those who have dominated our society since the beginning of the Cold War. In today's public schools Dewey's nightmare is more often the rule than the exception. Advocates of minimalist, or essentialist, education have imposed standardized tests designed to encourage a stifling uniformity of achievement and minimal intellectual development. In many schools education has been narrowed down to teaching only for the test. Still, Dewey's proposed methods and his vision of education and its purpose offer the best hope for democracy to triumph over the spirit of elitist individualism and the hierarchy of wealth that increasingly characterize our society.

V

Dewey developed his ideas at a time when colleges and universities were the almost-exclusive preserve of ruling class and upper-middle-class children. Colleges were training grounds for professionals—medical doctors, lawyers, engineers—as well as places where few other than wealthy young men became acquainted with the cultural traditions of Europe from Greek and Roman times onward. Like DuBois, Dewey, too, had benefited from this system, but unlike DuBois his educational theories had little or nothing to do with higher education. Rather, Dewey aimed at the student's early school experience, which was universal and might more generally influence the kinds of lives they would live.

Furthermore, since Dewey's day, research and experience have proven that education is vitally important for children below grade school age. The years from two to five are crucial for brain development, especially for language skills. Thus pre-school programs are essential for poor communities if we are to provide equality of opportunity in later life. Universally available supervised child care and pre-school programs, therefore, must be guaranteed to all those who need them.

Today, higher education, although not universal, has become important for a much wider range of young people. For millions of youngsters the accessibility and quality of college education and training are decisive in determining their paths in life. That's why colleges and universities, municipal and state, have become battlegrounds for and against affirmative action and over the question of tuition. And it is why college education should be made available to all who wish either to become more highly skilled or simply to deepen their knowledge and understanding of things that interest them. To maximize intellectual development colleges should limit class sizes and provide full-time, well-paid professors or instructors and graduate student teaching assistants. Tenure systems should be strengthened rather than undermined, as is now the common practice, and the quality of teaching should be given equal weight with publishing and scholarly research in granting tenure.

The United States already has many great state universities and colleges. This has been one of the nation's most important achievements, but these schools have never fulfilled their promise of education for all. Indeed, in recent decades their democratic value has been undermined by inadequate funding, steadily rising tuition costs, admission limits, and emphasis on business education at the expense of the humanities. Public colleges and universities should be tuition-free, or require only token tuition as a measure of commitment on the student's part. Generous grants should be provided to help pay for tuition at private colleges and universities.

The need for lifelong educational opportunity, desirable in itself, is increasingly important in our society because fewer and fewer people are now tied to single lifetime occupations. Earlier forms of capitalism not only had company towns where everyone was destined, one way or another, to work for the local coal mine, textile mill, steel mill, or railroad, but also many industries that provided lifetime jobs handed down from one generation to the next. Now, not only are the children of industrial workers expected to disperse into other occupations—and other cities and states (thereby undermining family values)—but the very idea of a lifetime job is rapidly disappearing, both as a reality and as a desirable goal.

Full and free individual development, of course, can only rarely be achieved by anyone tied for life to a single employer, or even to a single occupation, especially if the work is routine and provides no opportunity for growth, creativity, or advancement. Traditionally, socialists would be asked, who will collect the garbage, work the assembly lines, or have other necessary but supposedly degrading jobs in their utopia. That's a good question that can only be answered in the real life of the future, not by anyone's blueprint or fiat. Still, one possibility is that such jobs, which are steadily on the decline, could be done for short periods of time as part of everyone's education, or simply as a short period of universal public service. Such an arrangement would increase everyone's understanding of the workings of society, while removing the social stigma (and feeling of personal inadequacy or inferiority) attached to such work—and it would enable those now relegated to them to live fuller and more interesting lives.

VI

Those who are unhealthy in body or mind are not likely to develop freely or fully. Nor are they likely to lead happy lives, or be stress-free and productive. That is why the public consistently ranks adequate and affordable health care at or near the top of its concerns. And it is why socialists espouse universal access to health care. Indeed, every country that has called itself socialist, or has had a social-democratic majority in parliament, has adopted some system of socialized medicine. Even Cuba—whose economy is best known for its failures—created an admirable health care system, one that is far and away the best in Latin America.

Socialists, however, are not alone in their support of health care as a human right. Like many other social reforms, the idea of universal health care as a right has intruded into mainstream thinking. For example, Chicago's Cardinal Joseph Bernardin, a Catholic middle-of-the-roader, saw health care as an "essential safeguard of human life and dignity." He believed therefore that society has "an obligation . . . to ensure that every person be able to realize this right." And even a Stanford University economics professor can see that health care is more important than the accumulation of things. "At the end of the day," said Paul Romer, capitalism "as a system is supposed to make life nice," but as a student of technological change he realizes that "computers don't do all that much to make . . . life happier." The source of his happiness, Romer told the *New York Times,* "is good food, a nice house and, most of all, good health."

This last insight, of course, was not an endorsement of universal health care. After all, defenders of capitalism never tire of pointing out that the American health care system is the best in the world. In a sense they are correct. Our system has the best of everything. Our hospitals are equipped with the latest and most sophisticated machines. Most American physicians and nurses are superbly trained. American medical research is first-rate. And Americans spend more of their gross national product on health care than any other nation. If you are a professor at Stanford and your employer generously supplies you with access to it all, what's to change?

But Romer is part of a lucky and shrinking minority. For as productivity continues to increase and employment in manufacturing continues to fall, there is a steady decline in well-paying union jobs, and an increasing number of workers without adequate health insurance. Today, in 2003, an estimated 42 million Americans have no health insurance at all, and many who are insured have limited coverage. Worse, preventive care and exploratory procedures are excluded or underinsured, so many with insurance are treated only after they have become seriously ill. These conditions, of course, affect lower-income people disproportionately.

Thirty-three percent of Hispanics and 21 percent of African-Americans and Asians have no insurance, compared to 11 percent of non-Hispanic whites. Not surprisingly, people without adequate medical care have shorter life expectancies than those with full coverage.

In the decade since President Bill Clinton mishandled the health care issue, health and maintenance organizations (HMOs) and for-profit hospitals have come to dominate the health care industry. As they have, popular insecurity about health care, and anger at HMO and insurance company control over medical decisions—which should be made by doctors and patients, not bureaucrats—has grown steadily. And since the World Trade Center bombing, the anthrax scare, and fear of bioterrorism, the dismal state of the American public health care system has emerged as a public concern.

Traditionally, while some patients may have complained, doctors staunchly defended the American system of free market medicine. Increasingly, however, as their control over decisions about medical care and procedures has eroded, doctors have joined other critics of medical insurance companies and HMOs. As Physicians for a National Health Program asserts, the "gratifications of healing" are giving way to "anger and alienation in a system that treats people as commodities and doctors as investors' tools." Private practitioners are especially burdened by the countless hours wasted in billing patients and fulfilling insurance company regulations. And they are increasingly unhappy when forced to avoid procedures, consultations, or medications if their insurance companies disallow them—or if their patients are uninsured.

In HMOs, under the surveillance of bureaucrats who prod them to "abdicate allegiance to patients" and to avoid the sickest patients because they may be unprofitable, doctors "walk a tightrope between thrift and penuriousness." Even in academia, where the free market is converting the search for knowledge into the pursuit of intellectual property, the traditions of openness and collaboration—so necessary in any scientific endeavor—are giving way to secrecy and the private ownership of cures.

"The underlying problem," Marcia Angell, former editor-in-chief of the *New England Journal of Medicine* told the congressional black and progressive caucuses in 2001, "is that we treat health care like a market commodity instead of a social service." By providing health care based on ability to pay rather than medical need, the United States has become "the only nation in the world with a health care system based on dodging sick people." Insurance companies and HMOs keep costs down and profits up by stinting on medical services, by not insuring high-risk patients, by limiting the coverage of those they do insure, and by denying as many claims as they can.

Indeed, to keep costs down, insurance companies seek to attract the affluent and healthy and avoid the poor and sick. Called cost-shifting, this requires lots of paperwork and many intermediaries, as well as creative marketing. As a result, the American medical system has the highest overhead costs in the world, and American health care is the most expensive in the world. On average, Americans pay twice as much per person as citizens of other developed nations, and the gap is growing. This is not because Americans are sicker or more demanding (Canadians, for example, see their doctors more often and spend more time in hospital than we do). Nor is it because the American system produces better results. On the contrary, Americans' life expectancy, infant mortality, and immunization rates, which are the usual measures of health, are worse than those in other developed nations. Why is this? Because, Angell concluded, "there is something about our system—about the way we finance and deliver health care—that is enormously inefficient."

Indeed there is. Here is how Angell traces the health care dollar on its path from insurance policy-holders to the doctors, nurses, and hospitals who provide the actual care: First the insurance companies skim anywhere from 10 percent to 30 percent off the top for their marketing and administrative costs and profits. What's left then passes through "a veritable gauntlet of satellite businesses that have grown like fungus around the health care industry. These include brokers who cut the deals, disease management and utilization review boards that advise the insurers about allowing treatments, drug management companies, legal services that defend against patient suits, marketing consultants, billing agencies, etc." All of these parasites drain pennies from the patient's dollar, which, "by the time it reaches the actual providers of care, is cut in half."

Is this inevitable in a health care system organized on free market principles? If it is not, and if there is an alternative way to organize the provision of health care, what are the underlying principles on which it should be based? First, it seems to me that access to comprehensive health care is a human right in a society as developed as ours. The preamble to the United States Constitution, which states that one of the purposes of forming the Union was to "promote the general welfare," supports this view. Second, in a free society, patients should have the right to choose and change their physicians. Third, while the public may appropriately set overall health care policies, individual medical decisions should be made by patients in consultation with their personal caregivers.

Physicians for a National Health Plan has proposed one such national health insurance program (NHI). It would build on the existing Medicare program by extending coverage to all age groups and expanding the program to include all medically necessary services as well as mental health, dental care, and preventive measures. Prescription medications and long-term in-hospital and home care would also be guaranteed. Such a system would structure payment mechanisms to improve efficiency and guarantee prompt reimbursement to physicians, hospitals, and clinics. Health planning would be aimed at improving availability of resources wherever needed, while reducing bureaucracy. Under such a plan patient co-payments and deductibles would be eliminated.

To guarantee a uniformly high level of care and to end the current disparities in treatment between rich and poor, various ethnic groups, and rural and urban communities, private insurance that duplicates public coverage would be eliminated. Investor-owned facilities would be phased out and for-profit hospitals would be bought out by the government or by not-for-profit medical associations. This would minimize the complexity of billing and administration that now exists and raises costs in HMOs and in private practices. (Unlike private insurance programs under which even the most efficient HMOs consume 14 percent of premiums for overhead, both the Medicare and Canada's national health insurance program spend less than 3 percent on overhead. In both of these systems, 97 percent of the cost goes to doctors, hospitals, or clinics.)

There are several reasons for disallowing private insurance of duplicated service. First, because they could not compete with an NHI system that cost nothing and provided first-rate service, private insurers, if allowed, would lobby ceaselessly to sabotage the public system. (This has happened in England, where private insurers now have regained a part of the market by undermining the public system.) Second, if the wealthy could turn to private coverage, they would also lobby against being taxed for the public system. Third, private coverage would encourage doctors and hospitals to provide two classes of care, much as they do now.

To avoid the expense of billing for services covered by NHI, payment to hospitals, physicians, and outpatient providers would be made directly by the government. Hospitals would be paid a monthly sum to cover their operating expenses. The amount of these payments would be determined by annual negotiations based on past expenditures, previous financial and clinical performance, projected changes in levels of services, wages, and other inputs, as well as proposed new programs. Hospitals could not use operating funds for excessive executive salaries, marketing, or major unbudgeted capital purchases or expansion. This arrangement would greatly simplify hospital administration and free up money to enhance clinical care. Prohibiting the use of operating funds for capital investments or profit would eliminate the incentive for excessive interventions or skimping on care, since neither inflating revenues nor limiting care could result in institutional gain.

Payment to physicians and outpatient facilities could be made in one of three ways: fees-for-service; salaried positions in institutions; or salaries within group practices and in HMOs that operate on a per-capita basis. NHI and representatives of fee-for-service physicians (perhaps state medical societies) would negotiate a simplified and binding schedule of fees, and, like hospitals, all investor-owned HMOs and group practices would be converted to not-for-profit status.

Patients would never be billed. Instead, physicians would submit bills directly to NHI on a simple form or via e-mail, and they would be paid within thirty days. Salaries within hospitals, health centers, group practices, and home care agencies could be paid from the agencies' global budget for delivery of care, education, and prevention programs, and practitioners would be paid by their institutions.

Capital allocations for expansion of existing health care facilities or the construction of new ones, as well as for major equipment upgrades, would be appropriated from the NHI budget, but such decisions would be made by regional planning boards of experts and community representatives. NHI would pay owners of currently for-profit hospitals, nursing homes, and clinics a reasonable fixed rate of return on existing equipment. For-profit HMOs would receive similar compensation for clinical facilities and administrative equipment. Private donations for major capital projects would only require approval if they entailed increases in future operating expenses.

NHI would also pay for all medically needed prescription drugs and medical supplies. An expert panel would establish and regularly update the formulary of medicinal substances and procedures, and NHI would negotiate drug and equipment prices with manufacturers, based on their costs of production (excluding marketing and lobbying expenses). Suppliers would bill NHI directly.

The savings under this proposed system would allow all those now uninsured or underinsured to be covered without any increase in the percentage of GNP absorbed by the health care industry. All patients would receive a uniform, high standard of treatment, free drugs, and preventive care. That in itself would reduce the need for expensive treatments that are often required by today's uninsured by the time that they finally reach a hospital.

Through Medicare and insurance plans for federal workers, the government already pays out 65 percent of all health care costs in the United States. Additional funds would be required for NHI, but they could be raised efficiently and equitably through a progressive surcharge on income taxes, or as transfers from the current military budget. Under this plan, the vast majority of Americans would get better care and pay less than they now do for their private insurance.

This is an ambitious plan, but it is not pie in the sky. It has been endorsed by Rodney G. Hood, M.D., president of the National Medical Association, an organization of 25,000 physicians of African descent, by Sindu Srinivas, M.D., president of the American Medical Student Association, the nation's largest such association, and by several prominent physicians, including Marcia Angell, Elinor Chistiansen, president of American Medical Women's Association, and Merlin DuVal, assistant secretary of health under Richard Nixon.

VII

Many benefits would flow from the adoption of the two sets of proposals suggested above. Improvements in education and health care are the obvious ones and would improve the lives of millions of Americans. But the reforms would also strengthen our democracy by providing a better educated and healthier citizenry, people who would be able to improve their own lives and to be more involved in the life of their communities. Then, too, these industries, unlike manufacturing, are both labor intensive. In privately owned industries the goal is to increase productivity and profits by producing more goods and services with less human labor. But in education and health care the goal should be to increase the well-being of students and patients—and, thereby, of society as a whole—by increasing the amount and satisfaction of people engaged in socially useful and creative work.

Investment in these fields will lead to the employment of millions of people who have lost their jobs in manufacturing and other capital-intensive industries and are now working two or more low-paying jobs with no security or futures. Jobs in education and health care, on the other hand, would generally be more satisfying and provide both security and opportunities for personal growth. In short, these are more than do-good reforms for poor people. If presented courageously to the public they have a good chance of gaining widespread popular support.

VIII

Recent electoral reform proposals, including the McCain-Feingold act, have focused on reducing the amount of private money poured into election campaigns, either directly or indirectly, as a way of reducing the corruption of our democracy. Some reformers have seen this as woefully inadequate. Instead, they propose full public financing of federal elections. That would be a step in the right direction—assuming it covered primary election contests as well as third-party candidates and provided clear minimal standards for eligibility. Still, public funding would entail significant expenditures of taxpayer money, as well as the creation of yet another government bureaucracy.

More important, even this reform would do little to change the way in which election campaigns systematically degrade public discourse and evade intelligent consideration of the issues that most concern the potential electorate. The issue, in other words, is not so much who pays for the thirty-second TV sound bites that now are such a key factor in elections. Rather, it is—or should be—the way in which such campaigns pander to media-created opinions and prejudices and serve to confuse or turn off potential voters. Electoral reform should aim to raise the level of political discourse by forcing candidates to address the issues and the principles that underlie their positions on public policy. In short, as democratic theorists going back to Thomas Jefferson have repeatedly pointed out, true democracy is impossible without an informed citizenry. And one of the reasons that we do not have an informed citizenry is that election campaigns increasingly depend on methods designed to keep serious public policy issues out of sight and mind.

Fortunately, there is a solution that is in line with left principles. It is one that would force candidates to discuss issues in some depth, cost the public nothing, and avoid the creation of yet another bureaucratic regulatory agency. And the answer is: Free air time for all candidates for federal office who can meet a minimum standard of popular support. This solution is based on the fact that the airwaves belong to us all, that broadcasters can operate only by securing licenses from the federal government, which has the right to impose any conditions we wish for the privilege.

It is true, of course, that such a reform would cost the giant media companies something in lost revenues—while public financing might be a bonanza for them. But so what? The corporations to whom we grant licenses make hundreds of millions, if not billions, of dollars every year by using our airwaves, yet we derive little social benefit from their bonanza. As a people, it is our right to set whatever conditions we deem to be appropriate for the use of our property. Limiting media corporation profits in order to benefit us all is not only possible, but highly desirable. What could be more important in a democratic society than using one of our public resources to educate and inform our own citizens—to benefit us, rather than the media corporations to whom we have given this bonanza?

Here's how this might work. Thirty-minute (or fifteen-minute) blocks of time would be distributed to all candidates who meet legislatively defined levels of support. This would open the political process to many candidates and groups now excluded from effective participation in the political life of our nation. Equally important, such blocks of time would replace the usual distorted slanders and innuendoes of thirty-second sound bites with coherent (or at least sustained) discussion of issues. Candidates would find it more difficult to avoid addressing and examining issues intelligently. A true diversity of views could be placed before the voters for a healthy change.

Some say that federal bureaucrats would be needed to decide who gets the best slots, but if the legislation is properly drawn federal bureaucrats would have no role. Who gets what time slots could be decided simply by drawing lots, and disputes could be handled by the courts, mandated to act expeditiously. Some also argue that free air time would be yet another subsidy to wealthy candidates. There is some truth to this, but by eliminating the cost of television advertising, and by providing substantial blocks of time, the level of public debate would be raised and the advantage of personal money would be reduced. This would facilitate popular participation and reduce the current corruption of our democracy. In short, a win-win idea.

IX

In addition to education, health care, and electoral reform there are several other areas that should be dramatically supported with public money. The most obvious are cultural. A federal arts program, (similar to the New Deal Works Progress Administration) is now sorely needed. Autonomous theater and video workshops, art projects, concert studios, and halls should be federally funded on a long-term basis. Such arts centers should have permanent locations and staffs, governed by local community boards. They should not be dependent on individual grants or require the obeisant requests and favoritism that foundations and the National Endowment for the Arts now do. They should be open to any group that demonstrates serious interest in one of the arts, some degree of talent, and some community support. Funding should pay for rent or purchase of premises, staff salaries, and stipends for talented long-term members and groups.

On a more general level, adequate federal funding should be available for public ownership of services that cannot adequately be provided by private investment, for example, urban rapid transit systems. Most large cities have some form of rail transit—subways, els, light rail. Most of them are now publicly owned, many because the private companies that built them could not make a profit and either went bankrupt or arranged to sell them to the city (often at inflated prices). These systems still run at a loss, but they are mandated to operate as if they were for-profit enterprises, so they are starved for adequate operating funds from municipal, state, and national government and are forced to raise fares and provide less service even though the city's poor and working populations need them most. I would propose instead that urban rapid transit be heavily funded, that service be upgraded and fares reduced and eliminated for students, seniors, and the unemployed. Many European countries have such transportation systems, and Cuba, a poor, badly managed country, experimented with free fares after its revolution. Surely, the richest country in the world could do as much.

Similarly, interurban train service, generally phased out after airlines made railroads unprofitable, should be heavily promoted. High-speed interurban trains and even long-distance passenger trains have a role to play in a balanced national transportation system. Those who argue against such a system point to the failure of nationalized rail in countries like Britain. But in Britain public rail service was starved by Margaret Thatcher until it fell apart, and then the parts were sold to private companies at deep discounts. That, however, created true chaos. The rail system in Britain today is a series of disasters, some of them of unprecedented scope.

In the United States something similar occurred. When Amtrak was set up, it too was mandated to act as if it could be made profitable, even though it replaced failed private systems. In the attempt, it, too, was starved and forced to downgrade service (except in its busiest corridor between Washington and Boston) and raise fares. Of course, as service got worse and schedules less convenient, Amtrak lost riders. But, especially in this time of airline congestion, a high-speed rail service between cities like Chicago and Detroit, St. Louis, Indianapolis, or Minneapolis would be entirely rational.

In general, public ownership of utilities is criticized (or slandered) on the grounds that it destroys the incentives for efficiency and innovation that market forces exert on private owners. There is some truth in that, especially in competitive industries with evolving technologies, such as telephones. But in others, such as water, electric power, and gas, municipal ownership has proven just as efficient as private ownership. In fact, in city after city public utilities provide services at a much lower cost than private utilities. This, too, should be looked at, especially in areas of artificially high energy prices.

Finally, there is the failed war on drugs, which like Prohibition before it, has stimulated consumption and created a major criminal industry. Even though the rate of drug use is as high or higher in middle- and upper-class communities, the drug industry is manned at the street level largely by inner-city youth, and the victims of this war are almost entirely poor, African-Americans and Latinos, a large percentage of whom have been thrown into prison for infractions for which white suburban youths are merely slapped on the wrist. This, of course, has also been the main engine behind the powerful prison-industrial complex and the misallocation of billions of dollars into facilities whose main function has been to produce hardened criminals. A courageous left would take up this issue and call for decriminalization of marijuana and the public regulation of the more dangerous addictive drugs, as well as for drug rehabilitation centers in place of prison.

There are many ways in which socialist principles, properly understood, remain relevant today. From a humane and democratic perspective some of these proposals are not only urgently needed, but also have existing constitutencies. Others are capable of winning constituencies now dormant and needing only a political movement to turn such still-private ideas into public issues.

10

ENTERING THE MAINSTREAM:
WHAT IS TO BE DONE?

I

TO BE SIGNIFICANT, AN AMERICAN left needs principles and programs that point in the developmental direction of our society and resonate with its historical possibilities and the social concerns already on the public's mind. And, to be viable, such a left will require an engagement strategy in harmony with our evolving democratic traditions and political institutions. This last requirement is the subject of my final chapter.

Over the past two centuries socialism in America has evolved and changed its strategies and policies in response to developments in the surrounding society. In the eighteenth and early nineteenth centuries utopian socialists created independent, self-sufficient colonies within the larger society in order to remain functionally and socially separate from it. For half a century or so these coherently Christian colonies came already formed from Europe. And because they were more advanced than the surrounding society they initially did well. But as the level of development in the more dynamic larger society overcame and surpassed these utopians— roughly in the mid-nineteenth century—the colonies began to dissolve. By the end of the nineteenth century, members of most utopian colonies had cashed in their assets and joined the mainstream.

Next, as the United States rapidly industrialized and Marx's ideas found their way to the New World, worker-based socialism emerged along with anarchism to contest for the minds of disaffected workingmen and women. In the initial stages of industrial development the anarchists—who rejected all cooperation or engagement with the capitalist state and its civic institutions—gave socialists a run for their money. This was especially true in Europe, where propertyless workers had few rights or legal protections. Indeed, anarchist strength in the First Socialist International was sufficient to induce Marx to close up shop in Europe and transfer the International's headquarters to the United States. Even here, however, especially among first-generation immigrants with few civil rights or little or no experience with our evolving democracy, anarchism flourished briefly as a political philosophy. But as trade unionism developed, and workers began to form their own political parties—and even to elect their members to public office—anarchists were increasingly marginalized. Some, like the Haymarket martyrs, began to understand the need, if only for practical reasons, to participate constructively as part of the labor movement. The Haymarket affair, however, and—fourteen years later—President William McKinley's assassination at the hands of anarchist Leon Czolgosz, spelled the end of anarchism as a significant contestant for working-class support in the New World.

Meanwhile, by the 1880s, millions of farmers and workers were organizing to oppose the increasingly oppressive power of Eastern banks, railroads, and monopolistic manufacturers. Both farmers and workers reacted to the emergence of large-scale industrial corporations and financial institutions by creating their own political parties. By the mid-1880s the Union Labor Party in New York City was able to outpoll the Republicans, and in hundreds of small cities and towns members of the Knights of Labor elected mayors and council members on labor party tickets. More importantly, in these years, Southern and Midwestern farmers alliances came together with labor to fight the railroads and Eastern banks by forming the People's Party. That party's greatest strength was in Kansas, where five of seven congressional seats, as well as four-fifths of the state legislature, went to Populists in 1890. As in Kansas, so in South Dakota and Nebraska, Populists (calling themselves Independents) elected members to office. In 1890, the farmers' revolt swept a Democrat into the Nebraska governor's office for the first time since the Civil War, and the Republicans lost all three of the state's congressional seats. Two went to Independents, one of whom was William Jennings Bryan, the "boy orator of the Platte" who six years later would win the Democratic nomination for president.

In 1892, the People's Party reached its high point. Its candidate for president, Civil War General James B. Weaver, got more than a million votes, swept Kansas, Colorado, Nevada, and Idaho, and won half of North Dakota's and Oregon's electoral votes (for a total of twenty-two). Weaver's electoral votes were the first any third party had won since the Civil War—and they would be the last a working people's third party will ever win. But the Populists' glory days did not last long. Only four years later they yielded to the inevitable and, following the Democrats' lead, also nominated Bryan for president. Bryan was almost a Populist. His inflationary platform called for the free coinage of silver and the regulation of monopolies. And he was greatly feared by the new corporate ruling class. In a contest viciously fought by the Republicans—a model for Richard Nixon's "dirty politics" a century later—McKinley was elected.

Many Populists saw this as a great defeat, not because Bryan lost but because their party broke up and dissolved almost immediately after the election. It seemed a serious loss because third parties had not been a matter of choice in the post–Civil-War years. As the great American historian Charles W. Beard explained in *The Rise of American Civilization*, the major parties were inaccessible to outsiders. They had become tightly controlled machines that "corresponded to the requirements of substantial owners of industrial property who ruled with the aid of the more fortunate farmers." In their philosophy, "doric in its simplicity," Beard wrote, a political party was a "private association of gentlemen and others who had the leisure for public affairs." The party's "functional purpose was to get possession of the government in the name of patriotism" and to distribute the spoils of office among "the commanders, the army, and its camp followers."

How the major parties managed their caucuses, conventions, and committees "was none of the general public's business." Leaders sometimes bought voters and marched them to the polls "but they were only doing unto others what they expected others to do unto them." In short, before the Populist revolt a major political party was "in effect a standing army." When in control of a state, or the national government, it "could make laws and carry on administration in caucuses and cabals behind closed doors without much risk of intrusion by the citizens."

Ironically, this party system had begun as a democratic reform when Andrew Jackson was president. Intended to make the electoral process more open, it provided for local, state, and national nominating conventions to which the delegates were generally chosen by party members in primary elections. Then, "fresh from the people," as Jackson was wont to say, the delegates would come together and choose the party's candidates. But as time went on and the process came under the tight control of party leaders, fewer and fewer of "the people" voted in primaries. Instead, the leaders saw to it that their captains, officeholders, and friends were selected as delegates. By the end of the century, as Beard observed, independent delegates fresh from the people were rarities at major party conventions.

As discontent with the laissez-faire status quo increased, however, working people began to insist that major party candidates be subject to the direct vote of party members. In this movement, Robert LaFollette, Wisconsin's future progressive Republican senator, played a leading role. In 1897, in a speech at the University of Chicago, LaFollette exclaimed: "Abolish the caucus and the convention; go back to first principles of democracy; go back to the people." Six years later, under his leadership, Wisconsin enacted one of the first direct primary laws (the first was passed in Mississippi in 1902). By 1910 two-thirds of the states, mostly in the West, were nominating their candidates for office by popular vote in direct primaries.

These changes in the election laws obviated the need for third parties as the only means of popular participation in the electoral arena. Now any organized group—or, for that matter, any well-known or wealthy individual—could run for office simply by registering in either party and then filing the petitions required of all those seeking to be nominated. In 1915, of course, that was the method used by the Nonpartisan League to win control of North Dakota. Many decades later, during the Reagan years, it was also the method used by the religious right to take effective control of the Republican Party.

II

Still, the third-party idea remained attractive to many on the left, as well as to individuals who already had a large personal constituency, or had the money to buy one. Such efforts, whether of an H. Ross Perot on an ego trip, or of Strom Thurmond and George Wallace making last-ditch stands in defense of racial segregation, have been ephemeral. Similarly, the left has had a continuing love affair with the idea of having its own political party, and this has created a serious impediment to the creation of a coherent and effective movement to humanize our society.

Aside from youthful impetuosity and ignorance, the urge to form a third party arises from an understanding of working-class politics in Europe. Because Europeans enjoy the more democratic parliamentary form of democracy, third, and even fourth parties are common there, and frequently play significant roles in affairs of state. In Italy, for example, governments have frequently been patched together by combining two or more parties. In France, which has a system of partial proportional representation, there have been ruling coalitions between the large Socialist party and the smaller Communist party. And in Germany, where the Social Democrats are now the largest party, they share power with the small Green Party delegation. This happens because in a parliamentary system governments are creatures of parliament, cobbled together by simple legislative majorities. When a party with the largest number of seats fails to get a majority, it must rely on smaller parties to achieve one. By providing the balance of power between two larger parties, in other words, a small party can gain influence greatly disproportionate to its numbers. In such a system, third, and even fourth or fifth, parties often make sense.

But the efficacy of European third parties rests on a system in which there is no distinction between the legislative and executive branches, and in which the party membership is ideologically coherent. In parliaments, the prime minister is the head of government who serves at the majority's pleasure. Thus a minor party in a ruling coalition can overthrow a government simply by withdrawing its support in a vote of no confidence. This system gives considerable power to the lucky small parties included in coalition governments.

Parliamentary systems are a good deal more democratic than the American system, in which the head of government (president) is elected separately for a fixed term of years by a nationwide vote. The presidential system favors the wealthy and powerful because winning a nationwide election normally requires massive amounts of money and a subservient corporate media. Of course, a political movement with a large, well-organized, popular network of experienced people dedicated to a long-range struggle, might offset that advantage. But such a movement can neither be created overnight nor be willed into being. In fact, there's only one way that a new third party can succeed in a presidential system, and that is not by the miraculous creation of a fully mature opposition party, but by the disruption or disintegration of one of the existing major parties.

This has happened once, in 1850, when the Whigs, one of the two major parties of the early 1800s, were deeply divided over the question of slavery's extension into the Western territories. That issue was of vital national concern. It divided the slave South from the more dynamic industrializing North. And the Republicans, who were organized in 1856 and stood strongly against admitting any more slave states to the Union, won the day with Abraham Lincoln's election in 1860. A well-defined split of that depth in one of the two major parties, however, has not occurred since, nor is there any likelihood that such a split will develop in the foreseeable future.

This point seems so obvious that it shouldn't require an extended argument. But the third-party mystique survives because leftists think only in terms of European ideological politics and do not examine the nature of their own system seriously. Also, the appeal of a party of one's own—one built around a clear set of principles, with general agreement on program, and not subject to the necessity of compromises with non-true believers—is very comforting.

The examples of the old Socialist Party and the Communist Party, each of which dominated the left in its heyday, has also served to reinforce the third-party mystique. As we have seen, Socialists were extremely jealous of their identity even though the party was ideologically diverse, in part because its founding leaders and members were themselves products of the years when the door to participation in major parties had been tightly shut. Their commitment to third parties, in other words, was congenital. Those Populists who helped found the Socialist Party were purists who came from the wing of their old party that had opposed the 1896 merger in support of Bryan. Eugene Debs, who had supported Bryan, came out of disillusionment with the Democrats, both when he was legislator and when the Democratic attorney general and president destroyed his American Railway Union. Morris Hillquit came as a leader of his half of the Socialist Labor Party, and Victor Berger also had a long history of third-party commitment. Furthermore, the Socialists were fortunate in having prospered better, or at any rate in having survived intact longer, than any previous or subsequent working people's party. They dreamed, therefore, of evolving into a major party themselves, and their initial trajectory of steady growth fueled that hope at least until 1912.

However, that illusion began to fade when the Socialist International collapsed after the war started in Europe in 1914. And it was struck a more telling blow when the party broke up after the Russian Revolution. Even so, the Old Socialists had a proud tradition to defend. Over a twenty-year period, they had won thousands of municipal offices in everything from small towns to the nation's largest cities, they had elected a hundred and fifty state legislators in eighteen states, and, most importantly, they had seen their ideas and programs enter national policy debates and help humanize the new corporate system. However, the party also had clear limits. Only two Socialists managed to become members of Congress in these two decades, and the party itself had been all but excluded from the national political structure. Furthermore, once the Wilsonian reforms began to draw people into the more fertile fields of mainstream politics, many on the party's fringes began slipping away. By the 1920s, even a stalwart like Berger began (privately, in letters to his wife) to question his party's viability.

Of course, in 1915, Arthur Townley had pinpointed the Socialists' outsider strategy as the source of their weakness. His decision to leave the North Dakota party and to organize the Nonpartisan League around almost identical principles brilliantly confirmed this insight. So, too, did Upton Sinclair's somewhat more eccentric campaign to End Poverty in California in 1934 as a Democrat. Nor were these the only defections. A steady trickle of other left-wingers abandoned the party of their hearts to play a more profitable—and effective—game under the major parties' big tent— among them a handful of House members during the New Deal years.

III

In any case, the Socialists were the last sustained third party, and they had all but faded away by the mid-1920s. They were followed by a number of fleeting intrusions into independent presidential politics, some of which are cited from time to time in justification of new would-be third party efforts, such as Ralph Nader's Green Party campaign in 2000. Of these, two stand out; Robert LaFollette's presidential campaign in 1924 and Henry Wallace's Progressive Party effort in 1948.

At first glance (which is usually all it gets from third-party polemicists) LaFollette's campaign appears to be on point. LaFollette did run for president in 1924 to protest his party's nomination of conservative, anti-labor Calvin Coolidge. But LaFollette insisted that he had no intention of starting a third party. Indeed, he explicitly forbade his followers from putting up candidates for any other offices on his ballot line. This was a one-shot protest effort. After the election LaFollette returned to the Republican Party.

Former Vice President Henry A. Wallace, on the other hand, not only ran as a Progressive in 1948, but intended to form a new party. Wallace was motivated by a desire to reverse the Cold War policies of the Truman administration, in which he had been secretary of commerce. He was popular among labor leaders and liberals within the Democratic Party. And because he stood for peaceful cooperation with the Soviet Union, he was viewed favorably by the Communists.

This is a unique case that warrants a close look, because the Communist Party, which was the main engine in the creation of the Wallace party, had long been opposed to such a move, and in their hearts must have known better than to proceed as they did. The CP's attitude to third parties had been developing ever since the mid-'30s when the Popular Front period began. They did not oppose third parties, per se. In fact, abstractly, they favored a new configuration of parties, one of which would be a party of labor and the left. But, as CP national committee member Jack Stachel wrote in the September 1947 issue of the official party journal, *Political Affairs,* it could be "accepted as fact that the Communists alone, and even with their left supporters in the labor and people's movement, will not and cannot organize a third party." Stachel viewed the existing third-party movement, "and even the Wallace for President movement, which is much broader than the third party movement," as much too narrow for a meaningful new people's party. He implicitly acknowledged that a third party in 1948 could only come into being if the Communists played a major role in the process. But, he wrote, the "genuine, broad, mass third party" that the CP advocated would only be permissible if it were "of such proportions that the Communists could not possibly dominate it even if they sought to."

This was not Stachel's personal view, or the view of a party faction, as another national committee member, Simon Gerson, made clear the next month, also in *Political Affairs.* Writing about the difficulty the third-party movement faced even in New York's American Labor Party, the largest and most successful of left coalition organizations, Gerson explained that "within the ALP and the progressive labor movement of New York there are people who wholeheartedly support the principle of a third party but are not convinced about the necessity of [even] a third ticket now." That was why the Communists had not urged a Wallace candidacy at the ALP convention in September of 1947. "It was," Gerson admitted, only by not pushing this issue that the ALP "remained united."

Had the Wallace for President issue been placed before the convention for a vote, he wrote, unity "would have been impossible."

This position received a rousing endorsement in late September at a gigantic rally in the old Madison Square Garden, where Party General Secretary Eugene Dennis proclaimed that Communists were "not adventurers." We are not going to isolate ourselves, he said. "We never did and do not now favor the launching of premature and unrepresentative third parties." Such moves, he continued, could only "serve the camp of progress when they arise out of the collective decision and united action of a broad democratic and anti-war coalition."

Yet, one month later, the Communists completely reversed themselves. This followed immediately on the heels of the Soviets' formation of the Communist Information Bureau (Cominform) in Budapest, in October 1947, and the publication of a manifesto declaring that the greatest danger facing the working class at the moment lay in underestimating its own strength and overestimating the strength of the imperialist camp. The manifesto was a clear instruction to the American Communists that opposition to forming a third party was now an impermissible error. It was an instruction to do exactly what the American party had correctly been warning against for many years. Literally overnight, the party frantically began to advocate and organize a Wallace campaign against Truman and to fabricate a third party.

The Communists' task now switched from putting the brakes on third-party initiatives to creating the illusion that there were sufficient forces to justify doing so. Launching a campaign to convince Wallace that there was broad popular support for a third party, they brought a steady stream of their most loyal members and supporters to his door. For his part, Wallace, who was already leaning in that direction, needed little persuasion. But the party he headed was so dependent on the CP that the Communists had to scurry to find non-party members to staff it. The Progressives that year put up candidates for many offices on their line, but instead of building a viable party, the 1948 campaign simply facilitated the Democrats' turn to the right and the left's expulsion from the mainstream of national politics.

In the end the Wallace party validated the Communists' earlier understanding. Wallace himself was permanently marginalized. Leftists and liberals within the Democratic Party—people such as Florida Senator Claude Pepper, former Minnesota Governor Elmer Benson, and California Attorney General Robert W. Kenny—were isolated. And in the CIO, support of Wallace led directly to the expulsion and destruction of eleven Communist-led or dominated affiliates—and to a stifling conformity on foreign policy questions within the labor movement.

That pretty much ended left-wing third-party activity until 1980, when environmentalist Barry Commoner formed the Citizens Party as a vehicle for him to run for president. That effort diverted a handful of scarce money and the energy of some well-meaning leftists from more productive activities. Ignored by the media and the public, the party disappeared immediately after the November election.

Then, of course, there was Ralph Nader's Green Party crusade. Nader, a well-known environmentalist and consumer advocate, has a large personal following and is a popular speaker. He mobilized tens of thousands of young people and held by far the largest campaign meetings of any candidate in the 2000 election. Still, running against two total duds, he barely garnered 3 percent of the vote. In the end, in the popular mind if not in fact, he is best remembered as someone who threw the election to George Bush II out of personal hostility to Al Gore. Nader's effect on the left, however, is less in doubt. Instead of building a constituency for his ideas, as he claimed to be doing, Nader divided an already existing constituency, and by so doing did a terrible disservice to progressives.

Clearly, support for Nader's ideas is much greater than the support for his candidacy. For every person who cast a vote for Nader, there were at least ten who shared his views on many issues but voted Democrat. It would seem imperative in a strategy aimed at building a new political force to pursue a path that brings supporters together. By dividing the potential constituency for his ideas and actions, Nader not only minimized the left's influence in mainstream politics, but also confounded and demoralized many progressively oriented citizens by making himself and his strategy, rather than the principles and programs he espoused, the subject of public debate. Claiming to be running in order to build a major movement in the electoral arena, he inspired a few thousand students to follow him. But he created a good deal more anger and recrimination among those on the left most consistently involved in political action. By running on the line of a party cobbled together for the purpose of his transitory individualistic campaign, he succeeded only in leading his forces into a blind alley. In short, it was a bad idea.

IV

There is, however, an electoral strategy that's better than butting heads into a stone wall. It is based on going with the flow of our election system. It is, of course, not a new idea. The left used it in North Dakota in 1915. Upton Sinclair used it in California in 1934. The Christian Right used it to further its conservative principles in the Republican Party in the 1990s. And Harold Washington used it in Chicago in the 1980s, when he became mayor of Chicago.

Washington was a lifelong Democrat, but when he talked about Chicago's two parties, he didn't mean the Democrats and the Republicans. To him, it was his party versus little Richie Daley's, both of whom were Democrats. Almost singlehandedly, Washington inspired and created a coalition of progressive Democrats that included an overwhelming majority of the city's African-Americans, a majority of its Hispanic voters, and a significant number of white progressives in and out of the labor movement. This is the natural left constituency and it constitutes a majority in many cities and some states. Unfortunately, however, Washington's first term was taken up largely with a battle against the old-line majority in the city council, and early in his second term, after he had secured a majority in the council, he died of a massive heart attack before he could consolidate his supporters into a movement capable of surviving him. Still, his administration changed the face of Chicago for the better.

The Nonpartisan League and Christian Right examples provide the clearest guides to a successful strategy for an emerging movement. The

Nonpartisan League aimed first at arenas where victories are easiest to come by. In politics especially, nothing succeeds like success. Following that maxim, Arthur Townley began at the state legislative level and after victories there moved on up to the gubernatorial and then the congressional levels. For North Dakota in 1916 that made prefect sense, and it got near-perfect results. But times, and our means of communication have changed. In 1916 it was difficult to reach much beyond the local level with leaflets and weekly newspapers; now, however, we have television and the Internet, which gives a national campaign some feasibility if it is done right and combined with a coherent local strategy. In other words, presidential campaigns can be useful. The fault of the Nader campaign was not that he arrogated to himself the right to run for president. Just the opposite, a person willing to take such an initiative is invaluable to a political movement. The problem wasn't what he did, but how and where he did it.

Consider Jesse Jackson, a man whose ego might give even Ralph Nader pause. Jackson, acting largely as an individual, ran twice for the Democratic presidential nomination, in 1984 and again in 1988. In his second campaign he participated in all the televised debates and consistently outshone his rivals. In the process he garnered some 7 million votes, won a primetime speaking slot at the Democratic National Convention, and made the meeting's best and most enthusiastically received speech. All this gained Jackson's progressive ideas wide public exposure, as well as proof of their massive popular support. Jackson proved that there was a large constituency for a left movement. And that's not all. He greatly enhanced the African-American community's visibility on the national political scene, which in turn stimulated a significant increase in the number of blacks running for and getting elected to public office.

Unfortunately, like Nader, Jackson started at the top and was pretty much a one-man show. Nor did Jackson follow up on his effort and consolidate his constituency. Even so, Jackson, Washington, and the Christian Coalition validate different aspects of the advantage of working within the existing institutional parameters of the American political system. And it is these examples—rather than eleventh-hour third-party campaigns that end up as little more than moralistic exercises in futility—that point the way to a strategy that might allow a left to become a recognized force in the nation's political life.

Still, a left entrance into the national political arena should not start with a presidential candidate. Left presidential campaigns are inherently episodic. Starting at that level greatly increases the danger of a pattern that has already plagued the left—one of indifference to national politics between presidential elections and then frantic, mindless efforts to do something when it's too late for anything beyond token gestures. And even if the effort creates a constituency it is ephemeral and quickly diffuses if not followed up with activities and campaigns for Congress.

V

Building a sustained national movement requires a commitment to continuous electoral activity, year-in and year-out. Single issue or interest movements—unions, environmentalists, civil rights groups, public health advocates, the kind of movements or organizations with which most leftists are familiar—can and often do function effectively as lobbyists. But the intensity of their issues tends to be episodic, and, of necessity, they work within the existing corporate institutional and ideological framework. Only rarely can they represent universal interests or principles. And because their success is based on getting a larger piece of a small pie, the interests of one progressive lobby frequently clash with those of another. In other words, a unified left cannot be built by putting together a laundry list of worthy causes in the hope of building a non-ideological coalition. How to unite people across lines of parochial interest and in favor of the general interest is what we will have to teach ourselves. But it is the only way to bring and hold together a unified constituency committed to humanizing our society.

In organizing such a new movement the left will have to think nationally—especially in terms of its program and critique of current government policies—but act locally and start modestly. Choosing an arena that is manageable but in which it addresses national issues and problems is essential. So is success, or at least the possibility of success. Therefore, the place to start seems clearly to be in the smallest constituencies concerned with national policy, which is congressional districts. And it is important to run in a way that least disadvantages organized groups with relatively little money, which is in the primary elections of congressional districts that do not already have a progressive representative, and in which the party it chooses to run in is not a hopeless minority. Generally, it makes more sense, other considerations being equal, to run as a Democrat (since one goal should be to gain or hold a Democratic majority in the House, in order to maximize the political clout of the progressive, black, women's and Hispanic caucuses, which are overwhelmingly Democratic). But the idea of running in a Republican primary should be considered, especially if there is a weak Republican incumbent in a largely working-class district. In any case, careful selection of a district is a good idea. Considerations include the social makeup of the district, its political balance, the incumbent's character and popularity, the forces available to begin the task of creating a constituency, and probably a host of other things. (In other words, not to be done lightly.)

There are several reasons for concentrating on congressional elections. First, presidential politics is dormant for three out of every four years. Engaging in campaigns like Nader's entails a start-and-stop politics that leads only to wasted effort and disappointment. Then, too, this style of *politicus interrurptus* requires starting at the top, which in turn requires a nationally recognized leader—someone like Jackson or Nader. But candidates as good as these are rarely available, and in any case a well-known candidate not of the left's own making may well tend to have a private agenda at odds with it. Finally, and most important, winning a congressional primary is relatively easy, and often tantamount to election. Few people vote in primaries—usually about 25–30 percent of the registered party members—so a solid base of as little as 10–15 percent of the eligible voters would make an odds-on favorite. That is a group that can be created by consistent work, and, if done right, can be immune from last-minute media blitzes by candidates with big bucks as their main qualification.

In short, a concentrated effort by a group of dedicated people working at the grassroots level—in the manner of the Christian Coalition—

can win a major party nomination for Congress relatively easily. Three or four such victories within the Democratic Party can gain national attention and encourage others to follow suit. So, if done well a sustained national constituency might be created independently of, but also in support of, progressive challenges in the presidential primaries every four years. Doing so will also increase the chances of finding and having some control over an attractive presidential candidate.

Of course, it's easy to put this on paper, but not so easy to test the theory in action. That next step is up to you.

BIBLIOGRAPHY

Adamic, Louis, *Dynamite* (New York: Viking Press, 1934).

Adams, Graham, Jr., *The Age of Industrial Violence, 1910–1915* (New York: Columbia University Press, 1966).

Alperpwitz, Gar, *The Decision to Use the Atomic Bomb, and the Archictecture of an American Myth* (New York: University of California Press, 1995).

Andreev-Khomiakov, Gennady, *Bitter Waters, Life and Work in Stalin's Russia* (Boulder: Westview Press, 1997).

Avineri, Schlomo, *The Social and Political Thought of Karl Marx* (Cambridge, U.K.: Cambridge University Press, 1970).

Ayers, Bill, *Fugitive Days* (Boston: Beacon Press, 2001).

Beard, Charles A., and Mary R. Beard, *The Rise of American Civilization* (New York: Macmillan, 1927).

Beard, Mary R., ed., *America Through Women's Eyes* (New York: Macmillan, 1934).

Bellah, Robert N., et al., *The Good Society* (New York: Alfred A. Knopf, 1991).

Bernstein, Irving, *Turbulent Years, A History of the American Worker, 1933–1941* (Boston: Houghton Mifflin, 1971).

Bernstein, Samuel, *The First International in America* (New York: Westview Press, 1962).

Boudin, Louis, *The Theoretical System of Karl Marx* (New York: Monthly Review Press, 1967).

Bruce, Robert V., *1877: Year of Violence* (Chicago: University of Chicago Press, 1987).

Buder, Stanley, *Pullman: An Experiment in Industrial Order and Community Planning, 1880–1930* (New York: Oxford University Press, 1967).

De Caux, Len, *Labor Radical, From the Wobblies to CIO* (Boston: Beacon Press, 1970).

Debs, Eugene V., *Writings and Speeches* (New York: Hermitage Press, 1948).

Draper, Theodore, *The Roots of Anerican Communism* (New York: Viking, 1957).

Duberman, Martin Bauml, *Paul Robeson* (New York: Alfred A. Knopf, 1988).

Dubofsky, Melvyn, and Warren Vantine, *John L. Lewis, A Biography* (Urbana and Chicago: University of Illinois Press, 1986).

DuBois, W. E. B., *The Souls of Black Folk* (New York: Henry Holt, 1953).

Dunne, Finley Peter, *Mr. Dooley, Now and Forever* (Stanford, Calif.: Academic Reprints, 1954).

Foner, Philip, ed., *The Autobiographies of the Haymarket Martyrs* (New York: Humanities Press, 1969).

Garros, Veronique, Natalia Kornevskaya, and Thomas Lahusen, eds., *Intimacy and Terror, Soviet Diaries of the 1930s* (New York: New Press, 1995).

Green, James R., *Grass Roots Socialism, Radical Movements in the Southwest, 1895–1943* (Baton Rouge: Louisiana University Press, 1978).

Harlan, Louis R., *Booker T. Washington: The Making of a Black Leader* (New York: Oxford University Press, 1972).

Hillquit, Morris, *History of Socialism in the United States* (New York: Dover Publications, 1971).

Hochschild, Adam, *The Unquiet Ghost, Russians Remember Stalin* (New York: Viking Press, 1994).

Holloway, David, *Stalin and the Bomb* (New Haven: Yale University Press, 1994).

Horn, Max, *The Intercollegiate Socialist Society, 1905–1921* (Boulder: Westview Press, 1979).

Howe, Irving, and Lewis Coser, *The American Communist Party: A Critical History (1818–1957)* (Boston: Beacon Press, 1957).

Isaacson, Walter, *Kissinger* (New York: Simon and Schuster, 1992).

Jacobs, Harold, ed., *Weatherman* (San Francisco: Ramparts Press, 1970).

Kotkin, Stephen, *Magnetic Mountain, Stalinism as a Civilization* (Berkeley: University of California Press, 1995).

Lewin, Moshe, *Russian Peasants and Soviet Power* (Evanston, Ill.: Northwestern University Press, 1968).

_____, *Lenin's Last Struggle* (London: Pluto Press, 1975a).

_____, *Political Undercurrents in Soviet Economic Debates* (London: Pluto Press, 1975b).

_____, *Russia, Soviet Union, Russia* (New York: New Press, 1995).

Lewis, David Levering, *W. E. B. DuBois: Biography of a Race, 1868–1919* (New York: Henry Holt, 1993).

Li Zhisui, *The Private Life of Chairman Mao* (New York: Random House, 1994).

Lih, Lars T., Oleg V. Naumov, Oleg V. Khlevniuk, eds., *Stalin's Letters to Molotov* (New Haven: Yale University Press, 1995).

Lindsey, Almont, *The Pullman Strike* (Chicago: University of Chicago Press, 1942).

Marx, Karl, *Capital, Volume III* (Chicago: Charles H. Kerr, 1909).

_____, *Capital, Volume I* (New York: Modern Library, 1936).

_____, *The Communist Manifesto* (London: Oxford University Press, 1998).

Mayer, George H., *The Political Career of Floyd B. Olson* (St. Paul: Minnesota Historical Society Press, 1987).

Menand, Louis, *The Metaphorical Club, A Story of Ideas in America* (New York: Farrar, Straus, Giroux, 2001).

Minehan, Thomas, *Boy and Girl Tramps of America* (New York: Farrar and Rinehardt, 1934).

Morlan, Robert, *Political Prairie Fire* (Minneapolis: University of Minnesota Press, 1955).

Mumford, Lewis, *Technics and Civilization* (New York: Harcourt Brace and World, 1934).

Noyes, John Humphrey, *History of American Socialisms* (New York: Hillary House, 1961).

Peterson, H. C., and Gilbert C. Fite, *Opponents of War, 1917–1918* (Madison: University of Wisconsin Press, 1957).

Pratt, Norma Fain, *Morris Hillquit, A Political History of an American Jewish Socialist* (Westport, Conn.: Greenwood Press, 1979).

Putnam, Robert D., *Bowling Alone* (New York: Simon and Schuster, 2000).

Reeves, Richard, *President Kennedy: Profile of Power* (New York: Simon and Schuster, 1993).

Rivlin, Gary, *Fire on the Prairie: Chicago's Harold Washington and the Politics of Race* (New York: Henry Holt, 1992).

Ryan, Alan, *John Dewey and the High Tide of American Lberalism* (New York: W. W. Norton, 1995).

Sale, Kirkpatrick, *SDS* (New York: Random House, 1973).

Salvatore, Nick, *Eugene V. Debs, Citizen and Socialist* (Urbana: University of Illinois Press, 1982).

Sanders, Elizabeth, *Roots of Reform, Farmers, Workers, and the American State, 1877–1917* (Chicago: Univeristy of Chicago Press, 1999).

Schlesinger, Arthur, Jr., *The Age of Roosevelt: The Politics of Upheaval* (Boston: Houghton Mifflin, 1960).

Schmidt, Regin, *Red Scare: FBI and the Origins of Anticommunism in the United States* (Copenhagen: Museum Tusculanum Press, 2000).

Sklar, Martin J., *The United States as a Developing Country* (Cambridge, U.K.: Cambridge University Press, 1992).

Stave, Bruce, ed., *Socialism and the Cities* (Port Washington, N.Y.: Kennikat Press, 1975).

Sudoplatov, Pavel, and Anatoli Sudoplatov, *Special Tasks, The Memoirs of an Unwanted Witness-a Soviet Spymaster* (New York: Little, Brown, 1994).

Weinstein, James, *The Corporate Ideal in the Liberal State, 1900–1918* (Boston: Beacon Press, 1968).

_____, *Ambiguous Legacy, The Left in American Poliics* (New York: New Viewpoints, 1975).

_____, *The Decline of Socialism in America, 1912–1924* (New Brunswick, N.J.: Rutgers University Press, 1984)

Westbrook, Robert B., *John Dewey and American Democracy* (Ithaca, N.Y.: Cornell University Press, 1991).

Wilde, Oscar, *The Soul of Man Under Socialism* (New York: Penguin, 2001).

Williams, T. Harry, *Huey Long* (New York: Vintage Books, 1981).

Williams, William Appleman, *History As a Way of Learning* (New York: New Viewpoints, 1973).

Woodward, C. Vann, *The Strange Career of Jim Crow* (New York: Penguin, 2001).

INDEX